THE HINSON BOYS OF ST. JOHN'S STREET

Harold T. Hinson

LANCASTER CREEK BOOKS

Copyright © 2023 by Harold T. Hinson, Sr.

All rights reserved. No part of this publication may be reproduced or transmitted in any form or by any means, electronic or mechanical, including photocopy, recording, or any information storage and retrieval system, without permission in writing from the publisher.

This is a work of historical fiction that takes place in the past, some remembered from lived experience.

Cover Design, Interior Design by Harold and Tom Hinson
, Author Photo by Harold Hinson
Hinson Boys Cover Photo by Aunt Lucy Hinson Packett
Girl on Cover is Cousin Gentry
Photos from the Hinson Collection
Sunrise on Lancaster Creek (Front Cover)
Sunset on Morattico Creek (Back Cover)

ISBN: 978-1-957928-34-0
Library of Congress Control Number: 2023904610

Printed in the United States of America

To My Brothers,
What Could Have Been, What Has Been!

Mama's Boys

The Hinson Family

Acknowledgements

Being a twin is a gift. I am blessed to be one. My twin Harvey Lee [Egg White] gave me the daily challenges to be the best. By my side when things got rough. We were alike, but different. The Artist and the Engineer. Left Brain – Right Brain. Those wonderful days – Ballers. Totally different paths to our futures. When things seemed not in our favor. Came out of it with lives fulfilled, got it done.

Brother Sammy. Life did not deal you a full deck. Gone so soon. You were the tough one. What would have been? Mother Barbara. Strict, loving, tough, giving all, you could, even with many hardships of life. The survivor providing a loving home. Every kid should have been, so blessed. We were your boys. Our father H. A. we strived to be like; even when our mother wanted us not to. We did not ask for anything, but love, knowing we made you proud. Warfield 'Little Sarge' for being in our life, a father to us. Taught so much. Many times, without saying a word. You began in the background, thank God not for long.

Teacher, Sarah Collins Honenberger, for the inspiration and guidance "To Tell My Story." Author of *Catcher, Caught; Waltzing Cowboys; White Lies; A Tale of Barbies, Vaccines and Deception.*

To Jan for the "Patience of Job."

My sincere thanks to the family for all of your input with your pictures and stories about our history.

A loving son and all the grands. Your Deo; Pop Pop loves you with all his heart and soul. The Family, without whom this story could not be told.

Contents

Hinson Twins Family History   1

Hinson's Lunch and Attic Bedroom   17

Family Times and Farms   23

Daddy Gone   29
Sammy Passes   31
Where is Mother?   33
Mother is Back - Attic Apartment   35

Bell Ville Lane – Hurricane Hazel   39
Warfield and Baseball   49

St. John's Street   53
Growing Up Grounded   59
Warsaw High School Baseball   69
After High School Graduation   75
Support Check   79

United States Air Force   81
Knocking Sound   93
Cuban Missile Crisis   97
Are You Mr. Hinson?   101
Commander-in-Chief   103
Key West Detachment   105
Reenlistment Date   111

Contents, Contd.

Tidewater Telephone Central Office   113
Showdown - Decisions   119
Joe Booher - Joe's Story   121
What is Going On?   125
Obligations   129
 I Never See You Out   131
Getting Out   135

J & L Tastee Freeze   139
All Good But!   141
What Have You Gotten Yourself Into?   145
Last Time?   149
Back Door Knock, Islington Road   151
First Show Cause   153
Second Show Cause   155

Do Not Have Job Here   157
Life About to Change, Move to Richmond   159
Job Listed, Richmond Sunday Times Dispatch   161
PS&C Union Shop   165
Confrontation   167

Richmond City Courts   171
Third Show Cause   175
Want to Talk with You   177
Job Change in My Future   179
Howard P. Foley, Custom Controls Shop   181
Fairlawn Townhouses   185
Summer Break Maine Vacation   187
Lobster Man   189
Friendship Sloop, Fishing in the Bay of Fundy   193

Contents, Contd.

Henrico County Court   195
ASA Softball   197
Life-Changing Decision   201
College Graduation   203
H.P. Foley Engineering   205

How I Met Shannon   207
Shannon's Parents   209
Engagement Ring   211
The Wedding   213
Thanksgiving 1979   217

Phillip Morris Employment – First Try; Second Try   219

Sparrow Drive   223
Our World Changes   227
Thomas Summer Job – United States Navy/Air Force   231
Erwin   233
Sparrow Drive Sold, Bromwich Drive   237
Waterfront Search - 1984 Closing   239

Shannon's River Journal   245
Our House Plans   249
Meet Joe Monk   253
Forty-Third Birthday Picnic   257
Construction Loan   261
House is Ours!   267
Ricky   269
Thanksgiving Rock Fishing   275

Help Honey - Broken Leg   281
President's Award   285
Screaming Animal   289
Admitted to MCV and Boot Hill   295

Contents, Contd.

Your Father Passed This Morning   297
Son's War, Ricky Home   299
Volunteer Separation, Will You Do Project?   303
Shannon's Health   305
Hurricane Isabel   307
Richard Dwayne Hinson, Sr - Quest for Answers   311
Datsun 260z Title   323

Last Gratitude Journal Entry, Medical Problems   325
Renal Failure   329
Regional Memorial Medical Center   335
Home Care   339
Riverside Hospital Emergency Room   341
Back to Medical Center   343
Intensive Care Unit   349
General Surgery Floor, Room 2176   355
Losing Shannon   357

Appendices   365
A. Obituary of Mrs. M.C. Hinson   367
B. Lucy Hall and Lewis Alexander Washington Hinson   369
C. Recipes   371
D. Hinson Genealogy   379
E. Letter from Warfield   383
F. Collage of Family Pictures   385

**Mama, Daddy, Dollie, Others
Washington, D.C.**

Aunt Dollie and Mama

Daddy and Mama, 1941

**Mama and Daddy
June 30, 1941**

Hinson Twins Family History

I was born on the fourth of July 1942, and I am not supposed to be here.

The location is Sibley Memorial Hospital, Washington, District of Columbia. Doctor B.C. MacDonald brings life at 3:00 o'clock P.M. to 'Baby A.' At 3:05 p.m. to 'Baby B.' Twins 'split' from the same egg! Born to Barbara Elizabeth Foti Hinson [20] and Harvey Alexander [HA] Hinson, Jr. [21].

Baby A is in poor health. Doctors believe he will likely pass. He is put into an Incubator.

Harvey. A name that has passed down for generations to each first-born son. The doctors called a meeting with Harvey Alexander and Barbara Elizabeth to update the twins' medical report. "Today you will take your baby B home. Before you do that, both sons will need to be named. Be aware of the health of Baby A, because of your family naming wishes, we do not suggest that you name him Harvey. Baby A may not survive." Our parents, after the shock, named us. Baby 'B' is given the name Harvey Lee. Baby 'A' named Harold Thomas. Lee for Aunt Dorothy. Thomas for Uncle Tommy. Barbara is with Harvey Lee at home. Her mother and sister Dorothy helping with the chores caring for a newborn baby boy. H. A. has returned to work at the Creamery. Weeks pass. When the phone rings at 831 N.W. Arlington Street, Barbara has a sick feeling in her stomach. Nurse Joy identifies herself from Dr. MacDonald's Office. "Your son made it. Come and get Harold." Barbara thinks, oh my God, the Twin's will be together again. Twins run in our mother's family. The journey begins.

December 2, 1942

**Hinson Twins
18-to-24 Months**

Our mother Barbara was born in Wheeling, West Virginia. She told the story many times. "The whistles were blowing at the coal mines when I was born." There were six siblings living in the Foti family.

Our mothers' father Samuel Foti Sereno was an Italian Emigrant born September 1893 in Reggio Calabria, Italy. Came to America at age twelve. None of the six siblings were allowed to speak English in the home. Speak Italian or get a slap across the face if they disobeyed. Mama knew some Italian; bad words came out when she was upset with us.

Grandfather Samuel with his brother like many others coming to the United States of America found jobs in the Coal Mines of

Ma and Sam, 1918

West Virginia. Our Grandmother on mothers' side was Irish. Betty Blevins. We called her Ma. She also had a twin sister Martha. Not much is known about our mother's family. Do remember that grandmother and grandfather Blevins lived to be 99 years old.

Annette, H.A., Garnett, and Lucy

Our father with all his siblings were born at the family farmhouse. Wellford's, Cobham Park Neck, Richmond County, Virginia. The homestead was the Hinson Dairy Farm with views of the Rappahannock River. During this period there were at least 100 dairy farms in the Northern Neck. The Town of Warsaw had the Northern Neck Creamery Processing Plant. Butter. Bottled Milk. Cottage Cheese. The first known Hinson in the Northern Neck of Virginia dates to 1652.

Our father moved to Washington D.C. after the sixth grade and lived with his youngest sister Lucy Packett and family. Daddy got a job at the Lucerne Dairy. Our mother and family moved from West Virginia to New Jersey. Then to Washington, D.C. Mama got a job at that same Lucerne Dairy. This is where our parents met. Mama told stories about when the Foti family moved to New Jersey to be near their father's

Steamer Lancaster at Wellfords

Italian family. Growing up not being able to take a bath. The bathtub was being used by her father to make gin. Grand Father must have been sent to prison for this. Mama did not give to many details on this account. She often said if it was not for milk gravy and homemade biscuits they would have starved to death.

Great Grandparents were William [Willy] Belvin Fones and Mary Sophia Catherine [Kate] Smith. The old graveyard is located near the site of the original Cobham Park Baptist Church. Our Grandmother Edith Rebecca named herself 'Big Mama.' Did not like the other Grandmother names. Big Mama's grave is in a Rod Iron fenced section. Burial grounds only for the Fones family. Our

Willy (1861-1945) and Kate (1868-1947) Fones

father's grave is up on The Hill. All Cemetery Property was owned by the Fones family.

There is a written history about Col. Fauntleroy and family.[1] Owned large tracts of land in Richmond County. Mars Hill and Crandall on the Rappahannock River. A third manor plantation of the Fauntleroy's was called the Cliffs, located North of the others. There is a graveyard there with many unmarked sites. Area known today as Naylor's. The Hinson ancestors came to the Northern Neck from the UK as white indentured servitude. Many of them located at the Cliffs. So many, the place was called Hinson Town. Also, history that the Hinson family are responsible for William and Mary College. It came about when the Pirate John Hinson was captured. Pirate Hinson's punishment was taking most of the loot and moneys he had.[2]

H.A. Hinson was drafted into the Army and sent overseas to serve in General Patton's 3rd Army 4th Armor Division. Mama remains living at Aunt Lucy and Uncle Russell's home in Washington D. C. until our father H. A. comes home when World War II ends.

Daddy Home After Basic Training

Daddy World War II German Motorcycle

---

1 Journal and Letters of Philip Vickers Fifhian 1773-1774 pg 24. See Appendix D, Hinson Genealogy; Jonas Hinson, Planter.
2 Pirates of the Cheasapeake Bay pg 29

**H.A. Hinson
Fort Bragg, 1943**

Uncle Pat Foti, WW II

Daddy, Everett and One Twin

Brother Samuel Allen Hinson was born August 10, 1944. Sammy is a stocky blonde headed, blue eyed, strong kid with a smile that would melt any heart. Sammy is named after our mother's father. H.A. came home after the War a proud man. There are three sons.

Daddy moved the family back to the Northern Neck and proclaimed he would never want to work for someone else. That is when H. A. Hinson decided to open a 'Lunch Room.'

Daddy got a loan from his father Harvey Alexander Sr. and his brother Garnett Lyle. Purchased an old General Store building on St. Johns Street. Remodeled the interior with a Kitchen, Counter, Stools, Booths, Tables and Chairs, Toilets and a Juke Box. HINSON'S LUNCH painted on the large glass window. Opened the 'Lunch Room' in the Winter of 1946.

Young Garnett and Leafie

Hinson Twins, November 1944

Original Front Entry

We boys spent a lot of time playing in the front yard of the home next to the Lunch Room. The grass of Rooney and Virginia Sanders. We did not have a front yard. Concrete and tar road was it. To the left of Hinson's Lunch was the Southern States Building. Further down St. Johns Street on the right towards Main Street was Dr. Handelman's Office and home. On the near side of the Handelman place was an old store turned into living space. Next was a Duplex Building with two homes on the far side. On the corner of St. Johns and Main Street was E.Y. Brooks store.

There was not much of a yard in the back of Hinson's Lunch either. No grass at all. There was a Peddle Car for the three of us. Many games to see which boy was the fastest. The starting line at the Light Line Pole edge of the sidewalk with St. John's Street, property line between Sanders and Hinson's Lunch. Finish line was at Pine Street located just pass the Barrack House. The REA property was located on the opposite side of Pine Street. The race always started out as fun. Soon ended with an argument as to which brother was the fastest. No stop watch. Then the pushing of one brother in the little car. "Go faster." Lots of screaming. "Go faster. Keep your feet off the petals." Then a wreck. Skinned up bodies.

Playing on the Sanders front step one day; we were seeing which one of us could jump to the end of the screen porch! Everything was a challenge no matter what. Am sure that I got pushed, most likely by Harvey Lee. Harvey did not like to lose. We were very competitive. Neither one liked to lose to the other. Harold hit his head on the porch flooring wood corner just above the right eye. Opened a gash over the eye socket. Dazed. Crying. Bleeding. Aunt Dollie was helping our mother in the Lunch Room. She heard the yelling. Came to us. "Stop running Harry." Aunt Dollie called Harold, Harry. She was the only sibling that did. "You are making the bleeding worst. I need to take you to Dr. Pierson." I stopped running. Harry trusted Aunt Dollie. Dr. Pierson's Office had that sterile smell. Was located at the family home on the left going West out of Warsaw. "Let me look at that, son" as Dr.

Pierson takes my head in his hands. "This is going to need some Pierson's stiches." Out of that chair I bolt. Out the door. Running. Do not know where to. Aunt Dollie is running behind me. "Stop running Harry. If you stop running. I will not let Dr. Pierson do any stiches." I stop and go to Aunt Dollie's arms. She gives me a hug. We walk back into Dr. Pierson's office. Doctor is waiting at the chair with a stainless-steel tray. "This really needs some stitches." I remained in the chair this time. "Dr. Pierson, I promised Harry that I would not let you give him any stitches. You will have to do something else Dr. Pierson." That was our Aunt Dollie. We left Dr. Pierson' office with a large bandage over my right eye. No stitches. Harvey Lee and Harold loved Aunt Dollie. She treated us like we were her children. *Life was good.*

Harvey Lee and Harold started the first grade in the Fall of 1948. Sammy was four in August. That first-grade class had twenty-six kids. We graduated with seventeen of them. Like brothers and sisters, we were. The first-grade teacher was Mrs. Lewis. Her daughter Dixie Lee was also in this class. Very strict person was Mrs. Lewis. Sometimes she would even spank Dixie Lee in front of the class. Just for affect, I think. One day Mrs. Lewis left the class room. All the classmates began

Mama and Dollie in Front of Hudson, 1948

to cheer me on! Had to be a good idea! The twin getting all the attention. In the moment. "Hey Harold, get up on the table and dance for us." Everyone is screaming. I am doing my 'happy dance.' No thought that Mrs. Lewis would be coming back. She did and was not happy. Come to think of it – do not ever remember seeing the woman smile. Mrs. Lewis grabbed the dancers arm pulled me off the table. Started dragging me out of the First/Second Grades building and down the sidewalk. As teacher was doing this – Harvey Lee was kicking her shins on the way to the steps for the next school building. If you did something to one twin – you had to deal with the other. Demanded Harvey. *"Get back to class."* Mrs. Lewis continued to drag me up the steps and into the building. Pushes me into a chair. Principal's Office. "You sit here until Mr. Perkins comes. He is going to take care of you." I peed my pants.

"Hey Hinson. What are you doing in here?" It was our first cousin Lyell Hinson; pocking his head through the Office doorway.

"I am waiting for Mr. Perkins to come." Trying to hide that my pants are wet.

"You get out of here, boy, right now. Go home. Tell Uncle H.A. about this."

I still remember standing by Daddy's side when he phoned the school for Mr. Perkins. "If you lay one God Damn finger on my boy, I am coming to that school to drag your skinny ass up and down those oiled stained floors." Then I got the belt whipping. Knew it was coming. Those memories about the belt beatings. We knew when one was coming. Was often. One Sunday morning H. A. and Barbara's only day of rest. The family bedroom was on the top floor of the Lunch Room. Hardwood Board flooring without any carpet or other cover. You could see through the board cracks to the rooms below. I am sure that Harvey Lee came up with the plan. "Let's go down to the Lunch Room, get some stuff to eat." Was not long before Daddy found us sitting on stools at the counter drinking soft drinks, eating Nabs and Candy Bars. Harvey Lee hears him first at the swinging door from the Lunch Room kitchen. Harvey Lee runs to hide in the Men's Room located left of the Bar.

"What did I tell you about coming into the Lunch Room?" He is mad and one of us is going to pay. Daddy grabs me by the arm. His wide belt in the other hand. I got the beating. Daddy was satisfied.

One time I was thinking faster than Harvey Lee who had run and made it into a bathroom. I looked up at our father. "Daddy. Why do you always beat me"? He looked down at me. Realizes who he has caught. "Where is Harvey Lee?" I pointed at the bathroom door. Daddy let go of my arm and headed for the bathroom located in the hall. There he found Harvey Lee with his pants down. Faking a shit. Harvey Lee got a good one that day. Maybe a little extra.

Aunt Nille, Shelby Dean, Bobby, Harvey, and Harold in Front of Dunnaways Department Store

Harold on Bicycle with Aunt Pammy

Family, August 1950

First Grade Class 1948-1949

Eighth Grade,
Warsaw High School

Hinson's Lunch and Attic Bedroom

Lunchroom was open six days a week for Breakfast, Lunch, Dinner. Typical days 'Open Hours' 6:00 a.m. to 12:00 Midnight. After closing. The Lunchroom, Kitchen, Bathrooms cleaned. The beer case repacked. Remember seeing Daddy empty a beer case box. Open the folded top, take out six bottle beers at a time. Three in each hand between the fingers. To bed after a long day around 2AM.

The typical Hinson's Lunch menu. Open Turkey or Roast Beef served over two slices of sandwich bread. Mashed Potatoes, Gravy, and a Green Vegetable. In season was Oyster Stew. Devil Crab deep fried in a cleaned Crab Shell. Crab Cake. Soft Shell Crab Sandwich. Hamburger. Cheeseburger. Hot Dogs. Egg Salad. Tuna Fish Salad sandwiches. French Fries. Potato Chips. Candy.

Raw hot dogs were loaded on spikes in a rotating cooker before 10AM. Dogs were ready by lunch time. There was a covered bin at the top of this cooker with two metal folding doors. Opened from either side. This bin area was loaded with Hot Dog Buns. The steam created from the Hot Dog Cooker below made the rolls soft and warm. You had to have 'one' to understand how good those Hot Dogs were. Most people ordered at least two at a time. Sometimes three. Fifteen cents each. Condiments were hand cut sweet onions, homemade relish in the double-sided covered dish. Bottles of mustard and catsup. Whatever your taste might be. Soft drinks including two of my favorites Neihi Orange or Root Beer. Square Nabs. Round Nabs. When you asked for a pack of nabs. "Do you want the square or round ones?" The square shape Cheese Cracker Nab or the Ritz Cracker Nab were in a pack of five with Peanut Butter filling. Planter Peanuts in a cellophane bag. All these items cost $0.05. A soft drink was $0.06. Ice cream bar was $0.06.

No scoop ice cream. Too much trouble. Bottle of beer $0.35. That ice cold beer was so cold there was a frost on the bottle. Could scrape it with your fingernail. Drink one fast. Instant nose burn. Another thing we did was put the bag of peanuts into a bottle of Coca Cola or Pepsi; after you took a good swag out of the bottle. Did not want to waste any because of the foam created from the salt.

On the bar was a large jar of Pickled Pig Knuckles. Each Knuckle cost $0.20; was served on a plate with two packs of Saltine Crackers. Butter knife and fork. After all the Knuckles were sold peeled Hard Boiled Eggs were added to the Pickle Juice jar. Also on the counter was a large jar of Little Red Spicy Sausages. Two for $0.20. Served the same manner as the Pig Knuckle. The Pig Knuckle took some time to eat giving more time for that second Beer. Can Beer did not exist in those early days. Daddy profited $0.05 on each Bottle of Beer sold. These were the days of no taxes on food or drink. Daddy could figure out the cost in his head.

Dinner meals were Pork Chop. Roast Beef. Steak. Fried Chicken. Fresh Fish. Fried Oysters. Ham. Home-made Soup. Crab Cake. Dinner Plate served with three sides. Mash Potato. Corn. Peas. Green Beans cooked with Ham. Butter Beans. Hand cut French Fries. Corn on the Cob in season. All home cooked. Seafood was depending on the season. Back then - Oysters were available only in months with an 'R.'

Daddy also did some Crabbing and Oyster Tonging in the Rappahannock River. When he caught a large Rock Fish, baked whole Rock Fish with strips of bacon on the top, stuffed with onions and carrots. Cooked with the head on. No waste. Rockfish cheeks are good eating.

And of course, the thing that Hinson's Lunch was famous for. H.A. Hinson's steamed hard crabs. Folks came from all over the Northern Neck, Northern Virginia out on Rt. 3/Rt 301, Rt 360 road to Richmond. Daddy had "his method" of doing Crabs. No one else had a Steam Crab like Hinson's Lunch.

Daddy made up a recipe from ingredients to create a sauce. Added to the potted steamed crab's minutes before he cut the gas off. He cooked two bushels of live hard-shell crabs at a time in a very large stainless steel bowl-shaped vessel. After the Crabs were done cooking; emptied them on a table to cool. Each Crab had a coating of the seasoning on it. No need to add seasoning after the crabs are cooked. Some of the 'Sauce' got 'sucked' into the Crab. Daddy put Brown Paper on the table. Brought a tray with how many Crabs ordered, dumped in the center on the paper. Saltine Crackers. Butter Knife for picking/breaking Pincher Craws. Roll of paper towels on each table.

Let us just say. A cold beer was needed. Maybe a beer for every other crab. That seasoning from fingers to mouth went well with a cold beer. My crabs are cooked using the method that our daddy did. H.A. Hinson style![3] Just in smaller batches. One-to-two dozen at a time. On Wednesday Night at Hinson's Lunch, it was all the crabs you could eat for $1.50. I questioned my father some years later. "How could you afford to do that?"

"Not about the crabs son." The beer. Hot Dogs. Hamburgers. Soft Drinks. Candy. Ice cream. These were family nights in Warsaw. Everybody came. Sometimes daddy would get a call from folks in Richmond. "H.A."

"We need three dozen."

"Going to be closing in a couple of hours. Find the grocery bag on the front steps. Leave the money under the rock." Money always there.

Hinson's Lunch was known for not a place where you got 'out of line.' No cussing or foul language tolerated. When H.A. said that you have had enough beer. That was it. "You want a cup of coffee; coke?" Worst thing that a person could do was mouth off to H. A. Hinson. Most locals knew that. When in the Army during World War II - Daddy was Middle Weight Boxing Champion in Patton's 4th Army. Something

---

3 Steam Crab Recipe back of book

Daddy was proud about. So were we. Daddy was solid as a rock. A country boy raised on a dairy farm, lifting Hay Bales. Big strong hands from pulling on those Diary-Cows tits. H. A. quit boxing when the Army Doctor reset his nose one more time. "Will not be good if you break that nose again."

There were times when the Town Sheriff Rockwell B. would call. "H.A. I hear there is a problem at the Lunch Room. You need any help?"

"No. I got it covered Rockwell." One story we heard was when daddy dragged this guy out of the Lunch Room door and kicked him from the curved front steps. Man landed on the other side of St. Johns Street.

There was another time we remember. Daddy and a person ended up in the alley between Southern States and the Lunch Room; near the back of the building where mama's kitchen was. Daddy hit that guy so hard that when he hit the building; knocked mama's dishes out of the cabinet. That is the truth. Cousin Jimmy H. told me about the event that day. "Your daddy was okay with his 'running around' but not if your mother did." You had to know, Jimmy!

Have had friends tell personal stories about H. A. Hinson. The times that Daddy would bring their own father home when he had too much. They never forgot that kindness. "Your daddy was a good man." We just did not know it then.

We remember the shared bedroom on the second floor of the Lunch Room. Most likely the attic of that old store building. Cold; drafty; dimly lit. The laughter; Juke Box Music and smells from the Lunch Room below. The dark staircase going up. Bare wood floors. No heat that we remember. Times being told by our Aunt Dollie. "Keep your feet under the blanket, or the rats might bite off your toes." Always kept the blanket tight, fighting over who had the most of the it.

There was a bathroom located in the hallway. Have tried to remember if it only had a sink and toilet. Do not recall a tub; there must have been one. Brother Sammy had a crib located in one corner. Twins slept together in a small bed on the opposite corner. Mama and daddy's bed was across the room just to the right of the window. There is a dresser with mama's makeup mirror. The door to the staircase going down to the Lunch Room kitchen on the opposite wall from the hallway to the bathroom. The door was near our bed. One night we were 'horse playing' as we often did. Harvey went under the bed to get something we were fighting over. Harvey Lee came out from under the bed screaming. He had a bad cut on his leg, most likely a wood floor splinter. Aunt Dollie came to us and cleaned Harvey Lee up. Bandaged his leg. Harvey wears that scare today. 'No stiches.' We stayed in that bedroom most of the time while mama and daddy worked in the Lunch Room. Do not remember what toys or games we had. TV was not invented yet. Remember getting scared about going into the hallway to the bathroom. Thoughts of rats. Started pissing out of the bedroom window. Piss went down to the Tin Roof over the air compressor and to the ground. The window screen rusted. Was not long before Daddy figured out what that smell was. Saw the window screen. Remember we both got a belt whipping for that one.

Harvey Lee and I got bored on one night being in that bedroom. Went down that staircase in the dark from the upstairs bedroom. Looking out for any rats. On a step was daddy's bottle of Miller High Life. He always kept his beer there; would not drink it out 'front.' Harvey Lee convinced me to see what was so special in that bottle. Whew. First sallow did not taste that good. Second one a little better. Now we are in trouble again.

Harvey Lee came up with a plan. I did not think that fast. "Let us add some water to the bottle. Daddy will not know that we drank any." We add water to the bottle. Problem was we could not remember how much beer was in the bottle before drinking it. Wrong. Wrong. I still remember that belt whipping.

Family Times and Farms

Those good Sunday times out together as a family. Westmoreland State Park; Sky Line Drive. Sundays were the only free day from the Lunch Room. Riding in the back seat of that big black 1948 Chrysler. Longer trips to Marion, Virginia for Christmas when the family could. All of mama's sisters and brothers; husbands; wives and kids were there. Our Grandmother Ma. Beckoned us to lay our head in her lap. "Let me check those ears." Ma would 'dig' the wax out of our ears with one of her Bobbie Pins.

"Ouch."

"Now you know I did not hurt you."

Harvey Lee and I loved to go flying with our daddy in a single engine plane at the Lively Airport. Mama would sit on the bench with a troubled look. Many times, Daddy would fly to Warsaw and land in the field in front of the Standard Garage on Hamilton Boulevard. Daddy and Mitchell Angolia – first cousins - took turns taking the plane up. Mitchell's mother (Carrie Ida Fones, b.1896, d.1964) was our Grandmother Edith's (b.1893, d.1979) sister. Flying around Warsaw. Landing back on that Bean field. One time flying with Daddy he climbed straight up towards the sun – rolled over - then dove straight back down towards earth. Up out of the dive. Stomach churning. Scared to death. Did not puke. Was quite a thrill. Then our Daddy quite flying. His best friend Wade B. was killed in a single engine plane that crashed at the Tappahannock Airport. As kids we remember hearing the story. Wade was flying with a person that found out Wade was seeing his wife. Crashed the plane on purpose. True. Do not know. Small town.

The days at Granddaddy and Grandmother's farm in Cobham Park Neck on the road to Wellford's Wharf, through Kennards pass Sanders Store. Sanders Store and home of Lola and Smith Sanders family: Norris, Kermit, Lucy, Joyce, Jimmy, Gladys, Josephine, Talmage. Lucy and Joyce baby sit us on occasion. Playing with our first cousins Russel Jr. – Freddy – Jimmy - Charles and brother Sammy. Cow pods for bases. Some- times there would be a cow pod that was not dry enough. We played barefoot and had stinky feet until washed under the yard hydrant near the barn.

Granddaddy Harvey always carried a plug of Brown Mule chewing tobacco in his pants pocket. We watched him cut off a piece with his Old Timer pocketknife. Begged him to be given a piece. "No boys. Your mama will skin me." Watched as he put a sliver in his mouth and soon started spitting brown juice. Copied this with Tootsie Roll candy. One day Granddaddy cut us a sliver. "Promise you will not tell your mama." He knew. The juice went down our throats. Puking Sick. Did not ask for that again. Remember him telling us not to eat all the cherries on the tree. We climbed it. Ate until we got sick. Our Grandmother Edith; [Big Mama] was what all of us kids called her; had a chicken house. Can see her now instructing us how to reach under the hen without getting pecked, to get the eggs. "Put the eggs in my apron. Careful. Do not break any." Big mama sold the eggs. That was her spending money.

Big Mama's Egg House with Aunt Annette, Franklin, Marian, Ann, Becky, Russell Jr. Teaching Us How to Collect the Eggs Without Breaking Them. She was much loved by us all!

Family Times and Farms

The wood burning cooking stove in the kitchen. Kept warm all day. Stove had a top section where there were always Sweet Potatoes and Biscuits. Homemade butter and preserves on the kitchen table. Better than candy. The times in Granddaddy's tool shed where he would crack Black Walnuts on the Anvil for us. He got upset with us when we were in the barn. Playing games on the Hay Bales. "You boys get out of that barn." Always did what we were told. Then went back again.

Harvey, Sr., Big Mama, Harvey Lee, Harold, Freddie and a Packett Lady

Many Sundays with the family at Islington Farm. The property was located on a well-kept long dirt road, passing the corn and bean fields, straight to the big house, towards the Rappahannock River. The end of the State Maintained hard top Islington Road. Daddy's brother, our Uncle Garnett, and Aunt Leafie's Dairy Farm. Sunday Lunch gathering after church with our first cousins Lyell – Everett – Bobby. What a fantastic cook our Aunt Leafie was. Her fried chicken and those pies. There is a shoreline and grounds to play. *Life was good.*

We were encouraged to go for it in Runny Sanders yard. Last boy standing got the fifty-cent silver half. Always Sammy. Lasting memories during an innocent time. *Life was happy, free, good.*

**Hinson & Packett Boys at the Farm
Cobham Park Neck**

Edith (Big Mama) and Harvey, Sr.

Family Times and Farms 27

Leafie, Lyell and Diane

Bobby and Everett Hinson

Garnett, Leafie and Sons

Aunt Lucy and Uncle Russell 1937

Washington D.C. Visit with Freddie Packett

Daddy Gone

Do Not know why.

Hinson's Lunch now managed by H.A.'s cousin Norris S. and wife Della. They live above Hinson's Lunch in the attic space we use to be as a family. They have a son Wayne and daughter Gentry Ann is our age. Wayne is Sammy's age. We are very happy to be with them. Having playmates right in the same house. Our life is different. We see the pain on our mother. This just going to be the beginning of change.

The four of us, now living in the back of Hinson's Lunch. There is a kitchen, table and chairs, small bedroom, and bathroom. We all slept together in that small bedroom. Harvey and me on a fold-up cot. Our mother slept with Sammy in the double bed. The cot had to be folded up in the morning to make walking room. Membered the cot end catches had to be placed on top of each other and would pinch your fingers. Only happened once. Made you very careful. Do not recall much about going to school during this time. Ever having a dinner with us together. What did our mother cook? When did she have time to cook? Those things seem very simple today. *What happened to our life?*

We were not made aware of how sick our brother was. Sammy did not play outside with us any longer. He did not leave that bedroom. Sammy was very ill.

The family country doctor could not determine what was wrong with him. Mama took Sammy to MCV Hospital in Richmond, Virginia. Test were done. Sammy was diagnosed with the deadly disease – Leukemia. The only treatment was Blood Transfusions. No cure. No drugs. Little known about the disease. Doctors just try to keep Sammy from dying. Josie and Arnold H. gave Sammy a white puppy to cheer him up. The family-owned Hinson's Super Market in Warsaw. Arnold's brother

Owen Doggett was the butcher at the market. Sammy named the puppy Skippy. Skippy was the only pet that I remember.

Mama and Sammy went to MCV Hospital often. We were never told what was wrong. Not told how serious it was. We just knew how upset our mother was. There was not a family car for us. Going to Richmond was a challenge for our mother. Do not remember how much our father tried to help. Our mother would take the Greyhound bus from Warsaw to Richmond. Back to Warsaw. The ride a two-hour trip in those days. Each way. State Route 360 was a two-lane winding road over three Rivers. Family and friends helped as much as they could. Everyone had their own lives. The truth is. We did not have any idea what was going on. How much this was taking out of our mother. Our lives. Why our mother had a short temper. Sometimes treated us mean. We were too young to realized what a life was hers. Just living. Taking care of Sammy. Trying to find answers. Sammy now Bedridden. Our daddy had moved back to Washington, D.C., he was driving a city bus. *His life changed also.*

Do not remember when it happened. Sammy went blind. Mama darkened the bedroom. Leukemia was fast taking brother Sammy's life away.

Sammy and Twins Skyline Drive

Sammy Passes

February a cruel, unforgiving month. Without good memories in my life.

February 5, 1951. We were suddenly awakened from sleep early in the morning. Our mother was screaming. A scream we had never heard before. Where is she? We found her sitting at the kitchen table, trying to hold the limp body of brother Sammy in her frail arms. Norris, Della, Gentry and Wayne came down to the kitchen from upstairs. They had heard mama. There are not many memories for me after this night. Della took us kids out of the kitchen, upstairs. She was like a second mother to us. Family.

It is a bitter cold harsh February day in the Northern Neck. Cobham Park Baptist Church is packed with family and friends. Snow was deep and still coming down. Mama wrote in Sammy's Remembrance Book - Age: 6 Years – 5 Months – 5 Days.

Do not remember when Sammy's little coffin was pulled out of that black hauler? Do not remember the service in the church. Did the brothers even go in the church? Did we follow the coffin, walking through the snow, towards that 'hole' up on the hill? Harvey Lee says we were kept in the back seat of Daddy's Chrysler. He remembered Mr. Sanders opening the door to check on us. Saying a prayer. Harvey Lee says that our mother was carried by her arms screaming. "Don't put my boy in the ground." I have no memory of that. The night brother Sammy died. The day Sammy was buried. Memories

Sammy's Window

stopped for me. What did *we* do each day? Gone from knowledge until age twelve. Lost forever. All memory gone. *Perhaps a blessing.*

Sammy, August 1950

PLEA FOR BLOOD DONORS TO AID SIX YEAR OLD

Little Sammy Hinson, age 6, of Warsaw in every respect appears to be just an average healthy youngster doing the usual carefree, happy things any youngster his age loves to do. This, however, is not the case, for the child is suffering from an acute attack of the blood destroying disease "Lukemia". A disease which for some reason causes one type blood corpuscle in his blood to destroy the others, gradually robbing the otherwise normal lad of that necessary life-giving property.

Little Sammy, son of Mrs Barbara Hinson, of Warsaw, has suffered from the disease since last March and in order for him to survive he must have frequent blood transfusions. Sammy has already had nine transusions requiring at least 2½ pints of blood each transfusion. The vitally needed transfusions suffice only for short intervals, but during which time Sammy can live and enjoy a normal life; but slowly after each transfusion, the fight becomes to great for the little fellow and fresh, life-giving blood must be found.

Fortunately for Sammy, the Blood Bank in Richmond has been able to supply some of the needed blood and a few individuals have made blood donations. The Blood Bank, however, must be repaid in six months for what has been withdrawn and the demand has been so great that Sammy's mother has asked this paper to make an appeal that anyone wishing to help please donate what blood they can to the Blood Bank at Richmond 820 W Franklin St and apply it to credit of Sammy Hinson. No particular blood type is necessary.

This plea we feel we must make in behalf of this small boy—the answer to which could mean the chance to live and defeat the strange affliction or otherwise suffer the inevitable

Northern Neck News

Where Is Mother?

We are with Aunt Dollie, Uncle Bob, Bobby, Dianne at their home. What happened to our mother? Where is She? Did mama be gone ever come up in conversation? Did we ask? No one talked about it.

Aunt Dollie our favorite living close to us. Always was looking after our well-being. Giving us lessons on how to be the best we could. Someday men. "Give whatever you are doing 100%. Then do 10% more. You will go far in life if you do that." Aunt Dollie was correct.

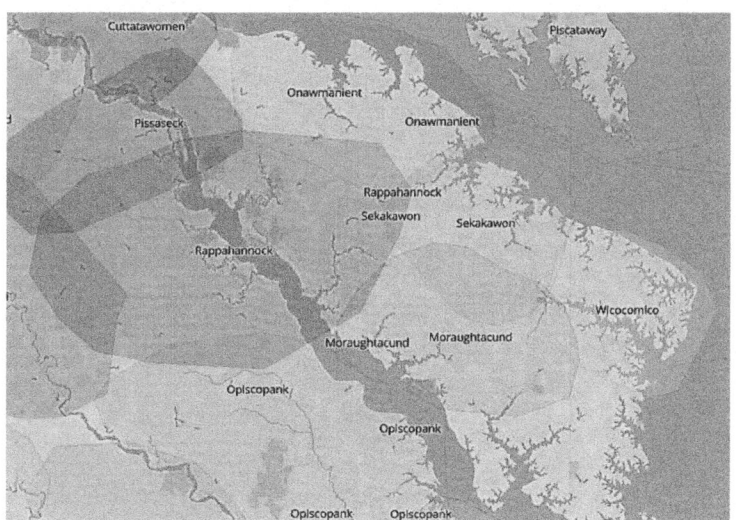

Indian Tribe Location. Now Indian Field Road
Photo: Richmond County Museum

The home is in the community of Indian Field outskirts of Warsaw about two miles. Indian Field dates to 1608 with a village. A mill pond near it. Now the first housing development in Richmond County. With its own water supply provided by the builder. How long were we living there? Had to be in the Winter 1951 and Spring 1952. No memory of

33

going to school. Must have. Probably rode on the school bus. It is a terrible thing not to remember these things. [Little Man in Head: *"A blessing, Harold."*] Okay, what was that?

Have some memory flashes on occasion. Mostly funny ones.

"Eat It." Our Aunt Dolly has just commanded us. The breakfast dish was 'White Paste.' We named it. Our Aunt's attempt at making milk gravy. [Little Man in Head: *"How you made glue."*]

We referred to Aunt Dollie as the 'Little Rooster.' Never to her face. Dollie had that way of getting her point across. There was a bedroom in the attic. Maybe the folding cot was there. Kids learn to make things adapt. Something we remembered. Uncle Bob always had to have mashed potatoes with every dinner. If there was cabbage, must be served with Cole Slaw.

Mother is Back
Attic Apartment

From where we never knew. Do not remember any mention of where she had been. We think that our mother had a nervous breakdown. Something not talked about. Mama started life over again. We have moved. Living in a small converted attic of the family home, our schoolmate Barbara Jean.

Family home is located on Rt 360 in the Town of Warsaw, across the highway from Bryant's Florist Shop. Different from living in Indian Field Community. Back to more like we grew up before our life was destroyed. Sidewalks. Lots of kids to play with. Familiar places to see. Things to do.

The attic space has a small kitchen; living room; bedroom. Open space down the center of slanted ceilings. Must walk in the middle of the rooms. Furniture up against the knee walls. There was one bed which we three slept in. No room for the cot.

The home's single bathroom on the lower level was shared by our landlord's family. Mother, Father, Barbara our classmate. The married daughter, husband and two grandkids came to visit, and it seemed like every day. Bathroom always busy! When the "piss" call came, we learned how to sneak quietly down the staircase. Open the door. Peak, hope nobody sees you. Exit the front door to the bushes. Sometimes to the back shed. Always mindful not to let Mrs. B. next door catch you.

Our Mama was in survivor mode. Mr. and Mrs. Smith treated us like we were their kids. Fun times learning how to play Gin Rummy. Food. Hugs. Mrs. Smith was a wonderful cook. She and her sister cooked at the School Cafeteria. They looked out for us when coming through the lunch line. All the food was special. Still remember the Spoon Bread and Fish Sticks on Fridays. Our favorite day.

Our mother started working as a telephone operator. She worked the day shift most of the time, so that she could be with us at night. If she had to pull a late night, she would take us. We stayed in the operator's break room. Did homework; slept on the sofa. There were many of those nights.

Our pocket money was from soda bottles picked up on the town streets and our quarter-a-week allowance. Pine Street was a favorite place for the locals to have a snort out of the brown bag bottle. Backed up with a bottle of Coke. The coke bottle got tossed out of the window into the tree line. One time we found a bottle with two rolled-up dollar bills in the neck. Someone was looking out for us. We took the bottles to Ike Halls General Store. Two cents for each bottle. Used the money to fill a small brown bag with penny candy. Some candy was two pieces for one cent. Squirrel Nut Zippers; Mary Janes; Tootsie Rolls; Jaw Breakers; Sugar Daddy. Self-serve yourself out of the Glass Jars. Each piece taken from jar carefully observed; dumped out of the bag; then recounted by the store clerk.

Warsaw Theater
(Photo, Richmond County Museum)

Those times living in Town. Going to the Warsaw Theater for the Saturday Matinee. It was the kids' place all afternoon. At least two movies. Roy Rogers. Hoppy Long Cassidy. Gene Autry. The Lone Ranger with Tonto. Mama gave us a dime for the movie. Whenever we slide the dimes through the opening at the ticket window, Mrs. Sanders would slide it back to us. "Buy yourself some candy and popcorn with this." What a sweet lady she was. Mama gave us a Jefferson; could have been a Buffalo in those days, to spend for snacks. We now had fifteen cents. That brought a lot of things, but never a Coca Cola. Waste of money. We purchased the Popcorn; Sugar Daddy; Juicy Fruits and Jelly Beans. This was a special time. Most of the school kids were there. Those Movie Shorts before the Main Feature. Flash Gordon. Dick Tracy with the watch on his arm. Dick talked to the watch. The spaceship taking off and landing back on earth.

Before we left home each morning walking to school - Mama gave us a clean handkerchief. She had tied a quarter and a nickel into one corner. The quarter was to buy Lunch. The nickel to spend at the School Store. We never took our lunch to school. Lunch was always a hot meal.

Mama did make the best Meat Balls with Meat Sauce. Our mother called it 'Spigets.' She took all the meat - chicken, pork chops - whatever was in the freezer, cooked into her sauce. Called this - "Cleaning out the freezer." The sauce 'cooking' started early in the morning. Cooked slow all day. The Italian way. Dinner by early afternoon. Our mother also fixed a store-brought loaf of Italian Bread with lots of butter. Mama's tossed salad. Made well ahead of time. Lots of Mayonnaise. Mixed the salad up with carrots; tomatoes; cukes; sweet onions. Put the big bowl in the frig. The tomatoes would melt down with the wilted limp salad greens. It was good.

One day J.A.C. and I were sitting behind the REA building beside an old Tanker Truck. J.A was poking a mound of dirt with a long stick. Out comes a couple of Yellow Jackets. "Just sit still, Harold. They will not bother you." When they started buzzing around my head, I took off running up the road. The Yellow Jackets started stinging. J.A. is running beside me beating the bees off with his baseball hat. "I told you to sit still." To my knowledge J.A. did not get stung. I got to the house back door. Covered with bee stings. Mama was not happy. We were close to J.A. and his sister Leanna. At this time in our lives his family rented a place at Hinson's Lunch. They moved later to the house over by the Richmond County Fair Grounds. We would all meet at his house. J.A. had found a hole in the wire fencing that we could crawl through. Get into the Fair Grounds without paying. This was some fun. He also found a way to pick up the bottom of that 'special' tent. The tent we were not old enough to go in. The Hoche Coche Girly Show. Never get caught, was the key. The Deputy Sheriff Mr. B. was always busy keeping the peace inside the tent. Getting a 'eye full.'

J.A. was our Hero. A big brother.

Bell Ville Lane
Hurricane Hazel

We have moved to a small house just off Main Street, connecting to Hamilton Boulevard. The street named for the Belle Ville Mansion containing a large tract of farmland, located on a dirt road off Hamilton Boulevard.

The Mundie family had lived in this house before moving to Indian Field. Parents and four brothers Billy, Michael, Dennis, and Ronald. Billy was one of brother Sammy's pallbearers. It is a new beginning for us; Mama, Harvey Lee, me. Our mother was a strong person determined to provide us with the best she could in our lives. Often told us, "It is only us now." We had not seen our father in a long time. I do not remember thinking about him, only our mother.

This is the awakening of my young life at 11 1/2 years. Pictures show the change from a sad boy to a smiling one. My mind now remembering some things. The house was small but had real ceilings in every room. Bedroom. Kitchen. Living room. Bathroom. Small porch on the front and back. Front and back yards. Room to play. Grass to cut. We never had grass to cut. Our bed is that folding cot. We slept - Harvey Lee facing one direction - me the other, with feet in the face. We are getting taller. To stop us

Hinson Twins

from fighting Mama provided us a blanket to wrap into. We did not like to touch each other. George and Zoa C. lived in a house behind us. No bathroom existed in that house. The outhouse was to the side just before Mrs. H's Chicken Coup.

Our fourth grade teacher was Mrs. Sanders. In that grade we were taught the Alphabet. Not a good time for me (undiagnosed Dyslexia). Still remember the letters on the wall above the blackboard. I was having a lot of problems. "Read to the class, Harold." Panic. I could not do it. Felt shamed, scared, and stupid all the time. One day Mrs. Sanders noticed that my shoes were untied. "Harold, come up here to my desk and tie your shoes." I went to her, but could not tie my shoes. Started crying. "You go home. Do not come back to school until you can tie your shoes." I walked home alone crying. [Little Man in Head: *"Going to be okay, Harold."*] Some things about yesterday's not forgotten. Harvey Lee spent time that night teaching me how to tie my shoes. Do not remember if our mother knew anything about this.

"I am going to cross this bridge. No matter what you say." The Tappahannock Town Deputy is closing the bridge to traffic linking the Northern Neck with the Middle Peninsula, connecting Essex and Richmond Counties, across the Rappahannock River.

**Downing Bridge, 1927
Richmond County**

'Hazel' has the Northern Neck in its 'eye.' The three of us are stopped in traffic on the Tappahannock side of the Downing Draw Bridge. Home is just seven miles away. To get there, need to cross the raging Rappahannock River. Mama is determined to get to Warsaw. Tells the Officer so. The 'Rapp' is high, with wind-driven waves, crashing over the top decking of the bridge. The 1950 Plymouth is pointed to the other side. Down the middle now.

Mama praying her heart out. Water begins to enter under the doors, soaking the vehicle floors. She drives on. No way to turn back now. Only one mile across to Richmond County. All the wrong things that could have happened that day did not. Prayer works.

For many years we had nightmares. We did not share this fact until later in life. Water all around us; entering the floor of that Plymouth. Wind; lighting and thunder. Did not know how to swim. Mama did not want us around water. Here we are. Never had swimming lessons

The Hurricane Eye came right through the heart of Warsaw. Lots of damage. The wind and rain were relentless. It passed. Remember that piece of wood sticking into the tree, right through the bark. That little house held up. Hurricane Hazel became the benchmark storm for the Northern Neck. Tide Levels never seen since 1933. It wiped out most of the remaining old steamboat landing structures still existing on the Rappahannock River. A lot of shorelines were redefined. Old cottages destroyed or in need to rebuild. The Microwave Tower at Tidewater Telephone came down. It went across Mr. B. Willard's brand new 1954 Chevy Sedan.

Christmas 1955 was the best that we ever remember. Along with Mama's annual Book of Life Savers was new bicycles. Timex watches. It was a warm Christmas day. B. Davis rode his bicycle to our house. We set out for Farmers Fork Road. Harvey Lee raced to the bottom of the hill, where the creek runs under the road. Makes a left turn, stops in middle of road. Bam. I T- Boned Harvey Lee, went airborne; landed on the Tar Road. Skinned up. Hurt. Pissed. Mad. "Why did you run into me?"

Christmas 1955

"Why did you turn in front of me?" I walked my bicycle back to Belle Ville Lane. Mama was pissed. Bent front wheel. Picked up enough bottles to purchase another wheel. Took a while.

We joined the Boy Scouts of America with our town friends. The Scouts met at the Old Richmond County Jail Building, still had the Jail Cell on the second floor. Who was the Scout Master? The night that one of the older scouts, think it was J. Tayloe, closed the cell door. Locked us in and left the building. The Scout Master returned sometime later. Unlocked the cell door. Boy Scouts did not meet at the Old Jail House again. Next meeting was in the basement at Warsaw Baptist Church Nursery. I was made the Senior Patrol Leader of Troop 203. At a meeting one evening, one of the boys would not pay attention when asked. The Scout Leader had left, putting me in charge. Before I knew what was about to happen, I picked up a wooden alphabet block off the floor. Threw a perfect 'fast ball.' Hit the boy just above his eye. He soon developed a big 'bump' on his forehead. I dismissed the troops. Walked the boy home. His mother answered the door. I told her what happened and how sorry I was. "No worry, Harold. He should have listened to you." 'Scouts Honor' lesson learned that night.

Bladen Hall
Third Great Grandfather

Grave Site. Our 3rd Great Grandfather Bladen Hall,[4] buried at St. Johns Cemetery, having not been allowed at Cobham Park Baptist

---

[4] See Hinson Genealogy, Appendix D. *Northern Neck of Virginia Historical Magazine*, December 1992, "Cobham Park, Kent, England and Richmond County, Virginia," Russell G. Brown, Page 4820. *Richmond County, Virginia 1776-1976*, Chapter VI, "Religion in Richmond County," Page 214, John C. Perry.

Church, was expelled from the Church, not allowed to be buried with the family. There are a lot of tales about Bladen Hall. The man liked to fight. One story we heard was how he would shave off all his hair. Smear his body with pig grease, show up on Court Day in Warsaw. Start or get in a fight. No one could hold on to him. Marking Bladen Hall's resting place is a Civil War Stone. Also, a Civil War Stone marks our 3rd Great Uncle Henry Fones' resting place in the Cobham Park Cemetery. 'Up on that Hill.'

The Southern States Store was on St. Johns Street separated by an alley to the Hinson's Lunch Building. The older guys, Billy M. and J.A. C., introduced us to the fun of sneaking into the back room, where the feed bags were stacked. We had a game chasing each other over the top of those bags full of grain, stacked up close to the ceiling. Sometimes a bag would fall to the floor. Burst open. The game changed to hiding, when we heard Mr. V. coming. "I told you boys not to come in here again." Hiding under the empty bag stack was not a good idea. My V. had heavy boots. It hurt when he kicked the stack. 'Run' out of the warehouse and up the street we would go. We were there on other days. Innocent fun, at least that is the way we looked at it. Mr. V. did not see it that way.

Mr. V. would check the chicken eggs under a lamp. He allowed us to watch. "If you agree not to run over the feed bags again."

"What are you looking for, Mr. V?"

"Making sure that the egg is good."

"What is a bad egg?"

"That would be when it has an eye ball."

"What?"

"Sometimes a whole chick will be in there."

"How does that happen?"

"Well boys…that happens when the roster gets to the hen."

Sex Education lesson. We did not even know what Mr. V. was talking about. We think Mr. V. liked us hanging around keeping him company. We stopped running on the feed bags. High School, we played baseball against his son. We attended different high schools together. Warsaw High School and Farnham High School. Just fourteen miles apart.

The day we got back at Mr. Leftwitch. He always shouted at us. "Get off the property." The lot behind the store where we pitched a baseball to each other. We never broke anything. Just playing catch. We found a crate of rotten eggs behind the Southern States Store. Put the crate in our wagon and pulled it to the parking lot. It was a Sunday. Warsaw is shut down on Sundays and after Noon on Wednesday's. One by one. We threw the rotten eggs on the building and into the air compressor. As far as we know, no one found out who did it. Now you all know. We stayed out of the store parking lot after that. Smell was bad from the sidewalk.

We were very close. In our young days we were seldom if ever seen apart. Most people called us 'Harvey/Harold.' Just to get it right. We were 'split from the same egg. Look alike. Talk alike. Walk alike. Do not think alike. Harvey Lee would say. "Harold; you think from a different side of the brain than me. You were always the one that fixed the bicycle when the chain came off." Seems that I am more like our father. Thing we always agreed on, how to play baseball, and look out for each other. If one of us are involved in a disagreement with some kid. That person had to deal with both of us. If we would disagree with each other. Turned into a wrestling match. We did not hit each other. Our mother would come home from work, the first words out of her mouth was. "What have you two tore up today?" We knew it was coming. We tried to fix whatever we broke, straighten up the house before she got home.

Harvey Lee did not like egg yolks. I did. Mama would fry two eggs over hard. Cut out the yolks for me. Other thing that Harvey Lee liked was Shredded Wheat with milk. Not for me. Was the equivalent of eating a bowl of hay. Good old Corn Flakes and/or Cheerios with milk. We drank a lot of milk. A half-gallon lasted about two days. Mama purchased a Spanish Bar Cake from the A&P every week. Started getting gallons of whole milk. The cake would be gone in three days. Mama would get us another one. Loved a slice with a glass of cold milk. I did not like the icing. Harvey Lee did.

We were always competitive. Everything we did became "who can do it better?" Many times would turn into a disagreement, followed by a wrestling match, followed by something getting broke in Mama's house. Harvey Lee was always right. If he thinks it is so. It is. Do not try to tell him otherwise. Sometimes one of us would lose our temper. Then it really gets rough. Broken skin. Cut lip. Bloody nose. Black eye. Just ask some of the boys we grew up with. These things could not be hidden from Mama. We were "Her Boys" as she always said. One day we decided to wash Mama's car. The old house on Belle Ville did not have an outdoor water connection for a hose. "I can do it, Harv." I tried to connect the hose on the kitchen sink facet. Turned on the water, started spraying all over the Kitchen. Mama kept the pop-up toaster plugged in the wall. I grasped it to get out of the water. Started getting electrocuted. Harvey Lee knocked me into the floor. The toaster came unplugged from the wall socket. We never told Mama what happened, just mopped up water in the kitchen and out of the toaster.

I was the twin always into Sports Cars. Pinned on our bedroom wall was a Renault Carville picture I found in a magazine. The Playboy. The Carville was a convertible two-seater from France. Nothing like it was manufactured in the United States. "I will have a sports car one day." Do not remember any other kids that we grew up with liking sports cars.

We wandered all over the place. One day we were walking on the dirt road leading to Bell Ville Manson. There was a swamp wetland on the side of the road where we found tadpoles, frogs, minnows, and other critters. One day there was this big turtle. Held a stick at its head, that turtle closed on it and would not let go. Hanging onto the stick, Harvey Lee on one side and me on the other. We picked the turtle up and tried to put it into Red Rider wagon with us most everywhere we went. It was wider than the wagon. We decide to go home with the turtle hanging over the sides. On the way home we cut over to St. John's Street.

Wanted to show off the turtle to our buddy W. Haynie. He was not at his grandmother Mrs. Barracks house. So, we head up St. John's Street and as we pass R. Sanders house, he came out of the porch swing and off the porch. "What you boys got there is a Snapping Turtle. Good thing you put a stick in his mouth. If that turtle grabs a finger, it will not let go until it thunders. You better leave him with me. I will take care of him for you before you get hurt."

Two days later we were on the way home after going on a bottle pick-up trip. We took a short cut through the back yards of houses on St. John's Street. Found the turtle shell laying in Mr. Sanders back yard against the chain link fence to the Northern Neck Electric REA pole yard.

We looked at the house; he was sitting on his back porch. "See you boys found that turtle. I got rid of it before it hurts somebody. Come on in the porch. Shucking some Oysters." We had to see how that was done. He is sitting on a five-gallon bucket with a bowl between his legs. Oyster knife in one hand. Every other oyster he shucked - he ate, right out of the shell, sucking the oyster down with the juices. "Want to try one?" I raised my arm. Mr. Sanders pries/works the oyster knife into the oyster shell edge until it enters inside. Then he works the oyster knife inside the top half until the oyster comes loose. He pries off the top half shell of the oyster, drops shell half in the basket. He slides the oyster knife under the bottom shell. "Have to cut away the oyster muscle while keeping all the juices in the shell." He hands me the raw oyster. "Just tip your head back and let it all slide into your mouth." I did. "Chew it up son." I chewed once. Gagged, but did not puke. Spit the oyster out. [Little Man in Head: "A*t least you tried."*] We head to the sidewalk pulling the red wagon and on up St. John's Street to Ike Halls Store, and cash in the bottles. Need some candy to get that taste out of my mouth.

Almost every day during the Summer we would be gathered with the other Town kids playing a game of baseball. B. Gould's dad, a retired Navy Officer, had a Sandwich Shop located inside R. Bryant's Citgo Service Station. Bobby at the grill counter where his dad would serve him a hamburger like he wanted it. Raw. We sat and watched him eat. Mr. Gould gave Bobby the money every week to buy a new baseball at the Carlins Western Auto Store, located on the corner, where the blinking yellow caution light was hanging. He was not the best baseball player, but he was the one with the baseball. Always included. We found a vacant lot to play the game and split up into teams. M. Packett's Aunt and Uncle Rice's home was just across Route 3 from Warsaw Baptist Church. There was a big vacant lot there. One day I hit a long fly ball that kept going. Went through the side porch glass door of the Rice home. Marion retrieved the ball for us.

We were also paper delivery boys for the Richmond Times Dispatch, the morning issue. Our buddy Barty had the Richmond News Leader Evening Paper. Most customers wanted their paper early in the morning to read with breakfast. Sundays were the worst day. It was not possible to carry all the papers at once. Bicycle would not hold them all. Harvey had one side of Warsaw and I the other. There were some customers that wanted 'special delivery.' "Please put the paper inside of the Storm Door." Weekdays this was not a problem. On Sunday with a basket full of papers, created a problem with the bicycle staying up on the kick stand. Sundays. Not the favorite morning for paper boys, but we tried to accommodate. Bicycle flops over, papers go flying. Rainey/snowy days were also not any fun. Each paper had to be rolled, put in a plastic bag. Took up even more space. Dreaded Paper Collection days. The customer would remind me that the paper was not in the place they wanted it, or no one would answer the door. Had to make more than one trip to collect. No tip. Was not enough money being a paper boy for me. Tips

Mama's Little Darlings

was what made the job worthwhile. Just for meanness I never put the paper where the 'non-tipper' wanted it. Not worth the Nickel. Started looking for another job.

Mama entered us into Talent Contests, dressed up like Cowboys. Aunt Dorothy Lee [Sauce] taught us a song. "The Beans and the Bacon." We must have been a couple of cute guys. Our cousin G. Sanders also sang in those talent contests. We never sang together. Gentry or us would win first place. Have never seen pictures of us on the stage. At the last school assembly before graduation, our classmates requested if we would sing that song. "The Beans and the Bacon." One more time?

Warfield Korea

Warfield And Baseball

Mama began dating this guy Edward Warfield Sirles. Warfield was a clean-cut military-looking man. Always had a crew cut. No facial hair. Smoked a pipe. This was after the Korean War.

After graduation from Warsaw High School in June 1942, he entered the United States Army. It was World War II. After the War ended, Warfield joined the Reserves, when told that he would not be called back. He was called back for the Korean War. The man we called "Little Sarge." Never to his face. He did not talk much; but when he did, you listened. He told us he should have stayed another ten years and retired. Warfield was in the Army during two Wars, a total of ten years. The Korea War changed his life. Warfield came home and continued his career with the National Biscuit Company.

We always had plenty of cookies. Oreos. Nutter Butter. Ginger Snaps. Chocolate Chip. Mac-a-Roons were our favorites. Warfield had a sales meeting in Richmond every month. There he would pick up a case of samples. "What do you boys want me to get this time?" Still remember those Fruit Cakes during the holiday season. The nice metal cans cakes came in. Warfield would put a cut apple into the center hole of the cake. Said that it kept the cake from drying out. [Little Man in Head: *"Did cake ever last that long?"*] Growing up with Warfield around was interesting. He was there most of the time and we looked forward to seeing him. Warfield rented the lower level of a house next to the Tidewater Telephone Company. There was a large screen porch where he kept a "Flying Squirrel." Warfield was always playing jokes on us. I can see him laughing. The time a bowl of Chocolate Covered Raisins appeared on the coffee table. "You boys eat all you want." In a short time, the bowl was empty. "How did you like those

Chocolate Covered Ants?" The time at the dinner table when Harvey Lee sees the fly in an ice cube of his glass of Ice Tea. Was fake of course. Harvey Lee pukes. When Warfield would remind us how much Milk cost. We drank a quart each day. Then one night at the dinner table. "How does that Milk taste?" [Little Man in Head: *"What has he done?"*] Next day we started looking through the cabinet under the sink. Found it. A Powdered Milk Box inscribed "Good as real milk." Directions: Just add water. Warfield got us again. We had discussed – "did not want to try Powdered Milk." Must give him credit for the effort. Warfield was mixing the powdered milk with half whole milk. Do not know when he started doing this, but the Powered Milk Box we found was almost empty. Warfield always wanted to know; "Is the Peanut Butter better on the bottom of the jar?" Someone was digging to the bottom. We ate a lot of Peanut Butter and Jelly Sandwiches. Warfield made "his" Home-Made Fudge. Think the recipe was on the package. Semi-Sweet Chocolate and a Jar of Marsh Mellow Sauce. Does not matter. Fudge with Marsh Mellow and English Walnuts. "Boys, do not eat all of it at once." Warfield liked for the Fudge to "age." Get crumbly on the edges. Not a chance of that happening around us. We think that he always made two batches. Hid one stored in a Fruit Cake Tin. Warfield would on occasion cook dinner for us when mama was working. One of his favorite meals was Mashed Black Eye Peas in a cast iron pan. He cooked down Diced Tomatoes into a Puree. Served the Black Eye Peas with the Tomatoes on top. Do not knock it. It was simple and good. Nabisco Ginger Snaps with Peanut Butter. Nabisco Gram Crackers with Peanut Butter. We would have never thought of these combos. Warfield did. Three pound and Five pound. The cakes were always good. We looked forward to the Cake Season.

This man, Warfield, became more of a father to us, than the one who lived just one street over.

July 4, 1953. Warfield gave us Stan Musial Baseball gloves on our 11th birthday. The glove only had three fingers and a thumb. Two middle fingers went into the center. This was our first glove. Warfield taught us how to play baseball. He was a star athlete in Baseball and Football when attending Warsaw High School. A catcher and halfback. He came by one day with a catchers mitt. The old style with only a hole the size of a baseball in the center and a lot of padding around that. When we started playing organized baseball, Warfield wanted me to be the pitcher and Harvey Lee to be the catcher. Harvey Lee did not agree to that at all.

WNNT Radio Station was built on the outskirts of Warsaw. That brought D. Loudy and his wife Mildred to Warsaw. They came from up north Illinois, where they had Little League. Had to be sanctioned to be called a Little League Team. In

Dean & Mildred Loudy
Pee Wee Team Organizers

Harvey and Harold Hinson
Pee Wee Baseball Twins

1954 Mr. Loudy, with other Northern Neck towns, started a "Pee Wee" league for 12-14-age boys. One day Dean came by the house to ask our mother if he could take us to the ballfield to test our skills. Who knew. We were natural baseball players. These two skinny kids made the team. The Warsaw Wildcats.[5]

Baseball became the gel that glued our twin lives forever. We had natural talents untapped until Warfield came into our lives. Warfield honed our skills:

---

[5] *Close Ties,* Vol. VI, Richmond County Intermediate School, A Whole New Ball Game, Midgets in Warsaw?

hitting; bunting; throwing; running the bases; sliding into bases; situation plays. Taught me a knuckle curve ball. Harvey in the outfield. Me a pitcher. The first year our team won all the games. We were two of the youngest boys on the team. Our mother never attended a single ballgame. "I do not like to see you sitting on the bench."

A Pony league team from Maryland was brought to Warsaw. The Warsaw Wildcats Team played in Tennis shoes. Maryland team showed up in metal spikes. This game was to go on. The ballpark was packed with 500-plus baseball fans. Mr. S. [Seward's Hardware] had the team from Maryland taken to his store where they fitted each player with tennis shoes. The game went on. Warsaw won that game. At season's end the town of Warsaw gave a big celebration event for the team. Each player was given a "Gold" Baseball. The year 1954. Sometimes we played baseball against another two kids. B. Bradshaw [LH] and A. Edwards most times playing at the High School ball field. Each team had a pitcher and a player in the field. The ball had to be hit only to one field. Left or right fields were determined by the split down the middle of the pitcher's mound. A left-handed batter had to hit to right field. We were around thirteen. A disagreement started over a ball that was not hit in the field it should have been. Things got heated, when Abe takes a wooden bat and crushes my left leg. I went to the ground in agonizing pain. A big bulge appeared below my left knee. Could not stand up. If I got to my feet, I fell. Could not walk. They took off to their homes on Hamilton Boulevard. Harvey Lee helped me get home. It took weeks to walk again. The country doctor Mr. Pearson said that the kneecap was not broken. The hit was below the knee cap in the 'Enos Slaughter' area. "Harold will be okay in a couple of weeks." Always had trouble with that bulge.

St. John's Street

We are living in the first rental house with a bedroom for Mama and one for us. A bathroom, back yard to play ball, screen front porch for sitting. The house is one of four in a row, three doors from Hinson's Lunch. The back yard was small. Bordered with the ten-foot chain link fence with barbed wire along the top, enclosing the pole yard for Rural Electric. We passed this house many times when living on Bell Ville. We practiced hitting in this confined space. One pitching to the other. The small space taught us how to hit the ball sharply on a line drive; always minding to keep the ball from going into the "pole yard." Sometimes it did. Many times, then not. Ended up in an argument, as to who was going to get the ball. "You did not pitch it right."

"You go get it."

"I had to get it last time." Sometimes the ball would stay where it landed. Neither one giving in. We are happy. *Life was good.*

Harvey and Harold with Mama

St. John's Street – 1950s and 1960s
(Photo, Richmond County Museum)

Daddy is back at Hinson's Lunch with his new family. Our house three doors from the Lunch Room. Sometimes that seems like a mile. He does not pay much attention to us, even when we walk past the Lunch Room. He would be standing, leaning in the doorway in his white shirt. Cuffs always rolled up. Daddy would not issue a sound. Neither did we. Do not to this day know why it was that way. Could have to do with our mother always bad mouthing him. What we would have given for a hug. We just continued up to E.Y. Brooks store on the corner, turned left, crossed Main Street, headed to the Western Auto Store to get more BBs. Sometimes we continued in Clemens Drug Store next door to the Western Auto. Read the Magazines. At least until you got caught by A. Angolia. She is family and mother to our cousins Jimmy, Brenda and Wayne. Brenda started the First Grade with us. On the way back home, we would stop at Syd's Soda Shop. The time that Brenda, Barbara Jean and the sisters Patsy and Nancy A. were throwing what we thought to be water balloons from an upper window in the home. Found out it was Mr. A's condoms.

We had BB Gun battles. Made forts out of refrigerator cardboard boxes found behind E.Y. Brooks store. The agreement was not to shoot above the waist. If you stayed behind the box, you did not get hit very hard. We had Red Ryder BB Guns, not powerful enough to shoot through the thick cardboard. But W. Sanders came with a Pump BB Gun. Lots more power. His BB shots did go through the cardboard. Tried not to get in a battle with him.

H. Barnes worked for the J. E. Wilson International Tractor Store located between the Citgo Service Station and Warsaw Baptist Church. On the back of the property were open front sheds where the tractors and farm equipment were stored. "Hey boys, I will provide you all the BB's you need. Just want you to kill all those English Sparrows in the sheds. Just do not hit any of the tractors and equipment. I am getting sick and tired of washing the *bird shit* off." We would spend the day with one on each end of the sheds, picking off the Sparrows in the rafters. We got very good, after learning how to adjust the shot for the drop of the BB. Many days we would have a tomato basket almost full of Sparrows. Happy gave us the money to keep going back to the Western Auto Store for more Daisy Copper BB's. Five cents a tube. On a day I went to catch up with Will. "Will is over across the field, Harold." I crossed the field and found him. He had been practicing 'quick draw' with his Ruger .22 Revolver, from a holster strapped to his right leg. Fuller P. had taught him how to do it. "I shot myself in the leg. The gun went off before I drew it." Will weighted about 170 lbs. Me a skinny 125 lbs. He wrapped his arms around my neck. I dragged him across the cut-over corn field back to his home. Mr. and Mrs. Sanders stopped at our house on the way back home from the hospital. "Will is going to be okay. He will not be doing 'fast draw' again." Wonder if his parents knew about the times Will and we shot an arrow straight up overhead, wondering where that arrow was going to come down. We liked going over to Will's house to shoot his Winchester Model 59 Pump .22 Rifle. The boy had a lot of toys.

The Cat Point Creek Bridge wooden span was gone, taken out by Hurricane Hazel. The new bridge span not built yet. We had to sneak out to go fishing; Mama forbade us to be around water. Best not letting our mother know what we are doing. Rode our bicycles through town toward the school buildings, took a left on Farmers Fork Road behind the Grayhound Bus Station, past our third-grade teacher Ms. Crabbe's home, seventh grade teacher Ms. Tayloe's home, then a left at Mr. Forrester's house. At the next intersection, Newland Road, take a left, further down a distance, take a right on Naylor's Beach Road. This road leads to Cat Point Creek. Taking the back roads was the safest way, keeping us off Rt. 360. Our fishing poles tied across the handle bars and a tackle box lashed to the seat. We are going fishing. A crabber had a soft crab shedding operation on the side of the road at the Creek, just before the bridge, now shut down to traffic. The crabber asks a dime for one peeler. Left our bicycles on the roadside and went out on the bridge to where the center span used to be. This gaping space to other bridge side, leading to Naylors Beach. Cut the peeler up and baited our hooks like Warfield had shown us. Lots of Catfish hung around the deep channel passing in this area, ambushing the minnows as they pass the bridge pilings. Was scary looking over the span edge to the fast-running water below, trying to keep the baited hook close to the piling. We caught many Catfish and Stiff Back Perch. Put the catch on a fish cord. We attached one end of the cord to the bridge railing. Threw the fish back into the water to stay fresh. Constantly watching the time, which seems to always fly when fishing. Need to be back at St. John's Street before Mama calls or comes walking down the sidewalk. Gave the fish to the crabber when we left for home. Never brought the fish home. Was never about the fish, just fond memories fishing.

Finally started not dressing alike our freshman year at Warsaw High School. I had to wear whatever Harvey Lee or Mama chose for years. It was not worth the argument. Mama went to Richmond once a year to buy school clothes. She always parked in the Rayless lot. Walked through the Rayless Store and onto Broad Street. Thalhimer's was right across Broad Street from Rayless. Miller & Rhoads was on the opposite corner of Broad. The basement is where Mama took us. That was what Mama could afford. We did not know any difference. We were well dressed for school and church.

Each Summer up to high school and summer jobs, we spent two weeks in Marion, Virginia, with Mama's youngest sister Dorothy Lee and Uncle B. They were young with no kids yet. Fondly remember those days. The drive-in movie nights, sitting in the back of the pickup truck. All the Pop Corn – Candy. That Orange Push-Up Ice Cream. On the trip back to the Hollow Uncle B letting each one take turns to drive the pickup sitting on his lap. We had control of the steering wheel and gear shift. Uncle B pushing the pedals. The night Harvey Lee almost drives us off the hillside. Who can forget the times that Uncle B and his brother Howard would grab us – fold our arm and rub it hard – twisting all the

Summer Mountain Time with Family
Grand Dad Blevins; Uncle Pat; Aunt Rose; Darrell;
Uncle B; Aunt Sauce; Barbara Lynn; Warfield; Mama;
Twins

hair into a ball. And Uncle B if we would be walking past a wire fence, he would grab one of us by the arm, then grab the electric fence wire. Stayed away from him around wire fences after that. Those were some wonderful times in Harvey Lee and Harold's life.

Traveling on St. John's Street from Main Street, our house was on the left next to the Barrack house. Just before the road beside the REA building. On the right side of St. John's Street were fields. Mrs. Barrack, if seeing us playing in our backyard, would come out of her kitchen to her back stoop. Call us over, holding a large cast iron pan. In the pan was what she called "Hoe Cake."[6] She would break the cake and give each one a half. Always wondered what that was. Remember she raised Genies in her back yard. Strange looking bird, shape, and colors.

Harvey Lee had to have his Tonsils out. Before I knew it, Mama had decided. "Doctor, might as well get both of them at the same time." By both, she meant me. Nothing was wrong with my Tonsils. Mama was probably thinking of the time we would need to heal. She would know where we both were. That first swallow. More Ice Cream, please. Uncle Tommy Foti came to stay with us as we recouped. The Rice Tommy cooked for us. Was like a Rice Soup with lots of Butter. Mama always served any vegetable dish without the juice. For our birthday he brought us a Six Transistor Radio, Brand Name Petite, in a leather case. Went to sleep many nights listening to music with the radio. NY radio station WKBW. WLEE in Richmond. Had to be after sunset when WNNT went off the air to receive those signals. Amazing how that happened as soon as WNNT went off the air.

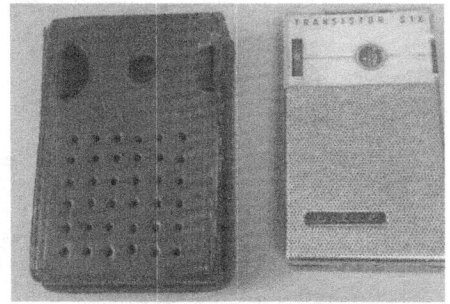

Six Transistor Radio

---

[6]Journal and Letters of Philip Vickers Fithian 1773 – 1774; A Plantation Tudor; page 74. Hoe Cake, so called because baked on a Hoe before the fire

Growing Up Grounded

There was not a lot of money in our little family. Mother often said, "It is us three and we need to look out for each other." Do not remember asking for things or wondering why our other friends had more than we did. Never came to mind that they were living in homes their parents owned, or we lived in rentals. Our Italian Mother worked every day to provide for us. She made simple dinners after a long day. Meals we enjoyed. Baked Can Biscuits, Cube Steak with Onions, Milk Gravy, Mashed Potatoes and Peas. Beef Liver was cooked same way. Sometimes other meats when she was rushed. Fried Boloney. Fried Spam. Homemade "Spigets," mother's word, she often fixed on a Sunday. Italian sauce started in the morning in a large covered pot. She made fresh meat balls using a combo of ground Pork, Italian Sausage and Ground Beef, Eggs, Bread Crumbs, Italian Seasoning. Cooked in the large cast iron pan until brown. Large pot of Pasta. Combined Meatballs and Pasta, let that marinate a while. Then Mama's Salmon Cakes. Open the can, dump into a large bowl. Mix with one egg and chopped onions. She did not take the time to remove the skin and bones. We ate it while picking out the bones and other parts trying to keep her from seeing us. The day walking home down St. John's Street. "What is that smell?" We were three doors from our house. Already could smell it. Chicklings. At the small dinner table with four chairs, under the open kitchen window. Warfield keeps telling us. "I cleaned them good. You must try it. They will melt in your mouth." Melt was not the right word. Not even close. I found the smallest piece on plate. Popped it in my mouth. Started chewing. The more I chewed, the larger the small piece got. I ran to the garbage can. Spit it out before I started puking. Warfield is smiling the whole time. He had also pulled one of his jokes on Mama.

A whole kernel of corn came out of a Chickling on her plate. Harvey Lee, not participating in the meal, almost lost it at the table.

The time with classmates sitting together at lunch in the Warsaw High School Cafeteria. Boys and Girls were not allowed to sit together. Wonder why. Fresh Collard Greens was served that day. Harvey Lee was enjoying his greens when he bit on something crunchy. Split out half a Bumble Bee.

Those Fourth of July Family Outings to Westmoreland State Park. The boys and men would go early with Uncle Bob in his Ford pickup truck. Hauling galvanized tubs filled with drinks and ice. Some of the food. Our early purpose was to pick out the spot and move picnic tables for the family. Those times floating in the Potomac all day. Meeting girls from other places. Washington DC, Maryland, Richmond. These girls were a lot more grown up than we were. Afterwards - having to stay in bed for a week, under Doctor's orders. Really bad sunburns. The family from the mountains would come for the Fourth. We did not get to see them often enough. Brother Sammy would have loved these times.

The memories of our fishing trips linger today. Warfield chartered a fishing boat Captain to carry us out of Saluda, Virginia, on a Chesapeake Deadrise in the Fall, before we started a new school year. Warfield purchased at Seward's Hardware in Warsaw for us, short Metal Rods (two feet long) with Ocean Pacific Bait Cast reels. Warfield taught us how to fish. "Release the Clicker - free the Bail. Keep your thumb on the reel. When you feel the sinker hit the bottom, stop the reel rotation, set the Clicker 'on.' If you do not do that you will get a 'rat's nest' back lash." Lot of time not fishing to straighten a back lash out. Before we met the Captain at the Deadrise - Warfield would stop at the Hardware Store in Saluda. Purchase a 40-gallon Galvanized Trash Can with lid and bagged ice. That was our "fish cooler.: Set the can in the Deadrise and iced it down. Do not remember if we kept count of how many were caught. Warfield's brother Bill and wife would also go with us. There was always a lot to eat and drink. What is it about being on Salt Water and not getting enough to eat? We cleaned a lot of fish when we got back to shore. Gave fish to our neighbors in the Town of Warsaw. Mama was a fisher woman. We were amazed that she always caught the Flounder. Many years later I learned the method how to catch a Flounder. When you feel the 'bite – nibble' – Do not set the hook too soon. Let the Flounder take the bait into its mouth. Chew a while. Now, set the hook. Mama was doing it the right way, even if she did not know it. When she pulled up on the rod the Flounder was hooked.

We found summer jobs when we were fourteen. "Go-For" on bread trucks. The day started before sunrise. Took about an hour to unload the Bakery trailer from Richmond. There were Restaurant Pies (no box) that were put in a pie rack. Plastic trays with bread; Hot Dog Buns; Hamburger Rolls; Dinner Rolls. Special Sesame Seeded Hamburger Rolls only for Little Reno Casino. The day ended back in Warsaw around 4:30 p.m. Harvey worked for Bond Bread and me for Mother Herbert's Bread. The route was the same for both companies. Service Hinson's Super Market; A&P; Ike Hall's; B&B Lunch; Hinson's Lunch in Warsaw. Head up Rt. 3 hitting each country store on the way to Montross. Turn off Rt. 3 at Oak Grove and on to Colonial Beach. Summertime, lots of sites for these young eyes, all the girls in the bikinis. [Little Man in Head: "*Life is good, Harold.*"]

B. Dawson gave me instructions on what to do, one that Harold never forgot. After loading the Bread Truck, we went directly to the Super Markets, always the first stop in the morning. Picked up all the bread products delivered the day before. "Put that in a special location on the truck." Bring in new product.

The day-old bread we picked up was left at every small mom & pop store. Sometimes sold at houses as we came back to Warsaw. One day Harold dropped an Apple Pie. "Wait Harold." Billy D. took a piece of cardboard and slid it carefully under the upside-down pie. Dusted the crust off. Blew on the pie. Later Billy sold the pie to a woman waiting in her yard for the bread truck to come. "$0.50, just a few cracks in the crust." The Bread Truck was empty when we got back to Warsaw.

Remember the day we were called into the Principal's Office. Deputy B. was there. "Where were you last night?"

"At home Mr. B."

"Let me see the bottom of your shoes." Our shoes had Ripple Rubber Soles.

"Your Mother works at night. You sure that you boys did not go out last night?"

"No sir, we were at home all night, just as our mother told us to be." Found out later that someone had broken into Warsaw High School. They caught him. The High School boy also had Ripple Sole shoes. Deputy B. was so sure that we had done it. Never did care for him after that. Warsaw had its share of characters.

There are teachers you always will remember. Mrs. Odessa S. was one of them. She was very strict. Catch you not paying attention in class-you were going to get a Black Board Eraser on your head. Odessa had quite the arm. Seldom missed. When she wanted to make more of a statement, she threw a piece of Chalk. That really hurt. Harvey Lee was a better student than me. Later in life I learned what my problem was. Undiagnosed Dyslexia. Was passed along with Harvey; no one tried to help. Just making the grades to pass each year. Had a real hard time Reading. Math, Spelling bad. If you cannot spell a word you are going to have a hard time finding it in a dictionary. Always adding a letter in the wrong place/not the right letter/not enough letters/not the right order. Most of the time spelling what looks like the word. Only to find. How did you think that was right? Little was known in the small school system we grew up in. Least no one seemed to care. [Little Man in Head: *"Not your fault."*]

We turned fifteen in July, 1957. Legal age for getting a driver's license. Months leading up to this day constantly reminding Mama. She would not hear of it. "No."

"Why?"

"Because I said so." One morning Aunt Dollie (Little Roster) decided that she was going to take us for the license in her 1955 Chevy.

Came by the house and picked us up. Mama was at work. We took the written and driving test. Passed. Aunt Dollie was asked to sign and then told she could not. "Get them to call their mother." I do not remember which of us called her. "We passed the Driver License Test this morning."

"You did what? I did not know you were taking the test. Who took you?"

"Aunt Dollie."

"Now we need a parent's signature."

"I am not signing it!"

After a pause. "I guess we need to call Daddy?"

"Put Dollie on the phone." The DMV was located where the Greyhound Bus Terminal was. Mama signed the papers required. Then explained what was going to be required for us to drive the 1955 Ford.

1955 Ford

One night Deputy B. was sleeping in his patrol car up on the "Knob." Could have been drunk. Some High Schoolers tied a rope to his axle. The other end of the rope tied to a galvanized washing tub, filled with rocks. It made quite a noise when Deputy B. went chasing after a speeding car that had just passed at the "Knob." Was not the Hinson Twins on that night speeding, but there was a night with Harold driving over sixty plus past the "Knob." At the bottom of the hill, left turn onto St. John's Street. Pull into the driveway. Rush into the house. Greet Mama and to bed. Moments later they hear Mama getting up to answer the front door knock. It was Deputy B. "Barbara, you tell them boys of yours if they do that again, they are going to be in big trouble." Must face Mama. "Get up, what did you do this time?" [Little Man in Head: *"Do not smile, Harold."*] We did not get the car again for a month. Kept it washed and waxed through. Mama only let us have the car once a month.

Warsaw "Knob" in the 1950s
(Photo, Richmond County Museum)

There was a place on the way to Montross where you could purchase Beer and Cigarettes without ID. It was on the side of Route 3 out there in the country. Nothing else in sight. Everybody knew where Sanford's Store was. Freddie B. would pick us up in his car on the corner of St. Johns Street by E.Y. Brooks Store. We would pool our money. Send Freddie in. Freddie was tall for his age with a deep voice. Harvey Lee and Harold started the first grade with him. We drove down all the back roads. Drinking two beers apiece, sharing the pack of smokes. Freddie dropped us off at St. John's Street. Mama was always awake, waiting for us to get home, checking the curfew time. "Let me smell your breath." Pow, Pow, slaps across the face. "Go to bed, I will deal with you two in the morning." Grounded again.

When we look back on those years, our mother kept us away from H.A. Hinson, our father. Do not know why, but she never had a good thing to say about him. For our sixteenth birthday Daddy gave us each Stevens Bolt Action 12 Gage Shotguns. Mama refused to let us to bring the guns into the house. Aunt Dollie intervened and our mother gave in. Fond memories when Daddy took us Dove Hunting down on the farm. He also carried us to the Local Trap Shoot. Remember the time while using Daddy's Winchester Auto we hit enough Clays for Daddy to be proud of us. "Those boys are pretty good, H.A." Seeing Daddy with that smile. Growing up at Cobham Park Baptist Church. The youth did not have much activity other than picnics. The ladies of St. John's Presbyterian Church held "sock hops" for the young people. They had a turntable playing 45s. Punch and cookies. These events were all teens had, except for school functions. The time I got grounded and did not get to go to the dance. We were required to be in the house fifteen minutes after school every day. "Answer the phone." Our mother got off work at 3:30 from Telephone Company and this was her way to keep us out of trouble. She did not want me seeing Byrd, who lived just up St. John's Street. One day not answering the phone. I sat on the front porch where I could hear the fun and music from St. John's Church.

We did not have pets. There was this stray Tabby cat that showed up at our house. "I do not want any pets in this house!"

"Why?"

"Because I said so." We would let the Tabby inside after mama went to bed. He slept with us. In the middle of the night we would hear, "Who let you in?" Tabby was in the front room next to Mama's bedroom. Pulling down on the venation blinds, asking to go out. Mama was hanging clothes in the back yard. Harvey Lee throws me the keys to the Ford. "Mama said we can take the car for a box of candy at Clements Drug Store…You drive!" We picked up Barty on the corner. He left his bike at EY's. We proceeded the long way on Farmers Fork Road…I wrecked Mama's car. When I phoned her from the house located on the curve, she dropped the handset. "I did not know you had taken the car!" I beat the hood instead of Harvey Lee!

Homework at the kitchen table in that small kitchen. The next room was where Mama and Warfield would be watching TV. We spent a lot of time sitting there listening to the TV. This was how it had to be.

Our Stepmother Evelyn was always good to us. Remembered us on our birthday and Christmas with presents. They will have three daughters, Linda, Sandra and Wanda. One of my favorite pictures is Wanda and Linda with Daddy's Gold Buick Limited, sitting in front of Hinson's Lunch. Must be a Sunday. The day I went with him to see Wanda at the Children's Hospital in Richmond, was the first time I saw Daddy break down crying. All our sisters are beautiful blond heads with blue eyes.

Linda and Wanda in Front of Hinson's Lunch

On Sunday's Daddy would take us all fishing on his deadrise. It was custom-built with a Chevy V8 under the motor box. Daddy kept it moored in Simonson. There was always plenty to eat and drink. Homemade sandwiches. Candy. Nabs. Potato Chips. Daddy knew how to fish the Morattico Oyster Bar and surrounding area. He always cut up the first Peeler Crabs for us. "Next time you do it, Son." The fish tackle was Bait Casting reels on six-foot medium rods. No need to cast, just open the bail on the reel and drop the weight and bait to the oyster bed bottom. Keep your thumb on the rotating reel to stop the rig when the sinker gets to the bottom. Forget, a backlash. First time Daddy would fix it. Next time, "You have to fix it." Being told once is enough.

One day Daddy took us with Cousin Everett (Uncle Garnett's son) fishing on the Morattico Bar. My fishing rig got hung on the oyster shell bottom. That happens a lot. Must be ready for it. I was not. Took the fishing rod right out of my hand. Daddy's fishing rod. He would not let up with his anger for losing his fishing rod. Cousin Everett. "Dam it H.A., I am getting tired of hearing your bitching. Give Harold a break." Everett jumps over the side of the deadrise and comes back to the surface holding the fishing rod. Was no way I could have done that. Everett grew up on Islington Farm right on the Rappahannock River. He had learned to swim. Bless our mother, she did not want us near the river.

One of our Birthdays, Uncle Tommy came with a two-foot wooden boat. The boat had an outboard motor that used two D-size batteries for power. We took the boat to the Revere's Pond to run it. I decided that the outboard needed more power to run faster. I took apart one of Mama's desk lamps. Unwired the electrical cord from the light socket. Wired the electrical cord to the battery terminals in the boat. Plugged the lamp cord into the wall receptacle. "Boom." As I remember this event, the motor did run faster, just before the whole thing caught fire. I am the twin with the "Left-Thinking Brain."

On the day December 1959 Mama asked us, "What do you think if I marry Warfield?"

We were seventeen. Harvey and Harold in unison, "What has taken you so long?" Warfield had been in our life since we were twelve years old. He was a father to us.

Mama and Warfield, Wedding Day

Warsaw High School Baseball

We grew up playing with the upper-class Warsaw High School Baseball team members. There was always a practice at the 'old Ball Park on any given day. We were always included. The older guys used us in the outfield to chase the balls. Throw the batted balls back. We did not look at it as being used. A chance to be included with the big boys like brothers Bobby, Chuck, Howard, JA, John, Jimmy, Junior, OMO. We were thrilled. Honing our fielding and throwing skills. We looked up to those guys. They were like big brothers.

When we were in the seventh and eighth Grades; the team asked Coach Seward if we could be the batboys? What an honor. Thrilling. Not allowed to travel with the team for out-of-town games, but were included whenever the team had practice. There are many good memories of those times. Many battings practice. Remember Coach Seward would tell J.A. not to "step in the bucket." J.A. on the next pitch would "step in the bucket" and hit the ball over the left field fence. Then look at Coach with that grin on his face. That Warsaw High School Baseball Team in 1956 went undefeated.

In the ninth grade we started playing on the Warsaw High School Baseball Team. Harvey was the Center Fielder and me one of the Pitchers. We did not get to start a game as Freshman. Juniors and Seniors started most games. We were used for base runners and sometimes got to pinch hit. No problem. It was playing baseball. When the upper class graduated in two years, we had our opportunities.

The Baseball District then was Warsaw; Tappahannock; Farnham; Montross; Colonial Beach; Oak Grove; Lancaster; Northumberland.

The schools played each other once in the regular season. There are many memories when we were seniors.

Opening season in April 1960 at home in Warsaw. I was the starting pitcher and Harvey the center fielder. The first game was against Northumberland High School. It was a cold overcast Spring day. Even had a snow flurry.

The Northumberland third baseman Leon D. was being highly recruited by Major League Scouts. The word was that baseball scouts were at this game. One thing I learned over the years - you did not want to throw Leon a fast ball. My fast ball was not that great in speed but it had movement. I used it to set up my good stuff - called "junk." Never thrown over the middle of the plate. Always inside; outside; high; low near home plate. On the corners. The "call" depended on the umpire's view. Knuckle curve. Four seam grips on the fast ball. The "stuff" was never in a straight line. You hope.

I spent hours at the ballpark pitching to Mac L. He was a freshman catcher, his mother our history teacher. Our favorite teacher. The ninth-grade kid that wanted to be my catcher; but was not going to get the chance! We worked on those "junk" pitches including a three-finger curve ball. Pitchers today call it a "circle change" (only three fingers – middle; ring; pinky grip the ball – the index and thumb create the circle). Warfield taught me how to throw the "knuckle curve." I threw these pitches most times because of the lack of a good fastball.

The game opening the season. I do not remember being nervous. Realized this game was my first start for Warsaw High School. Leon was batting cleanup. I frustrated Leon and the Northumberland team with all my "junk." Leon never hit a ball out of the infield. Keep him off balance. No timing was the thing to do. Harvey says that I struck him out twice. I do not remember. My mind was in the zone. Warsaw won the ball game 10 to 1. Last at bat for Northumberland - only long ball hit - was over Harvey's head in center field. Remembered what happens when the thrown pitch goes straight. Tiney Man Hall. - one of the fastest people on a baseball field. By the time Harvey retrieved the ball and rifled it from center field, Tiney Man had crossed home plate. Harvey had an arm and he cut down many a player with it. Not this time!

Oak Grove on their home field. The ball field is in the back of the school building. The center of State Route 3 is about 220 feet from home plate. The ground rule: if a ball hit bounces over the road, it is a ground rule double. If a ball is hit in the air and over the road, it is a home run. Outfielder is not to go after the ball. We won.

Colonial Beach game at Warsaw. Our first baseman Melvin M., a tall lanky guy batted clean-up. Melvin hits a home run over the score board in right field. Harvey comes to bat next inning. Hits a home run to left center, his favorite spot. I come up next and hit one over the left field fence. As I cross over third base the coach from Colonial Beach rushes in between third and home; grabs me by the arm. Proclaims to the umpire that the same player batted twice.

Coach Giles Hudson escorts Harvey to home plate. "This is his twin brother." Enough said. Been confusing people for years. My "junk" was working. Remember Harmon Bell calling out from the crowd. "Strike him out, Harold. I will give you a dollar." Started to leave the mound to get my dollar. Did not. Warsaw won the game.

Game at Montross home field. Their coach Billy Walker a legend in the Northern Neck. Four games in four weeks. Warsaw has won all of them. Farnham has also gone undefeated. We are the only two out of the seven teams undefeated. Then the Spring rains came. The game-a-week schedule now in trouble. One game already rained out. Two games now scheduled the next week.

Warsaw High School, 1960

Coach Hudson. "Harold. You will only be able to start one of the games scheduled for the following week." High School rule not letting a pitcher start two games in the same week. On the schedule are Tappahannock on Monday and Lancaster on Wednesday.

Game against Tappahannock at their field. The guys across the "rivah." There is a long history with these two teams over the years. Never good in Warsaw if you lose to Tappahannock. Never good in "T Town" if they lose. Coach Hudson starts the game with Harvey on the mound. Puts me in center field. Coach Hudson's had no choice. Maybe Harvey can get us to the second inning. Then Harold on the mound. Everything looks normal. A twin pitching and a twin in center field. Problem was Harvey thinks that his fastball down the middle of the plate

Harold on the Mound

will get him through one inning. Did not work. By the time the coach called Harold to the mound, score was 7-0. Warsaw lost that game 7-6.

Warsaw 4 wins - 1 loss.

The next game is at Lancaster High School. Harold started the game. Warsaw was winning in the top of the six innings by 1–0. I was in that zone; do not believe giving up a hit. Lancaster at bat. An error in the infield puts a runner on first. Lancaster next batter gets a hit to the shallow outfield. Two runners on - first and second. Two outs. Warsaw catcher Jimmy D. decides on the next pitch that he can pick the runner off second base. Bad idea. Jimmy throws the pickoff into the outfield. Runner on second scores. Runner on first to second. Next pitch another hit. Now the score is 2–1. I strike out the next batter to end the six. Warsaw does not score in the seventh. Lose the game. Remember our first baseman Melvin M. after the game. "I just saw Harold pitch the best game ever and we lost it on a 'bone head' play." Warsaw is now 4 wins – 2 loses. Win the next game against undefeated Farnham is all I could think of.

Farnham High School at Warsaw High School. The ballpark is packed. People took off work to be there. Does not get better than this. Our father H.A. Hinson was there. Daddy being told. "You need to go see your boys play baseball today." Do not remember our father ever coming to a ballgame until this one. Warfield was aways there when he could from the Pee Wee days.

The boys from Farnham and the boys from Warsaw were members of the same Pee Wee League team when growing up. That team was undefeated. Teammates. Some family cousins. Friends. Attended the same churches. Aunts; Uncles; Grandmothers and Grandfathers in same families. The communities are just ten miles apart. What a dream team that would have been in our High School Days. That did not happen. Now we face off knowing a lot about each other's abilities.

B. Hanks the Farnham pitcher now and when we played Pee Wee. Billy was taught a slider pitch when he was young. Now we are going to face him in a game we want to win just because Warsaw lost its chance to go on in the district with the loss at Lancaster.

I was the starting pitcher for Warsaw. Harvey Lee in Center Field. Tim Brown, Joe Bowles the only teammates for Warsaw that we played Pee Wee with. The game was tied at end of the fifth inning. Top of the sixth for Farnham. Two outs. No runners on base. D. Douglas catcher is next batter. Donald was the third baseman when we played Pee Wee. Tough guy to get out then. No different now.

I threw all my junk. Donald kept fouling each pitch off. More than 10 pitches. Then I threw a three-finger curve ball inside. Broke like a screwball into Donald. Do not think he tried to dodge it. Hit Batter. Donald looks at the mound on his way to first base. Next batter walks. Two on – two out. S. Barrack (first baseman on the Pee Wee team) the next batter. Hits a knuckle ball to Left field. Ball glances off our cousin

Owen's glove. Two runs score. Next batter strikes out. Warsaw does not score a run in the bottom of the 6th or the 7th. Lose game 5 to 3. At the final High School Assembly, Mr. Hudson our baseball coach and math teacher was giving out the Big Red 'W' to the Baseball Team. *"Harold Hinson."* The last player he called up on the stage. "And if it was not for this guy, we would not have had a Baseball team." That was special. We play *Ball* that Summer on separate church teams, Harvey Lee Warsaw Baptist/Methodist, and me for Cobham Park Baptist. *Life is separating us.* Has happened too soon.

KNEELING: Mac Lowery, Bat Boy; Linwood Gordon, Harold Hinson, Graham Balderson, Jimmy Davis, Oscar Delano; Boyd Clements, Bat Boy. BACK ROW: Charles Hale; Mr. Giles Hudson, Coach; Tim Brown, Orren Hinson, Melvin Mozingo; Roland Brown, Captain; Freddie Barrack; Walter Morris, Co-Captain; Tom Eastham, Bernard Davis.

Warsaw High School 1959 Baseball Team

FIRST ROW: Chris Sanders, Batboy; Harvey Hinson, Bobby Shrader, Melvin Mozingo, Charles Hale, Mac Lowery. SECOND ROW: Tim Brown, Harold Hinson, Graham Balderson, Edward Delano, Joe Bowles. THIRD ROW: Mr. Hudson, Coach; Aubrey Lee Edwards, Orren Hinson, Jerry Parr, Boyd Clements, Jack Davis. Not Pictured: Jimmy Davis, and Bobby Croxton, Batboy.

Warsaw High School 1960 Baseball Team

After High School Graduation

June 1960. I knew what I wanted to do after graduation. Get a job in the Central Office Tidewater Telephone Company. Saw this 'equipment' in the Central Office on a senior field trip. Was fascinated with how it worked. I made an appointment with Mr. Pulley at Tidewater Telephone Company. I caddied for him on occasions at Woodside Golf Club in Tappahannock, Virginia. My P. was an oversized man. Not much of a golfer as this caddie remembered.

The meeting went like this. "Well, Harold, we would like to give you a job in the Central Office. You will be eighteen soon. The Army is going to draft you. Why not do your military commitment. Then come back and see us. We will talk about the job then."

That dream job busted in less than five minutes. Existing situation. No money for college. No full-time jobs available. Not married. Going to get draft notice soon. Doing what in the Army? Big decision time. Truth was. I did not want to go to college.

I contacted Gay Packett at the Draft Board located in the Saddlery Building next to Brodearst Jewelry Store near Clement Pharmacy, as all eighteen-year-olds were required to do. She arranged an appointment with the Military Service Recruiters. Cousin Owen and I had a plan to go together. On a mission. Enter the service of our choice. Pick a career we want. Have some choice with location. Make sure to get a long tech school. Come out of the Service with a skill level. Job opportunities for the future. A lot of things to take on for an eighteen-year-old. Warfield helped me make some decisions. This was the time in our life that Harvey Lee and I went on different paths. *Forever changes for our futures.* Too young and numb to realize that then. On the following Tuesday a week after graduation I was at the Draft Office to meet with the Recruiter SSGT. He explained what was required. Battery of tests in different knowledge areas: reading, writing, math, science. Took around three hours. The result was I tested the highest in Mechanical Skill Level. Electrical Skill a close second. "Those scores allow you to choose whatever career field you want. Except Radar." Turns out that I was smarter than I gave myself credit for.

With my Electrical Score not high enough to go into Radar, the longest tech school, I choose the longest tech school in the Electrical Field. "Aircraft Electrical and Missile Repairman 42230 looks like the Career for me."

"A good choice. You will like it. The tech school is for six months at Chanute Air Force Base, Champlain, Ill. You will be assigned to Chanute A.F.B. after completing six-to-eight weeks Basic Training."

Then SSGT Dixson explained about Basic Training at Lackland Air Force Base, San Antonio, Texas. "Proper timing is important." As he put it. "One hell of a hot place in the Summer." He suggested starting Basic Training the first week of March 1961. "You will be out of Basic before they hand out the Safari Hats. Ten days leave to go home. Six months of tech school that Summer in Illinois. Great weather in the summer." Then the SSGT explained the military induction requirements. "You will be notified to report for Physical Exams by letter in a few weeks."

Now to find a job while waiting. The A&P Store located in the *Bottom* was where I headed. Talked with Mr. Tom Smith, the manager and Mr. Pete Brown, the Produce Manager. Pete was looking for a way to get more time off. He became part of the conversation. Tom. "I can teach Harold everything that he needs to know. Then you can make Harold the Assistant Produce Manager." You have to love small towns and the people. Done. Pete got off every Thursday after 12 Noon, Friday, and Saturday. I worked thirty hours a week at $1.50 an hour. A&P was closed on Sundays. I was proud of my Produce Department. It was a fun job working with Barty, Chuck, Leslie, Dicky, and Howard. Tom was a good manager. One other job at the A&P was putting new stock on the shelves. The instructions from Tom. "If a bag of candy gets damaged, write it in the book, and enjoy it." We liked candy.

I also filled in as a grocery bag boy during lunch shifts. That was nice because you got to go outside on occasion taking the groceries to the vehicle(s). Most times you got a tip. Dimes added up in those days. A gallon of gas was $0.27 cents. Some things seen outside of the store. Deacon tooting his horn, calling over the man sitting on the stool in front of the ABC Store. Money exchanged. Man goes into the Liquor Store, comes out with a brown bag. Deacon gives man a tip. Man returns to the chair waiting for the next horn to blow. [Little Man in Head: "*All well at church on Sunday morning."*] One day Tom called me into his office. "Sorry, but I will need to cut back your hours." Was not long after that when the A&P Store closed in Warsaw. I think this was when the new shopping center opened just outside Warsaw town limits. The main store being Hinson's Super Market.

I found another summer job as a runner on the Northern Neck Creamery Delivery Truck with Mac Tignor. The job started at 3:30 in the morning. Six days a week. Loading the delivery truck at the Creamery before heading out. Glass bottles of milk; Butter; Cottage Cheese; Five Gallon Boxes of Milk. The truck made deliveries in Warsaw and Tappahannock. In town houses got served early in the morning. My job was to run from the truck with two metal crates. Through the yards in the dark watching out for the scrubs. Many houses had a 'Milk Box' on the front stoop. Mac loaded the wire baskets and sent me off. "Take out the empty milk bottles, leave new product." Had to remember which house got what. Was glad when the sun came up. By 8:00 a.m., we hit the other stores, Mom-and-Pop Food Markets and Restaurants. By 3:30 p.m. we were back at the creamery unloading the truck. "Harold, take home all the milk you want." My pay was $40.00 for the six-day week. Mac gave me $20.00, Lawrence Altaffer $20.00. Pay was always in cash. I gave $20.00 to Harvey Lee each week. Not a lot of pay but better than nothing.

Support Check

Each Saturday morning one of us went to Hinson's Lunch to pick up the support check. Our memory of this still baffles to this day. Why did we have to go get the check? Many times, this turned into an argument. "I did it last week."

"You go." Then the tussle would begin. Ending with one of us going. Next week. All over again. You not me. We always tried to go early in the morning. Only one person would be sitting at the counter with his first beer, 8:00 a.m. He was always at the counter to the left on the last stool, next to the hallway that led to the Men's Bathroom. That bathroom smells. Cigarette smoke and piss. We go in through the front door. Continue past the table, chairs. Booths to the right side of the counter. Daddy was always standing there on the serving side of the counter. Guess he got use to Harvey and me coming at 8:00 sharp. When you arrive at the counter and stand behind a stool. He would spin around. Push "No Sale" lever on that old manual cash register. Reach in. Turn back around with the check in hand. Made out to Barbara Hinson, $25.00. No words were ever exchanged. We just take the check from our father's hand. Turned. Walked back out of the door. *Son, would you like some Candy? How 'bout a pack of Nabs? Bag of Peanuts? Coke? So proud of you and Harvey Lee for graduating High School. How about a few bucks? What are you plans? Hey why not work for me?* Words we would have loved to hear. Not spoken.

July 9, 1960. Eight o'clock early Saturday morning. We turned 18 on the 4th of July. That day was a Monday. After the weekly discussion, who must go get the check. I gave in. Walk down St. John's Street sidewalk, up the curved steps. Enter the Lunch Room. Mr. B is sitting in his usual spot having a beer. Our father just standing there. [Little Man in Head: *WTF?"*] He has not moved as I continued to the counter and stand behind a stool. Waiting. Our father starts talking. "What the hell do you want?" [Little Man in Head: "O*h shit."*] "You boys have turned eighteen. You are not going to get another God damn cent." I turned and walked quickly out of the Lunch Room. Tears in my eyes. Do not recall what I said to Mother when back home. *Without the check.* Mama uttered something in Italian. The memory of that day stayed with me for many years. More years than I wanted to remember it.

United States Air Force

February 1961. "Bend Over and spread them cheeks." The USAF process center in Richmond, Virginia. Physical. Passed and waiting for the upcoming date. Saying goodbyes to girlfriend, family, and friends.

March 1961. Our mother and grandmother Ma took me to the Warsaw Bus Station. My ride on a Greyhound Bus to Richmond. The Airman in charge, A3C Ed G. ROTC, hands me a package containing military orders and the plane ticket. "Memorize your Service Number; Chain of Command before we get to Richmond." The bus drops us off at the Induction Center. Proudly sworn in. "You belong to Uncle Sam now." From there we board a military bus and travel to Byrd Field to the Eastern Airlines plane waiting on the Tarmac. This was my first time flying on a commercial airplane. That takeoff experience and views were amazing for this country boy. The plane lands at the airport in Dallas Texas. I get off the plane; we were met by the USAF welcoming committee. A Sgt. barking out commands. "You Rainbows get in formation."

I raise my hand. "Going to take a piss Sgt."

"Get in formation. I will let you know when you can pee." [Little Man in Head: *"Ut oh."*] We board an Air Force Bus. First time seeing this dessert landscape. The bus of rainbows late getting to Lackland Air Force Base. When we arrive, there is a formation in place outside the barracks of other rainbows. Not a good way to start out. Throws the whole routine out of order. My group was to blame, so, we got special attention. *"Fall in you scum bags; long haired jerk offs."* Our first encounter with the [TI] Training Instructor Sgt. Wilson. Going to be this way for six weeks. Do as you are told. [Little Man in Head: *"Wipe that smile off your face, Harold."*]

We are instructed to march into the barracks, split into two groups. Stand in front of a bunk bed. Twenty-four on the upper level and twenty-four on the lower level. All lined up in front of the bunks. Split again, separated into groups of two. Airman on the left assigned the top bunk. Right assigned the bottom bunk. Airman Hinson's first day at Lackland AFB, San Antonio Texas, Basic Training facility for the United States Air Force. Top bunk. We are all *"Rainbows."* Still in civilian clothes. Fresh meat for the training instructor who has just ordered us. "Empty your baggage on top of your bunk. Things that you will not be allowed to have: candy; knives; weapons; pictures of your girlfriend; pictures of your mommy; cigarettes. If you have those, declare, give them up. Drop them in the sack when I come to your bunk." I am looking into the TI's face within inches of mine. "You got anything to declare Airman?"

"No Sir Sargent."

"You see any bars on my uniform, Airman?"

"No Sargent."

"Do not call me Sir." Sargent begins flicking his Batton through the items on top of my bunk. And he found it. My half-eaten roll of Lifesavers. "What have we got here? What is this, smiley face? Where the hell you from Airman?"

"Warsaw Virginia, Sir." Did it again.

"I ain't never heard anyone talk like that! Only thing that comes out of Virginia are queers and steers. I do not see any horns on you." Sgt picked up my empty toilet kit bag, while he continues to detail his geographic knowledge of the United States. Gave me a slap across the face. Do not believe that my face had a smile the rest of Basic Training. It is just as Stepfather Warfield warned. "Going to try and break you down, Son." Warfield gave the bag to me when I left home.

The TI assigned me and another Airman to be the *"Latrine Queens."* This was an honor. The bathroom is where most of the *Gigs* occur. They add up and are used to judge one Flight against the other Flights. Each

United States Air Force   83

TI wants his Flight to get the Top Flight Award. There were fourteen each toilet, urinals. The first thing we did was to put all but two toilets and urinals out of order. Fourteen sinks left open, along with fourteen shower heads in one large room. The barracks had to use the latrine in shifts. Sinks. Two toilets. And the shower. Otherwise known as Shave; Shit; Shower. Each Airman given fifteen minutes. Forty-eight men every evening. The latrine had to be cleaned every night after the last airman was finished. Beds made up so tight that you either got in on your stomach or slid in on your back. Do not mess up the hospital corners. Airman slept on the top blanket with a second blanket cover.

That first night in the barracks. Sgt. Wilson had one A1C assisting him with the "Rainbows." Soon as we got bunked and asleep, lights out. Lights back on. Awakened with a noise still not forgotten. It came from the galvanized trash can lid being banged on with a baton by Sgt. Wilson. "Fall out scumbags. Drop your cocks and grab your socks." Airman heading for the same door. At the same time. Falling. Tripping. Outside in just their underwear. A1C barking. "Fall in Formation." Desert night air cold. Roll call.

"Here sir."

"All accounted for Sgt. Fall out." Back to our bunks. Asleep. Lights on. Banging on the garbage lid. "Fall out." Second Fire Drill. This went on all night, until 3 a.m. Finally sleep. At 5 a.m., SGT. Wilson gives us the wake-up again with different instructions. This time we dress in our civvies and fall out in formation. March to the chow hall. March to the barber shop. Head gets skinned. March back to the barracks for pay call. $33.50 in cash and a shopping list for the PX. March to the PX. "Get everything on that shopping list." Fitted for Air Force clothing, stuff into a Duffle Bag. PX purchases, razor, blades, comb, shave cream, bar soap, toothbrush, toothpaste, shoe polish, shoe brush, cotton balls. Total $29.50. March back to the barracks. "Give one dollar to United Way." $3.00 remaining out of pay. Trained to set up foot lockers. Inspected area and personal area. "Always keep locked when not at your bunk." Fold socks. Roll underwear. Clothes rack. Laundry bag. Shine shoes, one Dress and two Brogans. Sew bottom of fatigue length. March to the cleaners where the Dress Blues are dropped off. A night of sleep. March next morning to chow hall and cleaners to pick up clothes. March everywhere we go. Unless we are running. In two days, the weak Airman are gone.

One day a blanket party was requested by the TI for an airman that would not take a shower. After the barracks are settled down, everyone tucked into their bunks, four airmen, two with a bar of soap wrapped in a towel, led by the Barracks Chief. Two men hold down a towel around the dirty airman's head and the rest start hitting him. Towels swinging, airman screaming. Right after the beating the Airman took a shower.

I was assigned to be the 'Permanent Barracks Guard.' Each time there was a Barracks inspection, I had to get back to the Barracks before the Inspector came, on guard duty to let him in. Inspection things remembered was having to recite the Chain of Command forward and backwards. My personal area also inspected. I remember having to run from the PT field to the Barracks before the Inspector got there. Still in my PT shorts and tee shirt. Sweating. Officer knew this was the *'chosen Airman'* on guard. TI. tried his best to trip me up. Never did. After the Inspection. I run back to the PT Field and reported to the TI." No Gigs Staff Sargent."

"Great, Airman. Now give me two laps." Each lap was a mile around the track. Some nights we ran for hours in the dark. One week we had the PT Course Training; setups; pull ups; jump out and grab a rope; swing across a pond of water; climb up a structure, over it and down the other side. All of this was timed. Be within the limit or fail. Each Airman required to pass PT Training to finish Basic Training. Shooting Range, first time shooting a Center Fire Riffle. I made Expert Marksman with the M1 rifle. Different then Winchester Model 61 .22 from Seward's Hardware.

My first Easter away from home was spent on Kitchen Police [KP] duty, pots, and pans, and peeling potatoes. Twenty-pound bags of potatoes.

We were told only to wear our white tee shirts, PT Shorts. Marched to a Medical Building. "Form a single line. Keep moving forward. Eyes straight ahead." Waiting at a table were two nurses. One on each side of the line. Between fingers on the left hand were three syringes. The nurse gave a 'slap' on my left arm with this hand. Then the nurse used the right hand to push 'jam' down. Delivered the meds. The nurse on your other side of the line was doing the same thing. To my right arm. At the same time. Six shots. Some Airman passed out. "Step over him. Keep moving." I walked two steps. WTF. My arms felt like they were going to fall off.

At six weeks the barracks passed the PT Course Training. The next day two thirds of the airman we bonded with were sent to their permanent assignments. The ten remaining now located on the lower level of the barracks. Giving the airman leaving their goodbye; Sgt. Wilson came to each of us staying in Basic Training. Stepped on our spit shined Brogan shoe toes. "You Airman leaving be glad."

Was the best two weeks of Basic Training. Sgt. Wilson eased up. We started having some fun. Within reason. He formed us into a 'Monkey Drill' marching group. We washed his car one weekend when he showed up having too much to drink sleeping it off in his room.

Called together and the TI read, passed out orders. Each Airman got the assignment that they had choose. My orders are to report to Chunute Air Force Base in Champlain, Ill. on May 17, 1961. Assigned to Training 31051B, Aircraft Electrical and Missile Repairman. Air Force gave me ten days to go on leave. Home.

May 5, 1961. Landing at Byrd Field in Richmond. Walked down the gang plank. I see our mother, stepfather waiting at the gate. First time in eight weeks. She did not recognize me. The skinny kid that left home 5'11", 135 lbs. Now Airman 3rd Class standing proud. Weighting 165 lbs.

Betty did not make the trip to Richmond. Still in High School. The wedding was all arranged, waiting for me to get home to marry my childhood sweetheart. Honeymoon in a hotel on Broad Street. One night. Is not young love great or what.

May 16, 1961. Back on an airplane. Destination Chanute Air Force Base; Champlain, Ill. Report to Tech School. Six months. After the first week I was included in the group of Airman that moved to the second floor. The group that wanted to get away from the party guys on the lower level.

Home after Basic Training May 1961

Harold, USAF, 18 Years Old

The first week of Tech School included a week of Kitchen Police duty. Here to concentrate on the schooling. The class is a unit of nine airman. We march to school. March to lunch. March back to the barracks. Every one of them remembered. Brothers. The Tech School made up of six training blocks. Each block a month has a final test. Must be passed in order to move into the next block. Failure is not an option. Do not want to be set back a block. Every time I talk to Betty. "You have to get me up there with you."

That is what I did. Had to go before the military brass to get permission to live off base. Found a cottage with two rooms and a bath. The bedroom was also the living room/dining room. Very small kitchen. Bathroom is located behind a curtain. Toilet. Stand up metal shower. A mirror over the kitchen sink, where I shaved, brush teeth, spit. All for the price of $65 a month.

I had to pull extra duty every Saturday. Paint details; cut grass. Sometimes the same grass that someone cut the day before. Pick up cigarette butts. I was told living off base had it easy compared to the Airman living on base. Had to walk a mile every day from cottage to the barracks. Get in formation. March to school five days a week. The extra duty on Saturday. I got tired of continuing to bend over to pick up a butt. Decided to crawl. Crawled up on a pair of spit shined dress shoes. Looking up. Captain Bars. I snaped too. Salute the officer. "You trying to be a smart-ass Airman?"

"No sir. Just trying to do a good job, Sir. So many butts in this area. Did not want to miss any."

"Carry on Airman." [Little Man in Head: *"Fast thinking county boy."*]

I had to learn how to write fast in block letters. Notes taken the first day. Could not read them. Spelling has always been a problem for me. Every night I studied at that little dining room table.

We did not have much money. Rent, food, nothing for entertainment, except on payday. We walked to the Base Movie

Theater. Movie was $0.10 for each. No popcorn, no candy or soda. Just the movie.

Betty and an airman's wife in the other cottage behind, would walk to base to get groceries at the PX. Share a cab back home. There was never enough money. On a day before payday, I got home to find for dinner a meal remembered. There were two slices of baloney, some milk, bread. Betty was proud she made one of my favorites. Not the homemade gravy on bread that I grew up with.

I excelled in Tech School. The Rope (class leader) Gomez was number one. Me second. I missed by five points to get the diploma on Parchment.

10 Oct 61. Graduated Tech School. All classmates promoted to Airman Second Class. We are given assignment orders to report each permanent Air Force Base. I had chosen the East Coast to be closer to home. Was assigned Seymore Johnson Air Force Base in Goldsboro, N.C. Received travel pay to travel from Champlain, Ill. To N.C. There was not enough money to fly Betty home. *Tell me again, living off base was a perk?* I started looking into trains. Had enough funds to book two tickets to Washington, D.C. No frills. The train ride took twenty-four hours. Every time the train got up to speed. Started slowing down for mail pickup while moving. Mail bag hanging on a swing arm. Snatch and go as the train picked up speed again. If we had anything to eat, or water to drink. Do not remember. We slept where seated. Mama and Warfield met us at the train station.

**Tech School Graduating Class
October 1961**

I had fifteen days leave and good to be home. Mama's home cooking. Squirrel hunting. What I wanted for breakfast the first morning. "How about a six-egg omelet with cheese, bacon and can biscuits?" Mama fixed it without a word. Her boy was home. Looking like he had not had a whole lot to eat since the last time that she saw him six months ago. She was correct.

1 Nov 61. Another goodbye for us. Must report to Seymore Johnson, Air Force Base on or before midnight. It was Halloween weekend when my mother drove us down to North Carolina. We stayed downtown Goldsboro in a hotel. I reported per military orders the next day at the 482FIS Orderly Room. Then to the barracks. Said goodbye to Mama. She tried to give me some money. I would not take it. "I am going to be okay. Cot and three meals a day."

At the barracks an airman I remember while in Tech School, Joe Whitlock, from McLean, Va. He was a Rope in Tech School. Different class. Same Aircraft Electrical Tech School. "You have a room assignment yet?"

"No, I just got here." We became roommates. Two airmen to a room with a bathroom shared by the adjoining room. These barracks a lot more modern than Basic or Tech School.

On the first day at the 482nd Electrical Shop the NCOIC Sgt. Cagle takes me out the flight line. As the Sgt. is going over dos and don'ts the firetrucks start running down the edge of the runway. There are two Jet Fighters coming in to land. One of them is billowing black smoke. As the planes get close to the runway, a pilot ejects. Parachute does not fully open. The F-105 was not very high, then it crashed. The pilot died. What a first day at the 482 FIS Squadron. Sgt. Cagle. "This does not happen very often." It was my weekend to be on call, return to flight line for trouble calls. A Lt. had permission to fly a T-33 home for the weekend. Trouble call for plane not being able to start. What I found was a bad starter button on the stick. Went to supply to get a new part. There were none. Returned to the waiting Lt. standing by his bags.

Logged a Red X. "Plane is grounded sir." The young Lt. begging me to do something to make that switch work. "Can't do that sir."

Betty stayed in Warsaw living with her parents. Saving up money for a car and a place to rent. Joe also was married to wife Barbara living in McLean, Virginia. He was also going to look for a place to rent. Already had a car, a 1954 Ford. We worked it out, so that we could get a weekend pass at the same time. Travel to Virginia together. Share the gas. Mama would pick me up at the Holiday Inn on Route 1. Would meet Joe there as arranged for the trip back to North Carolina.

This was during the Cuban Crisis and the Air Force was building up. All military branches were doing the same. The order was to have three airmen to a room. A room only intended for two. We had to stack two bunks. Not wanting another airman in our room, but having to do it, Joe and I added an extra spacer section when putting the second bunk up. That bunk was eighteen inches from the ceiling.

We put our new 'roomy' John R. on this bunk. A lankly skinny kid from the hills of West Virginia. Turned out to be a great guy.

Joe and I split a six pack of Malt Liquid many nights. Cost was $0.85 at the PX, two buildings over from our barracks. We chugged two to get a buzz. Sipped one. John worked the night shift and would bring us Midnight Chow Passes. Ready for that meal early in the morning. Found an apartment building in downtown Goldsboro. Joe also looking for a place to bring his wife. Being Non-Coms, we were not allowed to live in base housing.

Betty's father Rudy heard at church of a car for sale, $550. The motor had just been rebuilt. I have been saving up money for months. Had the cash for our first car. A 1955 Ford two door. We need a car for the growing family. Betty is pregnant. Next time I go to Virginia with Joe. Will drive the 1955 Ford back to North Carolina. Rudy took me to see the car. Inspected it with me. The Ford had two batteries hooked in parallel. "To get enough amperage to turn the motor over." The old High School friend that sold me the Ford said it was because the engine is still 'tight' from just being rebuilt. Sounded right to me.

It was not long after we got settled into the apartment that Betty started having trouble with the pregnancy. The doctor said that it would be best for her to have bed rest. I took Betty back to Warsaw. Got out of the apartment lease. Moved back into the barracks with Joe. Betty has a miscarriage.

Two months later Betty was okay to come to North Carolina. Sgt A. from the Electrical Shop told me of a trailer for rent in Robbins Trailer Park. Just outside the Base Main Gate, where he lived with his wife. Not as nice as the downtown apartment, but the same affordable rent. I signed a lease on the trailer home. Traveled to Warsaw, brought Betty back to North Carolina. We got settled in. In a few months, Betty has another miscarriage. I took her to the base hospital with the fetus wrapped in a towel.

Knocking Sound

The seller was 'some right.' After 200 miles the car did not need two batteries any longer. At 500 miles the oil pressure drops to 0. Engine knocking. My car fixing experience was washing Mama's. Harvey Lee and I worked in the Gulf Service Station for GWG. We were sixteen. $1.00 an hour. Many ten-hour days plus. Until the underground gas storage ran out. Happened a lot on Saturdays and Sundays in the Summertime. Call GW. "Out of gas."

"Close the station. I will be by to lock up." Folks filled up their vehicle and boat on the way to the "rivah." Again, on the way out of the Northern Neck. Gas was $0.27 a gallon. Full-service station. Pump gas. Check the oil. Show the dipstick to the driver. Wash the windows. Check the tire pressure. Try not to get caught looking at the smiling girl in the backseat with her skinny Bikini. Sometimes GWG had us do a full hand car wash and wax job on Mr. El Sanders Buick.

I spent all our money on this Ford, so that we had something dependable that would last. My buddy Dennis from the Electrical Shop has a 1955 Ford with the same V8 motor. "Your engine has blown up."

"What, it was already rebuilt."

"Someone did not do it correctly." Dennis volunteered to help me with the engine. He lives in another trailer park with his wife Joann and son in the small trailer that they own. They are from Fredericksburg, Virginia. Dennis had all the tools required. He had rebuilt his motor while being stationed in Delaware. We pulled the oil pan. Looked at a couple bearings. Scalded. "Going to require another rebuild."

We tore the motor down. Dennis marked the bearing caps 1-5. Made the engine as light as possible so we could haul it out with an engine puller rented from a machine shop. Put the engine block on the picnic table. Inspecting the engine parts discovered will need a turned crank shaft, oversize bearing. Might as well new rings. Need a new engine gasket kit. Will be like new when finished. We make a list of parts needed to rebuild the engine. Decided to have the block boiled out before it went back together. Dennis knew what to do. I was a willing learner. Ordered all the parts. Engine Shop came and picked up the block and crank shaft. Invoice came to $125. Funds. I did not have any. Called Mama. Warfield sent a check.

Dennis and I worked each afternoon after getting off duty. Some Saturdays. Put the engine block back into the car. We tried to turn over the engine with a socket and long breaker bar. Engine would not turn over. Before the bearing caps were torqued. I called the parts store. "You sold me the wrong bearings."

"Has this engine ever been rebuilt before?"

"Yes, we marked the bearing caps 1, 2, 3, 4, 5 before we took them off."

"Then someone switched the bearing caps when they rebuilt it. The front cap and the back cap can only go in one location. The middle cap only fits in that location. Someone has switched the other two caps. Switch these two bearing caps and the problem will be solved." The parts guy was correct. Now it is understood why the car had two batteries.

The so-called friend would provide no help in recovering the cost. "I did nothing wrong." Another life lesson learned. The rebuilt engine back together. Running. It is a good one. I learned a lot by this experience and am forever grateful to my friend Dennis. Money for food, rent, gas in the car, car maintenance. No money for entertainment. Was a good day when Sgt. Davis in the trailer across the street would invite us to watch TV with his family.

One weekend Mama and Warfield brought us a GE black and white TV. God bless them.

The gas station just outside the Main Gate to Seymore Johnson was where I filled up the Ford once a payday. It was convenient to Robbins Trailer Park. The owner would keep me on the books. The agreement.

He would cash my paycheck every 15th and 30th of the month. Take out what I owed. Give back the rest in cash. Also in this location was a Mexican restaurant where Betty liked to get the Corn Tortillas. $0.25 each. Down the street was the North Carolina BBQ Joint. A heaping plate of North Carolina BBQ served with Hush Puppies, no bun, and a cup of sweet tea. $1.50 a plate. That was our dinner night out each payday. I played softball on the 482nd Squadron Team. That was our outing once a week.

Cuban Missile Crisis

October 16, 1962. A Monday. First Shirt Sgt. Jackson enters the training room. Calls over the teacher Sgt. Williams and begins talking in a whisper. Sgt. Williams motions for me to go out of the room with them. "Airman Hinson. Go home and pack a bag for forty days. Be back to the Flight Line by Noon. If your wife asks. We are moving some planes out of harm for the hurricane that is coming. You do not know when you will be back." Betty takes me back to the base.

Waiting on the flight line are A2C Booher, SSgt. Absher, SSgt. English, A2C Blackmon, A2C Carter, A2C Potter. We are from the Electrical; Instrumentation; Flight Controls and Radar Shops. Also are Sgt. Gaskins, A2C Jenkins, A1C Simmons from Ground Support. We all work together supporting the F-102 FIS Fighter Interceptor Squadron Air Defense Command (ADC). Some out of the same building. We know each other well. No one is talking. All of us know this is not good. Something is not right. Where are my written orders?

Joe Booher and Harold Hinson, Cuban Crisis

We are fitted with parachutes before boarding the C-23 Cargo Plane. The plane loaded with ground support Equipment. Air supply units; MD-3 power units; ground support ladders and chokes. Inside down either side of the plane are net seats for us troops. *No seat belts.* Only instruction we were given is to bail out if the plane experiences an emergency. "When do we pull the chute was not asked." What we knew about this plane was that, if/when, it lost an engine, it went down like a rock. This is not a luxury flight. On takeoff, the noise from the engines is deafening. Need to keep your earplugs in. No bathroom. Must piss. There is an open tube attached near the wheel well enclosure. We are in this two-engine hunk of metal. No windows. *What happened to the heat?*

The cockpit is open. We can see the pilots and flight engineer. Controls. The only view out of the plane is through the cockpit windows. Not much to see there. Without written orders, airman do not know where we are going. Flying for hours. Nonstop.

The C-23 starts to descend. Lands. First thing you notice is the temperature. Hot for October. As we exit the C-23, Joe points out the sign under the control tower. Homestead Air Force Base. We know where we are. A B-52 Strategic Air Command (SAC) Base. Not one B-52 in sight. Caskets lined up on the edge of the Tarmac. F-101, F-102, F-105 Fighter Jets parked wingtip to wingtip. Taking all the available space remaining. Joe said. "We may not be leaving here." City boy thinking faster than I. We boarded an Air Force bus that took us to the barracks. This is going to be home for the next forty days. Open floor space is packed with extra bunks. Little room between. Stacked three bunks high.

First Sgt. came to barracks and gave orders. "Be in the Day Room by 6:00 PM. President Kennedy is going to be on TV." We are glued to the TV. This is when airman and the world got news about the Russian Missiles in Cuba. Maybe Joe is going to be right. Realizing that this is not going to be a Florida vacation, our Commander calls a meeting and explains what is expected. The 482nd is supporting Operation Southern Tip known to the rest of the World as the Cuban Missile Crisis. Duty assignment, twelve on. Twelve off. Starting tonight at Midnight. Full F-102 support, twenty-four hours a day. Joe and I volunteered for Midnight to Noon. SSgt Absher and A2C Sims the Noon to Midnight. It was very intense. Do not remember worrying what could happen. Just proud and caught up in it all.

Some of the pilots were not much older than us, twenty. The look on their faces I will remember. Everything connected with a wire had to be working. Sometimes we would work on fixing a light bulb while the pilot was in the cockpit. Engine running. Ready to go as soon as that bulb lit. Had to be aware of the F-102 Engine intake. Twenty planes to maintain. No time to rest. Homestead Air Force Base now home to the Air Force, Army, and the Marines. A lot of Military.

The Air Force was housed in the Barracks. The Army and Marines were in tents on most every piece of grass on the base. Chow halls were overcrowded. Open twenty-four hours a day. Joe and I stopped at the chow hall before 11:30 p.m. Midnight Chow. Breakfast. On to the flight line by midnight.

Shit on the Shingle (SOS), scrambled eggs, bacon, sausage, milk, juice, fruit. If you liked your scrambled eggs done, wait until you moved to the far end of the flat top grill. That is where the eggs were poured on the flat top first. Had time to cook. Field jackets were worn because of many pockets. Fill each pocket with fruit and whatever else could be carried. Daylight. Joe and I went to the chow hall in shifts. Leaving one on the flight line Electrical Shop. Breakfast was the same food as Midnight Chow. And more crowded. Eat breakfast quickly. Filled the field jacket again.

Lunch was a crazy time at the Chow Hall. Noon. I found whatever could be taken in the field jacket and pants pockets back to the barracks. Too tired to wait in the long lines for a hot meal. Had a hot Breakfast for forty-two days.

Our jobs on the flight line continued. The 482 FIS flew one thousand sorties during the Operation Southern Tip. Did not lose a single plane or fail to take off on a mission. The 482nd had one hundred sixty-two Airman and Pilots that received the Arm Forces Expeditionary Metal. History will explain the Cuban Crisis and those thirteen days in October. My written Military Orders for Temporary Duty (TDY) for Operation Southern Tip were included in the discharge paperwork. Noted on the Orders. "There was not time to issue them then. Only time for verbal orders with written orders to follow."

On the forty-second day we were relieved by more airman from the 482nd. Given orders to return to Seymore Johnson Air Force Base. Arriving back to Seymore was eerie. F-102s had not returned to base. The B-52's (SAC), KC135's and F-105's (TAC) were not there. The base flight line was mostly deserted. It was a lonely feeling. I bummed a ride back to Robbins Trailer Park. Called Betty to let her know. "Back at Seymore Johnson."

Betty gets pregnant again and starts having problems. Her doctor put her on total bed rest. I take her back home to be with her parents in Warsaw. Remained at the trailer in Robins Trailer Park. I return to Warsaw on some weekends and three-day passes, saving up leave for when the baby is born. Betty called. "You need to come home. Soon." She was taken to Richmond Memorial Hospital on Kensington Avenue before I could make it home. I drove directly to the hospital. Did not see Betty before she went to delivery. Found a nurse. "Wait in this room, Mr. Hinson." In the small room were other fathers waiting to be told that their child had been born. I waited for hours and decided to go out on the front porch. Get some fresh air. Sat down in the rocking chair. Exhausted. Stressed. Worried. Fell asleep.

Are You Mr. Hinson?

A nurse is holding the front door to the Hospital open. Looking at me. "Yes, I am."

"We have been looking all over the place for you. Your son has been born. Follow me." Life begins for Harold Thomas Hinson, Jr.

I followed the nurse to the maturity ward. "When can I see my wife?"

"She is resting. Go back to the waiting room. We will come and get you later." View him for the first time through a glass window. Ward nurse holding him up. About an hour later, after seeing Betty, I traveled on to Warsaw. Have nine days of leave before reporting back to Base. Times are tough. Money for food, rent, insurance, now a child. Looking forward to the promotion testing for A1C E4. A pay raise.

A2C with Future Tech Sgt Son

After passing test for Grade 42350, I was promoted to A1C, E4. Purchased a 1959 Ford Galaxie 500 Two Door Hardtop. Dealer gave me $245 for the 1955 Ford. "We just want that rebuilt V8!"

Commander-In-Chief

I had just pulled up in front of the trailer. It is 3:30 p.m. in the East. Was listening to the radio. Just heard that the President had been shot in Dallas, Texas. Knew this phone call was coming. "Yes, Sgt. Jackson."

"*You need to get back to the 482nd ASAP.*"

I gave Betty and Thomas a kiss. "Do not know when I will be back home. Turn on the TV."

Twenty minutes later, arrive at the 482nd Electrical Shop. You can see the tension on our NCO TSGT. Cagle. "You are to report to the Flight Line for Missile Loading Duty." All airman from the shops in this building have been put on this duty. We had been trained if this time ever came. Never did we think this day would. The real test. Crews brought out the Missile Caskets. Loaded on a flat-bed trailer. Single row of two. A load of missiles was placed to side of each Fighter Jet. Our job was to remove a Missile Casket from the flatbed. Place one under each wing. Unsnap the cover. Remove cover. Sit the cover aside. Step aside. Do not touch the missile at any time.

Once that missile is positioned under the wing by loading crew, put the cover back on the empty casket. Get another casket. Preform same routine. This goes on for hours. When all the planes were loaded, we are sent back to the Electrical Shop. Wait for more commands. There are no chow breaks. We are to stay in place. The only food is from the vending machines located within the building. And plenty of coffee. Airman sleep on the floor. On bench tops with our rolled-up flight jackets for a pillow. Not the time to bitch.

Awesome site seen for the second time the F-102 and F-105 fully loaded for action. All B-52s aircraft were flying. Seeing a B-52 takeoff a site remembered. The B-52 stay air born for days refueled by the KC-135 tankers. What is happening? There was not a TV where we are located. Is America under attack? Is there a takeover in our government? Bay of Pigs payback? The Cuban Crisis? The radio reports that President Kennedy has died. Vice President Lendon Johnson has been sworn in. United States has a new President and the military a new Commander in Chief. Two days later the Alert is over.

Now the Missiles loaded must be unloaded. After that, Airman are dismissed to go home. "Remain on call." In other words, stay by the phone. The Dallas Police let the suspected gunman, Lee Harvey Oswald, get shot by a bar owner. Killed while being transferred. "How does that happen?" The Kennedy funeral was televised. Next week is Thanksgiving. Thomas is but five months old with a unknown future.

Key West Detachment

After the Cuban Crisis in October, the 482nd Squadron was part of the Alert Facility located on Boca Chico, Island, Key West, Florida, Key West Naval Air Station. Runway; Flight Tower; Hangers and special fitted trailers for the Pilots and Airman crews. The F-102's were always assigned. Navy and Marine Fighter Jets alternated each month. Three 482nd Airman assigned from Radar – Flight Controls – Instrumentation – Electrical – Ground Support – Missile – Crew Chief for an eight-hour shift.

Around the clock 24 hours a day, seven days a week. One trailer was set up to house the pilots and the maintenance personnel. Instructions given, when the 'Gong' sounds for an Alert - "Let the pilots exit first – then you follow." Aircraft was off the runway in less than three minutes.

F102 Delta Daggers

When not on Alert Duty we stayed in Navy Barracks.

One day the Navy posted on the bulletin board an invitation for three Air Force Personnel to go on a day cruise, a WWII Submarine. Will be on Saturday. Leaving at 4 a.m. Joe Booher, Mike B. and I signed up.

A Navy bus picks us up at 3 a.m. for trip to the Submarine Base. At the Sub Base we have a full breakfast. Navy has the best chow and we chowed down good. After breakfast we boarded the bus and arrived at the ship. Commander welcomed us and gave instructions/history. The Submarine call letters were US399. Known as the "SEA CAT." Commissioned but never saw duty in WWII. "Permission to come aboard sir." This was required before stepping on the ship. The sub was not that wide. Walking along the top of the Sub was strange. Directed to an open hatch. Climbing down the ladder into the Sub was a lot harder than it looks. Straight down. The Navy guys show the Airman how it is done. Held on to the side rails swinging over the railing, put their shoes on either side of the rails, loosen the grip, slid all the way down to the bottom, sixty feet. Airman were put in the forward Torpedo Room. Walking through the Submarine passing hanging hammocks on both sides, every square inch of space was utilized. The Captain instructs that the trip was not going to be done normally. "This is a Training Mission – we will have twenty more sailors on board than normal. We will be out fourteen hours – most of this will be on top of the seas." Being in the Sub was like an 'enclosed can.' I am already feeling it. *'O Shit'* Tight space with smells not familiar. Heading out of the Harbor was smooth, until we were in open waters. The Sub continuously rocked side to side. Was not long before I got seasick. A sailor pointed to the toilet. If sailor told me how to flush the toilet – did not hear it. Puked up that wonderful breakfast. Thinking those Navy sailors knew what they were doing. "Hey Airman; these Pastries are very good." Felt like 'guts' were included. Everything made it into the toilet. Never been so sick. I started turning valves. Water under lots of pressure came rushing in. Did not stop coming. I screamed for help, thinking I was going to sink "the boat." I mean "the ship." A sailor came rushing in and turned the correct valves. Gave me that look. Joe was next. Once back in the Torpedo Room a sailor hands us a sleeve of Saltine Crackers. Noticed sailor was also having crackers. "Do not feel bad about getting seasick Airman. I have been on these 'cans' for fifteen years. This is one of the worst days that I can remember."

GONG – GONG – GONG "MAN OVERBOARD MAN OVERBOARD." The entire ship jumped into action. Hatches open and the sea comes in. Sailors go up the ladder like monkeys. "All CLEAR – ALL CLEAR." Hatches shut and locked. DIVE - DIVE – DIVE.

The sub angles over and starts going down. Once the Sub leveled off - it was like sitting in a quiet room. No more rocking. Dead silence. A sailor asked us to follow him. "The Captain wants to see you Airman." We are escorted to the Control Room. Capt. Alexander greets us and welcomes us aboard and takes us on a tour of the "SEA CAT." Memory not forgotten. Feeling better now about this experience. Sailors were getting haircuts. Overhauling one of the engines. Kitchen staff cooking lunch. Sailors eating. Some sailors sleeping in the hammocks. *"No sailor has an assigned hammock. Grab whichever one is empty."* Sailors doing ship maintenance. Playing cards. Some reading. If you wanted privacy, being on a sub will not be good for you. Down time is called Shore Leave. Back to the Control Room where Captain showed the depth gauge. "Going down below 150 feet. That is required to issue each of you an Honorary Submariner Card." The sub surfaced. We must have been close to the Harbor area. It was not long before the hatches opened. Going up the ladder was even more difficult than coming down. Airman Brown did not get seasick until his feet hit the dock. Walking again took a while to get in a straight line. Felt like body was still going side to side. I kept that Honorary Submariner Card in the wallet for years. Back to the barracks everyone wanted to know. "What was it like? You guys had a lot of guts. No way going out on a submarine."

Some characters during Air Force time never forgotten. All the stories. Their memories. Some had served in the Korean War. Some spent a tour in Vietnam. Did not talk much about time in Vietnam. Some came back from Japan. Airman J.Z.F. left the Navy and joined the Air Force. John was assigned to be my Non-Com in training towards promotion to A1C Grade E4. John was a crazy Louisiana dude. One day he invited me to come by his home on my way home. "Have a beer and meet the wife." John's trailer park was out the back gate of Seymore Johnson AFB. Truth. Before John introduces his wife. "Do not be alarmed, Harold. I had all her teeth pulled right after we got married." *WTF.* I am speechless. We had more than one beer. John begins telling his story. "Grew up on the family chicken farm in Louisiana. My father could not understand how his chickens kept coming up dead. Why do they all have twisted necks." Looks at me with that grin. "Have to get that last drying quiver." I got the picture. *John Zackary, where are you now.*

The good thing about a Navy Base is the food. Some of the best chow I remember in the service. Sunday Brunch after 10 a.m. Eggs; Steak; Duck; Boiled Shrimp; Pork Chops; Chicken; Potatoes; Green Beans; SOS on toast. Also on the Naval Air Station was an NCO Club. A1C Rank in the Air Force is E4, Navy sailor E4 is Non-Com, allowed in Club. Just show your Military ID. Had quite a few nights drinking more than I should. Highball a quarter.

There was this Sargent who also transferred from the Navy. Sgt. Miller was from West Virginia. I am on one end of the shower room, Sgt. Miller on the other end. You could not miss it when walking into the shower room. BEWARE TWIN SCREWS tattooed just above Sgt. butt cheeks. A propeller on each cheek. Four of us go to Key West one night going bar hopping. Not a hard thing to do in Key West. Leave one – go twenty steps - there is another bar. Eventually we stay put in a bar that the bar maid/owner is a lot of fun to talk to. Bar, empty except for us. Sgt. Miller asks the lady if she minded. "Would like going up and picking some tunes."

"Please do."

The Sgt. comes back where we are sitting. "Cannot play without a pick."

"Try my Social Security Card."

The Sgt. flicks. "That will work." In half an hour singing, picking country music, bar is filled with people. "You guys are welcome back any night. Just be sure to bring that one." Pointing to the bandstand. "Where did the Sgt. go?" Need to get back to NAS before curfew. As we approached the Pontiac Tempest, pressed against the side window in the backseat were those "Twin Screws." We found Sgt. Miller. The following week Sgt. Miller is in the shower with his essentials soaking down in a coffee can.

Reenlistment Date

October 1964. Six months before discharge date. I will have to make the decision. Reenlist or take the discharge from the Air Force. A commitment for four more years. A career in the Air Force. Thoughts of what Warfield told us. TSgt Hutchings the Softball Team Coach advised me not to reenlist. "I have been in the Air Force for fifteen years. I am not going to reenlist." What does TSgt Hutch know? That evening I talked with Betty about family life in the Air Force. Being apart for long periods, possible going overseas. Betty has a "meltdown."

The family starts the drive to Warsaw and it is soon dark. On the highway just before Wilson, North Carolina, the Ford has a flat tire. I ease the car just off the highway onto the shoulder, removed the spare tire, jack and lug wrench out of the trunk, broke loose the wheel lugs. Raised the Ford up on the bumper jack. A tractor trailer rig comes flying pass, right beside the Ford. The rig "blew" the Ford sideways. I had just put the spare tire on, ready to tighten the lug nuts, enough to lower the car. The Ford is now "struck/leaning" with a twisted jack on the bumper, no way to operate the jack again. We are there for an hour. "Can I help." Someone had stopped. They had a bottle jack and were able to lift the Ford enough to remove the worthless jack.

Again, on the way to Warsaw running two hours late. On Saturday morning I go to Sam's Barber Shop. Need to look sharp. The Telephone Central Office manager Tom H. comes in. "Hey Harold. How are you doing?"

"Ok Mr. Hudson. Home on a three-day pass. Need to find a job or sign the reenlistment paperwork for four more years in the Air Force."

What Mr. Hudson says next is surreal. "I just put in the paperwork this week to hire another person in the Central Office. What job are you doing in the Air Force?"

"An Aircraft and Missile Electrical Repairman."

"If you think working in the Central Office interests you, meet me at the Telephone Office at 2 p.m. I will take you through the equipment and explain the job."

This was that dream job when I was in High School. Told to get the military done first. Here it is. Mr. Hudson offered the job at $78.00 a week with full benefits. That is double the pay from the Air Force. I reached out for his hand and we shook. Then asked Mr. Hudson to write a note to OIC Lt. Lewis. Mr. Hudson wrote a note on his letterhead. I put it in my wallet. [Little Man in Head: *"You are one lucky country boy."*] Never mentioned about tearing up the reenlistment papers or the deal made with Lt. Lewis. Now I will move the family back home to Warsaw. Even though Betty did not want to. [Little Man in Head: *"She will come around, Harold."*] The next "fork in the road" is looming.

Joe Booher and I were discharged on the same day. He decided to stay in Goldsboro and went to work for the local telephone company. Formed a band called the Four Counts. Put down roots in North Carolina. I am going home to my roots. We had a going away party with our friends in the trailer park. U Haul and the 1959 Ford were packed with the little we had. Moving back to Warsaw, Virginia. I never saw Joe Booher again.

Tidewater Telephone Central Office

March 10, 1965. Tom's Office. Three days after discharge. First day as a civilian with a full-time job, back in the hometown of Warsaw, Virginia. Man, it felt so good. Free and happy with not a care in this world. All the hard work sacrifices have paid off. A twenty-three-year-old young man in the place he wants to be. A place to raise family with family. Ready to take on this new life. Hunting; fishing; baseball; softball; church with family and friends. Not sure that the wife of four years wanted to be back in Warsaw. Do not know why? Two-year-old son Thomas near the family. A place to settle down. We will live with mother Barbara and stepfather Warfield. Just until we can find a place to rent or a home to buy. Must bank some dollars and establish credit.

Not much rental available in Warsaw. Could have looked over in Tappahannock. That would not be the same as living in Warsaw where we grew up. Betty did not want me to leave the service. Goldsboro, North Carolina. All her friends. I tried to tell her that all those friends were just as transit as we were. "They are not going to stay in Goldsboro."

Front Yard, Tingles

She put me through total hell every day. Crying. Pissed off. Whining all the time. Made life difficult. Me starting a new job. Pressure to learn the telephone equipment. A new life. Maybe more kids. Getting adjusted to the new routine without military structure.

Came home every day to Mama's house. "What did you do today? How was your day, honey?"

"Not much." [Little Man in Head: *"Going to be okay, Harold."*] Next "fork in the road" coming fast.

Tom introduces me to all the folks in the Department. It is like old home week. Bobby; Harland; Charles; Garland; Maywood; Bill. People that we grew up with; attended high school, church; community functions. It is a good day. I am eager to start this new job. Tom assigns me working with Bill B. He was responsible for the Private Branch Exchange (PBX) equipment and phone system installations at Dahlgren Naval Weapons Laboratory, sixty-five miles north of Warsaw on Route 3. Bill is a person well-known in these parts. He would give you the shirt off his back. Story said that Bill even delivered a baby once. I grew up in this town with him and his family. It made me very happy to start a career with this man. We traveled from Warsaw down State Route 3 to Dahlgren, five days a week. The same routine every day. I always drove the panel van. We left Warsaw at 8:25 a.m. sharp. First stop was the drugstore in Montross, Virginia. Bill picked up the morning paper. Bill had his nose in the Richmond Times Dispatch, only pausing to let me know. "Do not go to fast. We want to get to the Dahlgren Gate around 10:15."

Dahlgren front security gate; motioned through. Bill directs me to which building. Upon parking the van. "Get the tools; Materials and follow me." Inter a building and find the manager. Get instructions on which phone station desk to be installed. Bill knows every desk location in the building. Stops to talk to most everyone introducing me as the "new guy."

I opened the package, seeing this for the first time. Unwrap the Eight Line Pushbutton PBX Phone. Installation Instruction Manual. The building phone cable routed back to the mainframe installed earlier is at the desk station. Cable ready to be connected on both ends. There are eight sets of color-coded wires in the cable. One set for each line. Each set of wires has a different color code. Red with blue strip; yellow with black strip; solid black; solid green; solid red; solid gray; blue with yellow strip; red with blue strip. You get the picture. Get any of the bundle wires in the wrong location, phone will not work. Bill reaches into his coat pocket, brings out a handwritten document. "Here Harold, do not use the Instruction Manual. Hook the wires up as shown on this paper." The 'new guy' knows this cannot be correct. [Little Man in Head: *"Just do as you are told, Harold."*] Bill looks at his watch. "Its 10:30. Need to get over to the cafeteria for breakfast before it gets busy. Pack up everything."

After the forty-minute breakfast, we are back to the phone installation. Bill disappears. I begin stripping the thick outer cover of the cable. Separate out each of the bundle sets of wires wrapped with thin threads. Bill comes back to check my progress. Looks at his watch. "Its 11:40. Need to get to the cafeteria for lunch before it gets busy. Pack up." Forty-minute lunch. Back to the phone installation. Bill disappears.

While Bill is away this time, I look in the Instruction Manual not to be used. Compared it to Bill's handwritten connection color code wiring list. And there it is. No way to trouble shoot this mess unless you have Bill's connection. [Little Man in Head: *"Quite a first day, Harold."*] When Bill returns at 2:15. "Time to take our afternoon break." Back to the phone installation at 2:35. Bill disappears. 3:20, Bill is back. "You need to get packed up so we can start back to Warsaw." Off Dahlgren site by 3:30. At Triangle traffic light, Bill asks me to stop at the drugstore. Returns with the Washington Post. On to Warsaw. Bill has his nose in the Post. "Hey Bill, what is the news?"

No answer. Minutes later Bill looks out from the paper. "Harold, do not go too fast. We do not want to get to Warsaw before 5:00." That was my first day at Tidewater Telephone Company. Every day will be like this one. You could set your watch on where that telephone van would be. The eight-line phone station was connected. Tested. Working by Friday. Before 3:20 p.m.

There was a knock on my door one Saturday afternoon. It was Bill. "Harold, can you take me across town?"

"Sure, where do you want to go?"

"Over near Taylor Mill Pond Road. Just follow my directions." I turn into a dirt road off Taylor Mill Pond Road. Continued up a hill to a rundown house at the end of the rutty driveway. Bill gets out. "You wait here. I will be right back." Here comes Bill, gets in the car. Reaches into his coat and takes out a pint of Vodka. "You want a taste, Harold?"

"No thanks." Bill takes one. "Can I take you back home?"

"No, just let me out at your house." Months later, sometime during the night, Bill went to the Telephone Main Office. Needed a pack of smokes. He was reported to management the next morning by the Supervisor. Operators were the only employees allowed in the building after 5:30 p.m. Bill knew he should not be on company property after hours. Tom's Office at the regular morning meeting. Bill is not there. Nothing said. Bill had a drinking problem. That is the reason I was always the driver. I never mentioned Bills PBX phone connection notes.

Tom H. assigns me working with Bobby S. We are old friends from high school. Bobby being four years older. We still play baseball for the local Warsaw team and church league softball. This is the day I get to work on the Dial Exchange Switching Equipment. First stop Lively, Virginia. Asking Bobby some questions about the equipment and what we are to do. "I am not going to tell you anything. You are going to have to learn it the same way I did." Bobby is one of the good guys. Knew what he was trying to get me to do. Think.

Grad Stroger Switching Telephone School

Required with the job was on the-job-training for a year,

then attend the eight-week Stroger Switching School in Northlake, Ill. Downside to this was being away from family until the eight-week training is completed. Upside was attending the White Socks and Cubs baseball games on the weekends. Jump on the Loop close to hotel. Get off at the ballpark for $0.25 each way. The two Major League Games Harvey and I attended were with Cobham Park men. Dr. Robert Knight with other Warsaw Rotary Club members. The Yankees and the Orioles. Telephone training also gave the opportunity to get Betty back on track.

Showdown - Decisions

One night at supper Warfield has had enough. First time I even saw him lose his temper. We are having dinner. Betty says she wishes that we had not left North Carolina. Warfield takes his wallet out. Slams it down on the dining room table. "Take whatever you need. Get on a bus and go back to North Carolina." Betty burst out crying even more. Jumps up and leaves the table. I had no words. Knew why Warfield took up for me. His son, he has seen, has become a man. A son that was doing all he could to make a life for his young family. Without any support from his wife. When I got home after work the next day; Betty informs me that she had rented a place for us. No consultation with me. Remember where Mama and we were living at eleven years old. The apartment in a converted attic. So much for living with the family. Saving up money to purchase our own home place. Turns out Betty is not too smart. I already knew that. [Little Man in Head: *"Rethink this situation with the big head for a change."*]

    Whoever said "Love is Blind" knew what they were talking about. Should have included more instructions. Life growing up the way we did. The way we had to, was not our choice. Our mother did not want those choices in her young life. It hardened me more than Harvey Lee. I start thinking about my decisions. Whatever they become. How are choices going to affect my son Thomas just two years old. Still sleeping in his crib. Will Thomas be, OK? This was the beginning of a future not imagined. Why am I the only one trying to get ahead in this life. *That is how I feel*. I need to rethink some things. Beginning with her. Maybe we were too young to marry. Then we have Harold Thomas, Jr. Never had enough money. Living from paycheck to paycheck on a military salary. Always a struggle those days before the next payday. [Little Man in Head: *"Too proud to ask for help, Harold?"*]

A time the day before payday. I had thirty-five cents. The 482nd Squadron had to stand for a Commander Inspection to get our paycheck. The inspection is tomorrow, and I need a haircut. Cost twenty cents. Betty had requested that I pick up a quart of milk and a loaf of bread on the way home. That cost twenty-five cents in the PX.

Leaves a dime. Cannot do both. Need to pass inspection. A paycheck more important than food. "Where is the milk and bread?" Do not remember what was for dinner that evening. If there was dinner. Saturday morning, I passed inspection. Received my paycheck. Went to the PX.

I talked with Betty. "We will not be living in that attic apartment for very long. As soon as we can find another place to rent, we are moving. Ms. H. Scott has an apartment above her house, when it becomes available. We will move."

Joe Booher - Joe's Story

When working in the Warsaw Dial Exchange, each morning verifying the Long Distance Circuit Switch Board. Plugged into each of the long-distance circuits to test that they were functioning correctly. Everyone used call names. Mine was "H Henry." One morning I was checking the Washington D.C. circuits when the person at the Washington D.C. end answered. Do not remember the call name. I did know this voice. "Joe." No answer. "Joe Booher is that you? Joe, this is Harold Hinson."

"Hey Harold. Yes, it is me."

We talked about the lost years since leaving the Air Force. Joe and his wife Barbara had split up. He moved back to McLean, Virginia. Living with his aunt and uncle. "You would not know who I am. I am fat and bald headed." We exchanged addresses. One day I received a package from Joe containing a 45 Record. The Counts IV Band, including a song written by Joe Booher. This brought back memories of being in the barracks room and Joe playing his Les Paul Guitar. He would play a record on the turntable and pick the strings. Soon Joe would have it down. We promised to stay in touch. Did not. Life got in the way. Have regretted all my life that I did not make the effort to meet up with Joe again. Have those beers like we use too do? I got the feeling that Joe was down on his luck and did not want to see the only true friend he ever had!

March 1961. Basic Training, his name was Joseph Whitlock. Next time I saw Joe was at Chunute Air Force Base. Betty and I were in line for the movie theater. Our one night out on payday. Betty motions. "That is the airman that bothered me at the PX today." He sees Betty with me. Starts running. I chased after him as he goes into a barracks building. Tackled him just inside the door. We are trashing on the floor when I look up to see who is barking. "Get up Airman." A Red Rope standing over us. Nameplate. Joseph Booher.

"What is this all about?"

Then Joe recognizes who has entered his barracks. *"Airman Hinson?"* I explained the situation with Betty and Airman at the PX. Joe excused me to go. We did not talk about why his name had changed.

The next time I saw Joe was when checking into the barracks at Seymore Johnson Air Force Base, Goldsboro, N.C. Joe was walking up the hall in the barracks. "Have you been assigned a room yet?"

"No; I just got here."

"Why don't we take the same room?"

That is how we became best friends. Roommates. Assigned to the 482 FIS Electrical Shop. In the barracks one night after we had those beers, Joe told me his life story. Why he changed his name. Joe was raised by his Aunt Margaret and Uncle Joseph Booher. They had a daughter Nancy who passed away. At eighteen Joe was told the truth. Nancy was his mother and was a prostitute. He never knew who his biological father was. He decided to change his name from Whitlock to Booher. After he was finished with Basic Training. He told me I was the only true friend that he has ever had. Whenever Joe's aunt and uncle came to Seymore to visit, they always took me with them to dinner. Joe [Whitlock] Booher on most of my Military Orders. We received Honorable Discharge from the United States Air Force on the same date. The last time I saw him.

Spring 1966. Fred Pittman was the Rappahannock High School baseball coach. He and Shirley lived in the rented house next door to the Smiths. "You were a pitcher. Let me catch you and see what you have." Freddie invited me to throw batting practice. "Do not throw your junk. Just the fastball." Being on the pitcher's mound again with baseball in hand on this ballfield was the good thing I needed. I should be a happy man. Am not. Working forty hours a week. Attending Richmond Professional Institute two nights a week. The Algebra class taught in an Elementary School, starts at 7:15 and ends at 9:10. RPI is growing. I left the car at home with Betty when not driving to class. She had a waitress job at Lowery's Restaurant in Warsaw. Her mother and father looked after Thomas until she got off. Sometimes Mama drove her car. She went shopping. Picked me up after class. Home around 11:00 p.m. Long days.

On nights I did not go to school, Betty took the car to work. Rudy was a lineman at the Telephone Company. I would get a ride with him to Lowery's to get the car. Go to the Bryants for dinner. Take Thomas home. Start doing homework studies. At 9:00 we drove to Lowery's for Betty. After we got home, Thomas settled in his crib, me back to the books. Betty announces that she is going to the Warsaw Auto Treat to get something to eat. "*What*. We just passed it on the way home. You were around food and now you want to go get food? Does not make any since to me." This went on a few more times, when I started thinking. Not a good thing for Betty. *Trust?* I cannot leave Thomas in the house alone to go and see what she is up too. Busting my balls to make a better future for the family. [Little Man in Head: "*What is Betty doing?*"] Then she started accusing me of not going to RPI.

One Monday morning when waking. Picked up the phone and called Tom H. at home. "Tom; this is Harold. Sorry to call you so early in the morning. Need to take a personal day if I can."

"Harold whatever you need to do. See you tomorrow morning." I made a second phone call to my mother. "Mama; I will be coming over this morning if it is OK. Hope that you have something needed to get done." I roll over to face Betty. "I am going to see my mother for most of the day. I will be back before you must go to work this afternoon. I want you to think about this marriage and where you want us to be in it?" [Little Man in Head: "*Did not mention her actions, which are disturbing.*"]

During that day, Betty got a ride to see Attorney B.K. at his office. Files for divorce based on me deserting her. *Are you kidding me.* What could she have told Mr. King to believe that?

Being me, sometimes not with level thinking. Was all I needed. Called it...turning off the Hot Water Faucet. "Betty; you have convinced me what you want." That afternoon I packed a bag of clothes. Moved to Mama and Warfield's home. [Little Man in Head: *"What are you going to tell them*?"] "Just got to work out some things."

Word flows quickly in a small town. Never very long coming. Families are all members at Cobham Park Baptist Church. We were married there. Grew up in this church. Hinson family rest in the graveyard.

What Is Going On?

Was not long before Pastor J.P. comes to see me. I told him most of it. Not all of it. Soon, I was told Pastor John went to see Betty. She would not talk to him. Then Pastor goes to see parents. Margaret slams the door on him. They are good people.

Betty told lawyer K. that I was mean to her. Had kicked her. *Not true.* There were times I felt like I could. Events are out of control. There does not seem any way to get back to what was this marriage from here. Mr. Dabney O. becomes my attorney. He gave this advice. "You cannot cohabitate if you are going to get a divorce. What do you two own?"

"The furniture is on credit with Martin Sale in Tappahannock. The Mustang is financed with the Tidewater Credit Union. Payment comes out of my paycheck each month. A few dollars in Northern Neck Bank."

Small town of Warsaw is all a buzz. What people do not know, they make up in a story. Wait and see what comes back. It is what it is. All left to the lawyers. The result is that I have child support, Alimony each week. Rent each month. Betty gets all the furniture. I get the payments. The Mustang GT is mine to keep. Visitation rights on Saturdays. Pick Thomas up at 9 a.m. Bring him home not later than 3 p.m. Our six-hour visitation.

Let me say it now. Fathers did not get much of a break. If you think so, you needed to be one of them. Mothers always got the child. Handed them to the father like a piece of candy. Mothers are in full control. Fathers treated like the bad guy. It broke my heart to leave Thomas after a visit. He was three, standing at the top of the stairs. I would blow him a kiss. When in his crib, I would hug him and say good-bye. He would put his arms around my neck. "Daddy. When are you going to come back home?" [Little Man in Head: *"Be strong, Harold."*]

I had a place to go. Home with our mama and Warfield. There was not enough money left each month for me to find a place of my own. I worked every day. Went home. Did not go out even for a beer or a game of pool. Mama fixed dinner. Kept clean sheets on the bed. I helped with the food. Often, I purchased frozen shrimp from a truck that stopped at the Telephone Office, knowing mother liked them. Went home for lunch and we would have some together. We talked. "Why don't you try to get back with Betty?" I never told my mother the whole story. Aunt Dollie asked the same question. They did not realize for me, *it was done.*

The day I had a conversation with a so-called friend. Both worked at Tidewater Telephone Company. Drag raced their cars with other friends on weekends at the Colonial Beach Dragway. He was a few years younger. "Hey Harold. What do you think about me dating Betty?"

"Go for it." [Little Man in Head: *"Humm."*] Betty and Johnny got married soon after the Divorce was final. No more alimony payments for me.

Filing federal and state taxes the first year was not a good experience. Internal Revenue Letter. Report to the IRS Office for review of your tax return. I gathered the paperwork and reported to the Richmond address as instructed. Another day of vacation taken. Agent wants me to explain the filing status. Single with Dependent. "Maam. The directions for filing say right here." I point to the text on the Filing Instructions. If you are separated, file as a single person. She did not want to hear it. "Mr. Hinson. Just write me a check for the amount we find that you owe. Do not call your lawyer. Write the check." I wrote the check. Next filing year. Another Audit letter from IRS. Same result at this meeting. Had the same female agent as year before. I wrote another check. Third year filing. Another IRS Audit letter. The IRS Agent called my name. She is a young black lady. Looks over the paperwork. "Mr. Hinson. I see that you have been audited now for three years in a row."

"That is correct."

"Mr. Hinson. I do not find any problem with your tax return. I am going to make sure that this does not happen to you again." And it did not.

Obligations

During the little time I had to be with him, Thomas was my focus. Provide what he needs. Trying to make six hours a week a memory. On Saturday's during hunting season, we would go in the woods looking for Squirrels. I carried my Winchester .22 Pump. Thomas carried his Red Ryder BB gun. "Walk softly. Do not step on sticks. Pick your feet up and put them down. Do not drag feet in the leaves. Do not want to spook the Squirrels. Here is a good spot to sit." We put our backs to a Hickory Tree. Waited for the Squirrels. I always carried a nap sack with sodas, snacks, Saltine Crackers, Vienna Sausage, Can Ham, salted peanuts in the shell, wrapped candy, plastic forks. It is a day for this dad and his son. A short day. Never long enough. Saturday mornings Thomas was with me. Harvey Lee's first children were living with our mother and Warfield (Pop). We began calling him. Reasons for this will have to come from Harvey. Not my place to write it. Brian oldest, Karen youngest and Thomas middle in age. All one year apart. We played together. Always coming up with different games to play. There are a lot of pictures I captured during those days. I purchased a gas-powered airplane operated off the end of a wire line. We flew it in that large yard. We played simple baseball games in the front yard. On a rainy day we found indoor games. Monopoly was a favorite.

Thomas and Brian were with me many times. Squirrel hunting and walking through the woods. They carried their BB Guns. Hunting was never about the killing. It was a day to be with me in the woods, loving every minute.

Harvey had a new family. Brian was sixteen when he calls. "Uncle Harold, will you take me to buy a .22 Rifle?"

"Brian; I can do that, but why don't you ask your father to take you?"

"I would rather that you be the person with me because of your knowledge of .22 rifles!"

Life and time getting in the way. As the kids got older and advanced in school there were less days together. Friends and school events took over. The school Band. Baseball and Basketball. Cheerleading. Thomas and I did not see as much of each other. Time is flying. There is no way to slow it down.

I Never See You Out

I am working in the Warsaw Main Central Office. Location with the Telephone Operators on the second floor. In this building is the Long-Distance Switching Equipment. Town of Warsaw Dial Exchange and the Carrier Phone Equipment. Equipment lot location for telephone poles; phone installation equipment; phone repair shop; maintenance garage; bucket trucks and crew vehicles. For months I had done the same routine every day. Work. Home to Mamas. Eat dinner. Help with chores. Watch TV. Sleep. Attend choir practice. Church on Sunday. Back to work. This should not be normal for a twenty-five-year-old male. I was without self-esteem. A failure. Ashamed to be seen in public. People talking behind my back. No one to my face. Misunderstood. I did not feel like being around anyone.

Then the day I picked up a trouble call. A telephone operator had reported a bad switchboard cord. I entered the Operator Room. Sitting at Station 21 was a cute trim lady. Her name Margaret O. I had never met or spoken to her before. "Hi, which cord set is it? Yep. Need to change this out. Must go to the back of the switchboard. Will let you know what to do." The "fix" requires that a back wood panel be opened. "Pull up on the bad cord please. Thanks. Have it." Disconnected the three wires at the terminal block. Ring; Tip and Sleeve. "Might as well do both cords while I am here." I am enjoying the conversation. [Little Man in Head: *"No need to rush."*]

Back around to where Margaret O. is sitting. She is smiling at me. What a cute face. I pulled out the disconnected cords and fed new cords into the station. Went back around and connected the new cords. Back around to Margaret O. She is still smiling. I smiled back. "Go ahead and run a test." Margaret begins the "test" with me leaning over the station.

She speaks softly. "How come I never see you out?" [Little Man in Head: *"Wow, tell her, Harold."*]

"I have been seeking a divorce from my wife of over six years. Thought that no one would want to pay any attention to me."

Margaret speaks again softly. "I would like to go out with you." Hands me a Trouble Ticket. On it was her home phone number. [Little Man in Head: *"Oh hell, yes."*] I did not realize or care that there were twenty-five other women in the room.

That weekend I called Margaret. She told me about the Saturday night dance coming up at White Stone Beach. The Doug Clarke and the Hot Nuts Band are going to be there. Gives me directions to her home in Heathsville. Saturday. I pick Margaret up at her home where she lives with her parents. I know the family. We go to White Stone Beach. A pier leading to a building built out over the Rappahannock River. I have never been there before. How did I not know about this place? Was living a different lifestyle then. What a party it was. We danced a lot. We dated several more weeks. I was becoming the happy guy I used to know. One day I call Margaret at home. This lady answers the phone. Mother. "Are you that Hinson Boy getting a divorce?"

"Yes, mam, I am."

"Do not ever call this house again." Slams the phone down.

In a few minutes Margaret calls me back. Crying. Really upset. "My mother had no right to talk to you like that. Please come to Callao and meet me at the Tasty Freeze. I want to see you."

The following week Margaret calls. "Would you help me move to Richmond. I will share a apartment with Mary F. I helped move them the next Saturday. The Engraved Zippo Lighter she gave me. Still have it. We dated some more. Then Margaret tells me that she has gotten engaged to an old boyfriend she went to Northumberland High School with. She was not sure that she wanted to do that when she started seeing me. [Little Man in Head: *"Mother got to Margaret."*] In the Northern

Neck News, the wedding announcement. I am forever grateful to Margaret for getting me out of my funk.

Getting Out

I am out most every night now. Hinson's Lunch; B&B Lunch; with friends shooting Pool or cruising the highway from Warsaw – Tappahannock – Montross – Callao. One Tasty Freeze to the other. To Richmond on occasion. Mama and Warfield are not pleased with me coming in early mornings. "Why don't you go to church with us this morning?"

"Maybe next week." My head is splitting from the night before. Warsaw does not have a lot of things to do. Baseball and softball during the summer or shooting pool in the back room of B&B Lunch. Odd Ball was the game we played. The persons that had the "1" ball and the "9" ball were team partners. Ten ways each rack. Each Odd Ball was worth a quarter. Team with most Odd balls a $0.25; most balls a $0.25. Possible each game to winning team $2.50; payout gets exchanged discreetly; going out of your pocket or coming in. The "house" was paid ten cents per rack. I became a pretty good pool player when in the Air Force. Pool Tournament every Saturday in the Day Room. B&B Lunch provided many good memories with the friends that we grew up with in Warsaw. Hinson's Lunch did not have a Pool Table in those days. Jimmy told me latter that he made his car payment with the winnings. Junior, Jimmy & J.A., all Air Force Veterans, were very good pool shots. No cheating; our beers were put on the shelf in the pass way, between the kitchen and the pool room. ABC law satisfied.

The Vietnam War had intensified. Many of the men of age, not married or going to college are getting drafted. 7 March 67. My two years "back pocket orders" were over. I considered reenlisting after the divorce. What kind of deal would they give? Sign up dollars promised still available? Keep the E4 Rank or E5 promised? Did not take long to give up on that idea. Thomas needs his dad close to him.

One of my wild nights, I got two traffic tickets. One issued on the way to Richmond. One coming back to Warsaw. Letter arrives from DMV. "Send DMV your driver's license." License lost for six weeks. This was my wake-up call. Long overdue. After days of shaming, I let Harvey Lee take my Mustang GT to Richmond. I walked to work from Islington Road for six weeks. There were plenty of days. [Little Man in Head: *"How are you doing now, Harold?"*] Time to reflect and pray each morning with mile walk to work. Harvey Lee brought my Mustang back. DMV sends driver's license in the mail. Attended a safe driving class to reduce points.

I was a member of the Warsaw Volunteer Fire Department with my buddies and family. The team won five of the Annual Fireman's Competition Events held that year in Colonial Beach. [Little Man in Head: *"Life is good, Harold."*]

Warsaw Auto Treat

Traveling from town to town to the Tasty Freezes. Sitting, talking, eating, drinking. I carried a pint of Jim Beam, Dish Towel and Spoon in the Console. "Give me a Ginger Ale please." Back to the Mustang; mix one. Some nights we set up a drag race on one of the country roads. Wellford's had a straight stretch half-mile. Friends were coming home from Vietnam.[7] They had on order some of the 60s & 70s "Muscle: waiting for them when they got back to the States. Peeling out of the Auto Treat and not getting caught was a challenge.

---

[7] Richmond County Book, page 493. Men of Richmond County, Virginia, who served in the Vietnam War August 4, 1964-June 8, 1969.

J & L Tastee Freeze

One night in Tappahannock at J&L Tasty Freeze, I spotted this good looking long blond-haired gal. She was driving a 1958 Ford Thunderbird, white with red interior. We began talking. She was not attached to anyone and had graduated from Essex High School. There has over the years been this unwritten rule. Do not ask me why. Very few of us from the Richmond County and Essex County sides of the Rappahannock River dated. Other than being on the basketball court or baseball field, we rarely see each other. Except at the Tasty Freeze. Sound crazy? I knew very little about her but was eager to find out. We started dating and after a few months, she tells me she is pregnant. Is it time for me to settle down? What do they say, "Love is Blind?" Time passes. I know she cannot be pregnant. Problem was. I got attached. Not exactly a rebound after my failed marriage of six years. [Little Man in Head: *"Give this marriage thing another try, Harold."*]

When I would visit her at her home, there would sometimes be a vehicle drive up. The occupant would ask "Gerty inside?" Person would go in the house and come out holding something out of sight. Turns out that her mother Gerty has the biggest "Boot Leg" operation going in Essex County. She told me she would move to Warsaw. Get away from this situation she had nothing to do with. She had a job as an operator at Tidewater Telephone Company. Rented a room in a Warsaw Boarding House. Will not be around her family. I bought it. "Hook Line and Sinker." Was this fair? I could not go the next step in the relationship without it. [Little Man in Head: *"Okay, Harold."*] I was right about her not being pregnant. She told me it was a lie. A loving person. Sweet to me and Thomas. *Beginnings.*

We make an appointment with her Pastor and discussed it all. Being a divorcee with a son. "God forgives." Pastor agrees to marry us. All the family and friends were there on the wedding day. I find a rental house at Indian Field. Same area that Aunt Dolly lives with her family. We was still paying on the furniture from Martin Sale. [Little Man in Head: *"All is good, Harold."*] Change is coming.

All Good But!

I have returned home after two weeks in Charlottesville, Virginia, attending Modular Cross Bar Training. The latest electronic upgrade in Telephone Equipment. Will be replacing the Stroger Mechanical Switches in all Central Offices. It is Super Bowl Sunday. The New York Jets are playing the Baltimore Colts. Lots of Hype. The Game. Joe N., Jets Quarterback has been bragging for weeks that Jets are going to beat the Colts. Broadway Joe was not the only person that was thinking this way. It was something about Joe that I liked. I believed Joe Broadway could do it. Jets do not have a chance was all over the news. Wallace McG., a "die hard" Colts fan kept needling me until the bet was made. "Keep it up, Harold. Put the money where your mouth is. Joe Jet is going down. $20.00."

"Okay Wallace. Done." We shake on the bet.

Beulah asked her mother to come over to our place on Super Bowl Sunday, without discussing it with me. Gerty did not come to watch the game. I really wanted to. Do not remember who brought her mother. It was not long before Beulah and Gerty began instigating a plan for me not to watch the Super Bowl game. This was the first time I realized this family had a knack to stir up some *shit*.

I had just turned the Super Bowl on. Game just started. Beulah comes into the living room with that "look." She jerks the electrical cord out of the wall. Cuts off the electrical plug. [Little Man in Head: "*WTF?*"] The first time I saw Beulah go off like this. We had only been married two months. The look on her face. "I told you that you are not going to watch that game." Laughter is coming from the kitchen. They all are so happy causing this. [Little man in Head: "*What have you got yourself into, Harold?"*] *Number one.* I arrived to work on Monday morning ready to pay up. That is when Wallace McG. hands me twenty bucks. It was the biggest upset in Super Bowl history. I did not get to see.

The lease is running out on the rented house in Indian Field. The owner Mr. Wilkins offered it for sale, but I was not in financial condition to buy it. Not sure about woman married to. Car payment, furniture payment(s) child support. Set aside what I can for a rainy day. Not feeling good about it all. Daddy had just purchased the house next door to Hinson's Lunch belonging to Sanders. I stopped by one day and talked about renting it. Daddy said that would be great, but he wants to get the hardwood floors refinished before he rents it. I offered to do that for him if he got everything needed to do it. I refinished the floors, and we moved in. Daddy said he would let us live there for no rent, but he had to charge something. "How does $65.00 a month sound?" I had rented "dumps" for that when in the Air Force. This home with two bedrooms, living room; kitchen/dining, full bath, front porch, screen porch on the back was a nice place. On St. Johns Street. Two doors from where we grew up. I am a very happy man. Maybe this will make Beulah happy. [Little Man in Head: *"Hope it lasts, Harold."*]

Cousin Michael H. and I joined the Essex County Jaycees where Maywood E. was a member. We worked with him in the Central Office in Warsaw. Warsaw was approached by the Hanover Jaycees to form a chapter. They supported Warsaw through the process of organizing. In 1970 serving as the External Vice President, I wrote up a project to build a much-needed ball park. The only other ballfield available was the old Warsaw High School Baseball Diamond. If a softball game was played on this field, the bases and pitcher's mound had to be moved to softball measurements; a temporary fence installed; all put back to the baseball field dimensions. The Warsaw Jaycees submitted the project for consideration to the State and was awarded third place in the State; First place in the District. The Levi Factory donated the land needed for building the field next to the manufacturing building. Donations from businesses and private donations provided the needed funds. The diamond was built to softball rules with lights; fences and grandstands. Named The Jaycees Ballpark. We were host for the annual Jaycee Softball Tournament to be played at the High School Diamond. Beulah had one of her moments the night before; because I was spending the day without her. Went to her mother's. *Number two*. Michael picked me up and we started working at the Ballpark clearing the areas at the field. I was swinging a Brush Axe when I got into some ground bees. Stinging everywhere all in my long hair. Only thought was to get out of there. As I was getting away; stuck the Bush Axe through my left ankle. The ankle bone and ligaments exposed. I yelled out to Michael. He wrapped the ankle in my tee shirt and helped me into the back seat of his Buick. We head to the Hospital in Tappahannock, Virginia. The next hospital is fifty-plus miles away. The doctor in the Emergency Room poured Surgical Soap into the gash in my ankle. Instantly there was no more pain. Shot the ankle with pain meds. It took 150 stitches Internal and External to close the wound. The doctor said that I would never walk again without a limp. Too much damage was done. The axe had missed cutting my Achilles in half by a quarter inch. Michael carried me to Mama's house. I was totally out of my senses. Mama settled me to bed and later woke me up. "I do not think I want dinner."

"Made your favorite, Harold." "Spigets." I made it to the dining room table where Mama had put a plate for me. Began feeling light-headed. Passed out.

When I came to, Warfield was wiping my face. "They gave you too many meds, Son." I had gone face down into that dinner plate.

Brian: "I never seen Uncle Harold do that before."

Next day Beulah returned to the house on St. Johns Street. No Harold. She calls Mama to see if she knows. "Where is Harold, Barbara?"

"He is here." Mama calls me to the phone.

"Please come back home. I will do better." Warfield took me back to St. Johns Street and helped me up the front porch steps. During the continued mean spells, she threw my crutches out of the back door. Sweet woman. Then mean as a snake.

What Have You Gotten Yourself Into?

I was out of work on short term disability for a week home on St. Johns Street. Going back to work on Monday. That Friday, my friend L. Withers stopped at the house, pulling his boat. Came in. "Harold, let's go fishing."

"Do not think that is a good idea."

"I will get you in the boat before we launch. Come on let us go." At the Totuskey boat ramp, Larry helped me climb in the boat. We motor out of Totuskey Creek, take a left, enter the Rappahannock River. Continue down the river about six miles to the Morattico Oyster Bar. There was just a ripple on the water that day. The vibration on the bottom of the boat felt good on my feet. We fished for a couple of hours. Back at the boat ramp, Larry helped me out of the boat. I was able to put the left foot heel down on the ground for the first time since the injury. The boat ride was the best physical therapy I could have had. The vibration on my left foot did a lot of good. On Sunday morning I walked, with crutches to the nine-hole golf course, behind the Auto Treat. The location at the end of St. Johns Street across Route 360. I could only put the entire left foot straight down on the sole. "Posted Rules If we are not open; put a dollar under the pull up door." I carried a bag of ten balls; some tees; a pitching iron and a putter. Hit the bag of balls toward a green. Pitched and putted toward the hole. Continued to the next hole. Worked on putting the left heel down, stretching to my toes. I did this until the golf course was opened by the owners Flicklin and Carole. Strengthen. Must walk without a limp. Pain. Lots of it. I was determined to walk into the hospital the day the stiches came out. Without the crutches or a limp. I had no feeling in my left ankle. Just tingling. I played right field in the church league softball championship for Cobham Park that Fall. It will be years before I will get any feeling in my left foot. Life with Beulah is going ok. *For now.*

Harvey Lee has graduated from RPI with a two-year degree in Drafting and Design and has a job in the Planning Office at Henrico County. No problem with his job, but his home life is in trouble. We have not talked about it. All I know, Martha and Harvey Lee are separated. The Richmond County Draft Board was notified of the change in Harvey's married status and he receives the letter: "Report to the Draft Board in Warsaw, Virginia." Shortly the letter to report for induction into the United States Army. Our cousin Bobby H. got his notice at the same time. They are sharing a house with Wally M. in the Fan. They go to Boot Camp together. After Basic Training Harvey Lee is assigned to an Artillery Unit at Fort Hood. Bobby is sent overseas to Korea. God was looking over them. Harvey Lee and Bobby will not be sent to Vietnam.

Over a short time, Beulah becomes more unraveled. Possessive. Where is this coming from? What is going on? Is she going to continue to "go off" at any moment. She did not want me out of her sight. It never came to mind to seek some help for Beulah. How that even worked. I had gone to play a round of golf with an old friend Abe. He drove us to Woodside Golf Club in Tappahannock, just off Rt. 17 North. It was slower play than normal round. When we arrived at house on St. Johns Street, Beulah was in one of her moods. As I exited the car, she come out on the front porch, waving a butcher knife. With that look. Screaming. "Where the hell have you been all this time?" I told Beulah when we left that I would be back in four hours. It was now four and a half hours. "Harold, I do not have to put up with this *shit*." Abe was right. This will be the last time playing golf with my friend. We grew up together. I went in the house. Beulah had gotten Joe Booher's 45 record. Broke it in half. *Number three*. Why. Just for meanest? Minutes

What Have You Gotten Yourself Into?

later Beulah is back to normal. "I am so sorry Harold. I do not know what made me do that?"

If I went over to Hinson's Lunch to have a beer and Crab Cake and talk with my daddy when Beulah was doing some sewing that she liked, everything would be good when I left. Coming home after an hour, she would be all fired up. Cussing; bitching; hitting. [Little Man in Head: *"Do not hit back, Harold."*] I am feeling more and more. "What in this world have I got myself into?" We have been married fourteen months.

One Saturday I drove to Bell Ville Lane – one street over - where Thomas lives with his mother Betty and stepfather Johnny to pick him up for my six-hour visitation. Soon as we enter the house on St. Johns Street; Beulah "goes off," screaming at me with a butcher knife in her hand. To this day I do not know why. Six-year-old Thomas burst out of the front door. Minutes later the phone rings. It is Betty. "You will not be able to get Thomas again until I decide. Thomas came home all upset because Beulah was coming at you with a butcher knife. I do not want him around that. You need to get your life in order." I did not blame Betty. Not the place for Thomas around this. I feel hopeless. [Little Man in Head: *"Do something, Harold."*] *Number four.*

One afternoon I was washing the Mustang in the driveway. A Telephone Operator that lived down the street with her parents was walking past. She stopped to talk with me. "Nice car Harold."

"Thank you." She continued her way home. Beulah comes from behind the house holding my double barrel shotgun. She drops two high brass 12 Ga. Shells into the chambers. Closes the shotgun.

1966 Mustang GT in Driveway

Screams. "What were you doing talking with Gale?" [Little Man in Head: *"Get the hell out of here, Harold."*] Keeping my eyes on her; I slid into the Mustang and backed out onto St. Johns Street. Went to my mother's. Not long after getting there, the phone rang.

"Yes Beulah. Harold is here."

Mama hands over the phone. Beulah starts crying. "Please come back home." *Number five.*

Last Time?

Early Fall. 6 a.m. I woke up in our shared bed. Beulah is propped up on her elbow. Staring at me. Waiting for me to wake up. "You are one lucky son of a bitch. I was going to cut your throat as you slept last night." Beulah raised her pillow to reveal a ten-inch butcher knife. [Little Man in Head: "*Get out while you can, Harold*"]. *Number six.* This is more than just one of the "going off" moments. *Number six is premeditated.* I cannot take much more of this. Why? Pride. Cannot think. Small town talkers are going to love this. This time is more serious than the other five. What if she had cut my throat? How would this be written in the local paper; as Warfield called it Northern Neck News Nonsense. Headlines: Local Warsaw man had accident with butcher knife while sleeping. Planned! Get out of this situation before she does kill you. What about Thomas? Would she try to harm him? The last straw. Good thing we do not have any kids in this marriage.

[Little Man in Head: "*Do not panic, Harold.*"] Time to think. Time to keep a level head. She has the butcher knife in short reach. And that "look." Who knows what she might be capable of. And soon. I am determined that this will be the last time. Beulah's call will come. Not going to bring me back. I slide out of bed. Keeping an eye on her. Dress. Pick up car keys and wallet on the dresser. Ease out of the back door. Back the Mustang out of the driveway. Went for a long drive. Need to think this out: "What am I going to do? Good thing. I still have my life." How to tell someone. Who to talk with. I am lost. 'Only twenty-eight.' 'Can get over this.' 'Have a good job.' 'Making a good salary.' 'Have a lot of friends.' 'Well respected in your home place.' 'Grew up here.' 'One of the beloved Hinson Twins.' 'People have called you Harvey/ Harold ever since remembered.' 'Good thing she is not pregnant.' 'You

Cannot.' 'Will not go back this time.' 'Best thing would be for her to leave.' 'What a mess you have got yourself in.' 'You should have known that marrying her was not a good thing.' 'You thought that you could make a good life for her.' 'You have been hiding what you knew for years from your family' 'Too ashamed to let them know.' 'What the Hell was wrong with you.' 'Harvey Lee tried to get you to leave the church on your wedding day.' 'Pick your head up.' 'Quit blaming yourself.' 'You are a fighter.' 'Survivor'.

[Little Man in Head: *"Not even supposed to be here, Harold."*]

Two hours and 100 miles later, I return to the house. Beulah is not there. Has left. Gone. I went next door to Hinson's Lunch. Need to talk with Daddy. I did not tell him all that happened this morning. "Beulah has left. Going to change the front and back door locks. Letting you know. Will make you a set of keys." Daddy just looked at me. Never asked why. Old houses have thin walls. Believe that he knew.

Beulah has been gone to her mother's for a month. We have hired attorneys for divorce. Her attorney files paperwork for Alimony and Child Support. *WTF* Beulah pregnant? Not showing. Beulah has done it again. Lied? Attorney was slick. A day in court I will not forget.

Judge ruled, "This divorce will not be granted until the child is born. And you, Mr. Hinson will be responsible for taking care of this."

Back Door Knock Islington Road

Thanksgiving Day. The traditional holiday feast after a morning of hunting. I have taken Thomas home to Betty to be with her family. Our Stepfather Warfield gets up from the table. Goes to the back door. "Harold, Sheriff R.B. needs to talk with you." The man has known the family since we were little guys.

"Harold, your wife has requested to get into the house. Needs to get some of her things. You have changed the door locks and must let her in."

"Cannot do that."

"It is the law."

"There is nothing in that house that Beulah needs. She only wants to get in and not leave. My divorce attorney has advised me not to cohabitat in the same house with her."

"You must let her in. I will be out front of the house. Make sure that nothing happens." So much for a Happy Thanksgiving. Beulah is waiting out front. Her brother has brought her from Essex County. I unlock the front door. Follow Beulah in. She takes off her coat. Wheels around. Proclaims with that look. "I am not leaving. What are you going to do? Sucker." *Number seven.*

Sheriff Patrol Car is sitting across on St. Johns Street. "I told you what was going to happen."

"Well, I am sorry about that Harold." He did not offer any further help. I returned to the house. Packed some things. [Little Man in Head: *"What a shit day."*]

I went to the best place I knew. Mama's. Told her what had happened. "You can move back here, Son." That did not happen. Our Stepfather Warfield needed to teach me a hard lesson. "You can't be coming back home like this again, Son." I called Cousin Michael and his wife Mary Ellen. They offered a bedroom at home with them. Had moved into the family farm home once Mary Ellen's mother Elenore had passed.

First Show Cause

Deputy Sheriff George B. is at the door with papers. Summons for non-support. Show cause to be heard in Richmond County General Court; Tuesday; December 12, 1969; 9 a.m. Attorney T.T. goes with me. Beulah tells the Judge. "Harold has not sent the support checks."

"Mr. Hinson. Do you have proof that you are not in contempt of the Court Order?"

"Yes, Your Honor." The judge fingers through the cancelled checks in the Cigar Box that is handed him.

"Do not see anything wrong. Case dismissed." Two hours off from work without pay. More money to the attorneys. Less for me.

I started seeing a young lady. She invited me to have dinner with her parents in Haynesville. We have known this family all our lives. During dinner her sister noticed. "Hey; I just saw your Mustang leaving the driveway?" She was correct. Beulah had taken it. I reported the theft to the Sheriff.

"Do not do something stupid, Harold." Bonnie and I drove to Tappahannock. Beulah was stopped just after crossing the bridge into Tappahannock by town officer. She tells the officer that she needs the car to go to the doctor's tomorrow. They let Beulah keep the car. Next day we get the Mustang. It has been left at the Police Station in Tappahannock. There was not any doctor's appointment. I am paying all the medical bills. The woman is a devil. Anything to make my life as miserable as she can. Beulah is the master at it. [Little Man in Head: *"How did you get into this, Harold."*] I keep beating myself up over it.

Second Show Cause

A couple of months have passed. I was served again. Another trip to Richmond County General Court. Before the case begins, Beulah's Attorney Mr. J.S. calls for a meeting in the Judge's Chamber with all parties. As soon as we get seated, her attorney, Mr. Joseph S., looking at me, "got you" look on his face. "We are going to put you in jail today, Son." I was stunned for a moment.

My Attorney T.T. does not utter a word on my behalf. I looked at him sitting across the table from me. "You going to let him talk to me like that?" Silence from my Attorney. "You are fired. I can take care of this myself." Leave the Judge's Chamber. Take a seat in the Courtroom.

"All rise." A different Judge enters the Courtroom.

Beulah under oath claims. "Harold has not sent me the support checks."

Under oath answer the Judge. "Yes, Your Honor. Have my cancelled checks." Hand over the Cigar Box.

The Judge fingers through them carefully and asks the Clerk of the Court, "What is todays date?" Clerk answers. "Do not see any problem here. Case is Dismissed." Another two hours without pay, more money for the attorneys. Less for me. I am being harassed with the Legal System.

The Cigar Box for Cancelled Checks

Do Not Have Job Here

April 1970. Co-worker John E. is with me doing routine maintenance on the switching equipment at the Telephone Dial Exchange in Montross. "Harold, Otilia wants you on the phone." The office manager asked me to return to the main office in Warsaw.

"Harold. It is not good. Tom wants to meet with you at 2:30 in his office."

"How about John? We traveled together to Montross in the company car."

"They will send someone to pick John up. Harold, this is not going to be a good day for you." *"Shit."* [Little Man in Head: *"Knew this day was coming."*] I removed my personal tools out of the Company Tool Roll.

The meeting went like this. Tom had a box of telephones on his desk. "Your wife Beulah called here this morning. Said she had evidence that Tidewater Telephone should want to see. Sent a telephone installer to the house and removed these three phones. One was in the bedroom, one in the living room and the other in the bathroom. There was also a wall phone in the kitchen with a modified 25-foot handset cord. You know that you are only allowed to have one free phone. You pay for the others."

"Give me a break, Tom. Are you kidding me? All of us have installed more than one phone in our homes." No comment from Tom.

"Harold, you are one of my best people. If you were living in Richmond or some bigger city, would not be a problem. Nothing wrong with your escapades. But, in this small community of Warsaw. It is. Everyone knows everything. There was a reported problem two days ago. You were parked at 9:30 p.m. in the lot picking up a young lady. You had been told not to do that and to park across the street."

"Tom. It was pouring down raining." [Little Man in Head: "*Getting red in the face.*"]

"This town is not big enough for you. You do not have a job here any longer." Tom hands me a piece of paper with a name and phone number.

"Tom, who is this?"

"Mr. Evans is the Central Office Manager, Contel Telephone Company in Manassas, Virginia. I have talked with him. Told him about you. How good your work is. What an asset you will make. You just need to get out of this small town."

"So now, Tom. You are telling me that I do not have a job here after seven-plus years. Where to go. You blocked me from leaving Tidewater months ago when you found out that I had gone to C&P in Richmond to be interviewed. C&P offered me a job at the Dial Exchange on Stuart Avenue. C&P HR Department called me and apologized that they would not be hiring me. They told me about the call from you. How you felt that C&P should wait six months before hiring me. Because Tidewater Telephone Company had spent all that money training me." [Little Man in Head: "*Do not say it, Harold.*"]

"Wow, Tom. You have a nerve. You for one are not going to tell me what to do. Where to work. Where to go." I got up and walked out of Tom's office. Otilia is standing beside her desk. I give her a big hug.

I am a young man. Not yet thirty. Healthy. Full of life. Living in the small town of Warsaw. Home. Seeking divorce for the second time. Paying child support for two. One not even born yet. Was I that naïve?' Never was a cocky guy. Just confident in what I could do. Maybe having too good a time. They do not want to see me happy.' [Little Man in Head: "*Unable to grasp the situation, Harold.*"]

Life About to Change Move to Richmond

I received my final paycheck from Tidewater Telephone Company. Less the long-distance phone bill Beulah had run up. Removed funds from the Tidewater Credit Union Savings Account. I have a total of $150.00 remaining. Opened a savings account at Northern Neck State Bank. The 1966 Mustang GT paid off.

Did I mention Tidewater Telephone was an independent phone company? I was at the secret meeting one night with the Communication Workers of America [CWA] Representatives. The meeting was called to talk about what a Tidewater Telephone Company with a union would mean? Pay and benefits equal to what the workers just fifty miles away with C&P were receiving. The Communication Workers of America have done the work required to have the employees cast the votes. Question to make the Tidewater Telephone Company union. Select one. [YES/NO]. Union not voted in. Many of the employees at the secret meeting have been getting fired. Except for one. Was that person the "snitch" on the others to management? I have always believed so.

I went to the local unemployment office in Warsaw. The Manager, my second grade teacher's husband. Mr. A. "You do not qualify for unemployment. Tom said that you were fired."

"That is news to me. Tom wanted me to move to Manassas and work for Contel."

"Sorry son." [Little Man in Head: *"More of that small town shit, Harold. Think!"*]

For the next two months I coached a Little League team. Son Tom and nephew Brian, some other local kids made the team. What little money I had was getting slim. Fun time is over. [Little Man in Head" *"Need to face reality. Quit feeling sorry for yourself."*] Woe is me ain't getting it done. I must tell these little kids. They do not know how hard this is. "I am leaving for Richmond." Memories of that little black kid, Jackson. Grabs me around my legs. Begging. Crying. "Please don't leave us."

That weekend I packed the Mustang with little I had. Leaving this town for the second time in my young life. I do not intend on coming back. [Little Man in Head: *"How could it all go so wrong?"*] No job. No home. Should I go back and talk to C&P? [Little Man in Head: *"F... them, Harold."*] Harvey Lee has married Brenda. Living off German School Road where they rent a two-bedroom one-bath apartment. Have one child Lisa. I am sleeping on their living room sofa.

Every morning fold the bed up. Stuff the sheet and blanket under the sofa cushion. Shower. Hit the road. Job shopping. Nothing looks appealing. Not going to pump gas. Do oil changes. Wash and wax autos. Sell vacuum cleaners. Got a free lunch one day for that session. Too many brain cells for that. In there somewhere is "smarts." Just need time.

Job Listed
Richmond Sunday Times Dispatch

Company called W.I. McK. Wet Copy Machine product delivery driver. Repairman skills on the copiers required. $100 for forty-hour week. No benefits. My take home after taxes comes out to $75. I was making $175 a week after taxes with benefits at Tidewater Telephone Company. Man. This suck. Got to do it. I am broke. Kissing the bottom. Must make the child support, alimony payments. $65.00 next week. Every week. Asked the judge that day in Court. "How do you expect me to do that, Judge?"

"Son, you either do it or we will put you at Camp 17."

Some of my cocky just left.

[Little man in Head: *"Dig out of this bottom; only you can do it, Harold."*] People that have been at "the bottom," know what it means. The solution, right in front of me. Go back to college. Starting next Semester. Finish the Associated Engineering Degree begun in 1966 at RPI. Take full credits each Semester. Receive $215 a month on the G.I. Bill. Most classes held at night. Keep working forty hours a week to make ends meet. [Little Man in Head: *"Piece of cake, Harold."*]

Check the Sunday Paper every week for another job making more take-home dollars. Required court-ordered benefits for Thomas; unborn child. Medical; Dental and Vision. And me. Vacation. Holidays.

Sunday Morning Paper job listing. Power Systems and Controls. Hiring Wireman. Top pay with benefits if you qualify. I made an appointment with PS&C for the interview. Will do during a delivery with copy machine products. The parent company turns out to be Carter Caterpillar. PS&C are manufacturing Uninterrupted Power Supply [UPS] systems for the emerging computer market. The Main Office and

Manufacturing Shop are in a warehouse building off the Boulevard. Just up the street from where Bill's BBQ is located on the corner. The engineering staff developed and hold the patents for the UPS Equipment power for Computers, 24/7; 360 days. The days before Cell Phones, IPADS, Laptops. TV's and Radios required vacuum tubes. Phone booths located on the corner. Home phones required a land line. Manual Cash Registers. Vehicles have carburetors. I am on the leading edge of the future.

The shop foreman Bill F., a tall lanky Country Boy from Hanover County. With a high voice. "Come with me Harold and I will show you around the shop to see the work required." The job requires the assemble of two control panels mounted on a painted steel frame. At the base of this frame was a Motor and an Inverter. The taller panel had coated copper bus bars mounted in it. The instrument panel built by a group of ladies in another room were then installed and wired by the men in the shop. The bus bars connect the cable system from the Inverter to the Battery Rack. Some sheet metal cutting and drilling to get all this system together with a lot of wiring. The generated DC Voltage was used to recharge a group of very large batteries. I had seen these before. This type of Battery Rack was also used in the Telephone Central Offices. Telephone equipment requires 90 VDC. Each battery for the UPS system is four feet high by two feet square. You get the picture. This system of 90 VDC will burn your arm off if you make a mistake. Back in the Shop Foreman's Office. He was looking over my Resume. "United States Air Force Aircraft Electrician and Missile Repairman four years. Telephone Central Office Tech for seven years. What do you think, Harold? You ever done this type of work before."

"No Mr. Fetty. I have never done this type of work before. But you have not shown me anything I cannot do."

"Wow. I like your attitude. Can you start work next Monday?"

"Yes, I Can."

I finished the last deliveries to the Virginia State Office Building on Broad Street. Got on the elevator. When the door opened standing there were Tom and Bud. No one spoke. I drove the delivery truck back to the McK. Office off Horse Pen Road. "Friday will be my last day. Sorry about not giving you more notice. A better job has come up. More pay and with benefits. I need to act on it."

A new career working in A. Miller's crew. Job pays $125 for a forty-hour week. There is overtime on Saturdays. Turned out to be every Saturday. Coming ahead a little at a time. Regular take-home a week will be $110 with Medical, Vision and Dental included. Worked there less than six weeks when the Company made me a Lead Wireman with a pay raise. I have a crew of four people to supervise. A blessed country boy being part of this emerging technology. Been a scary year.

PS&C Union Shop

Power Systems and Controls made a completed Uninterrupted Power System delivered to New York City. The Union would not allow the shipment to be unloaded. New York is a Union Worker State. UPS had no Union Label. Not going here. Virginia is a Right-to-Work State. Union Labor membership not required. Power Systems Company had to have Union workers. The Company had to change. The Shop took a vote. I was voted to be the Negotiator with the Union Representatives out of Northern Virginia. Part of that negotiation. Get pay raises for everyone. More pay for the Lead Wireman. Workers keep the company Uniforms. Toolboxes. Increase benefits. Company to provide Floor Fans in the shop. A hot sweaty place in July/August. The Union was voted in. I was made the Union Shop Steward. Then the bickering started. One Friday just before the day was over, Shop Foreman Bill F. came and gathered everyone to make an announcement. "Shop must tell me today before you leave, if you want to 'buy' your Toolboxes that were furnished by the company." *What?* I reminded Bill that the Toolboxes were part of the Union Negotiation.

"I do not care. Just doing what I am told." [Little Man in Head: *"Do not say 'dumb shit,' Harold."*] "What are you going to do Harold?"

"How much is the Box going to cost, Bill."

"I Don't know; but you have to let me know now if you are going to buy your Tool Box or not."

"Are you kidding me?" [Little Man in Head: *"Do not say it, Harold."*]

I punched the Time Clock and left for home. I came into work on Saturday morning. Punched the Time Clock and went into the Tool Shed. Tool Box was gone. Someone had cut off my lock. Went to see Bill F. "Hey Bill; where is my Toolbox?"

"You did not tell me you wanted it. The Company sold it to the painter; Howard H." [Little Man in Head: *"Do not say it, Harold."*] I returned to the shop and sat on my stool. Crew members came for work instructions. "Go ask Bill F. Not going to do any work until the company gives back my Toolbox."

Out of the office charges red-faced Bill F. "What is this about Harold?"

"No Tool Box. No work. Read the Union Contract."

"You will have to bring in your own tools, Harold."

"Bill, you have a lot to learn about how Unions work." I punched the Time Clock for Lunch; punched the Time Clock after eight hours and went home. Only other time that I got off my stool was to go to the bathroom. This went on for two weeks. Upper management called me into the office. More than once. "Power Systems and Controls has to Honor the Union Contract." I did not give in. Another week. PS&C is contacted by the Union Reps in Washington, D.C. They had responded to my call. The issue went into Arbitration. I met with the Union Representatives with PS&C management. Explained the situation. Power Systems and Controls were found in fault for making the shop pay for their Toolboxes. All the money paid by the men needs to be put back in each paycheck. Sad thing was. I did not agree to buy my Toolbox. Howard got it for free. The company did not provide me with another Toolbox. I brought my own personal tool bag to work every day. Got off the stool and went back to being a Lead Wireman.

May 19, 1971. I get a call at work from Beulah's sister Elsie. "Harold your son has been born. He is at Richmond Memorial Hospital." That afternoon after work I went to see Richard Dwayne Hinson.

Confrontation

Bonnie moved into the same apartment complex off German School Road. Renting a two-bedroom apartment with two gals from Warsaw, Brenda, and Loraine. They all work in downtown Richmond Office Building on Main. There was not a phone installed in the apartment. One evening Bonnie wanted to call her mother. "Mother's Birthday." I drive Bonnie to the Gulf Service Station, located at the corner of German School Road and Midlothian Turnpike to a pay phone. It is Summertime with the windows rolled down and the radio blasting Rock and Roll. The Service Station is open. I am sitting back in her Mustang with the Radio on. Bonnie is in the phone booth talking with her mother. Something hard hits me beside my head. Standing there, Beulah with that look. On the pavement a full bent Budweiser Can. I get out of the car as Beulah rushes to the phone booth and joins her sister Virginia. Family calls her "Suga Pie." They were pushing on the phone booth door to get it open. The two of them start the beating on Bonnie. She crumbles to the phone booth floor. I run to the booth. Grab Virginia who is closest to the opening. Start pulling her out when a big dude wraps his arms around me. I look at him. "Who the hell are you, man; let me go. Got to stop this." I get into the phone booth and pull Beulah off Bonnie. Out of the booth. Wrestle her down to the pavement. Sit on her while holding her head down by the long blonde hair, hoping she cannot bite.

Soon Richmond City Police arrive. One policeman comes to where I am sitting on Beulah. The other Policeman goes to the phone booth. The Policeman at the phone booth calls for EMS. Bonnie is still crumbled into the bottom of the booth. "Get up off this woman. Show me some identification." I get my Driver's License.

"What is this all about, Mr. Harold Hinson from Warsaw, Virginia?" I explained what had happened. Beulah and Virginia were put under arrest for assault and battery. The big guy turns out to be Suga Pie's husband. An off-duty Richmond Police Officer. Not charged. I told the officers that he had only bear-hugged me and turned me loose when requested. Not involved with the beating. The police let me go without any charges and suggested that I should file an Assault-and-Battery Charge for that beer can hit to face. I went back to the apartment to tell the roommates what had just happened to Bonnie. Did not file an Assault-and-Battery Charge. [Little Man in Head: *"Just more trouble."*]

Bonnie was taken to MCV Hospital. I saw her that night after she was admitted from the Emergency Room. Both eyes were black. Lips cut open. Stitches. Nose broke. Bruised all over. I had a real bad headache and lump on temple. The following night Harvey and I had our league softball games. Two late games. I brought Harvey back to his apartment from the ballpark at Parker Field Annex. When I stopped to let Harvey out, Brenda called me inside. "The Richmond Police were here with an Arrest Warrant for you. They said that it would be wise of you to turn yourself in." *Crap.* I left Harvey's apartment still wearing my softball uniform and drove straight to the Richmond Police Station. Went inside to the Sargent-on-Duty window. Standing there was Officer Eric F. We attended high school with him and his brother Buck.

"Harold, why are you here?"

"I believe that you have a warrant for my arrest."

Sgt. looks through the paperwork in a file box. "Yes; here it is. What in the world is this about? It says here that you are being served for Assault-and-Battery on two women." I tell Eric the whole story as it occurred. "You know, I must book you in. I will walk you through. Try to do what I can for you." After the mug shots and finger printing, Eric takes me to see the Magistrate. "This is Harold Hinson, an old friend from my hometown of Warsaw. I know he could not be guilty of these charges. Can you do anything for him?"

The Magistrate reads the Warrant. Looks at me. "Do you have a dollar, Mr. Hinson?"

"Yes, sir I do." I gave the Magistrate one of the dollars in my wallet.

"You are free to go Mr. Hinson."

"Thank you, friend." Bonnie is released from the hospital after two days.

I will need much better representation this time. One of the girls renting the apartment tells me about an attorney that her mother knows. The attorney is a friend of the family. Mr. Dan B. She called her mother and was given Mr. B's. phone number. The next day I called the attorney. The appointment is set for the coming week. Bonnie went with me to meet the Attorney. I was quite impressed with the man. Mr. B. is far above the lawyers that I had been dealing with in the Richmond County Court System. Mr. B. listened to my story as it had happened. Agreed to take the case. Then provided instructions on what to do. Not do. "I will contact you with the date of the Courts."

"Courts?"

"Yes. There will be two Court appearances, because of a child. Will do what I can about my fees. Both Court appearances will be set up on the same day. Time allowed between Courts. Civil Court first. Then Juvenile & Domestic Court. There will be a different Judge in each of the Courts. Again, I will do whatever to keep the cost down." I was not worried about the money at this point. A few weeks later I am served with the summons to appear at two Courts in Richmond, Virginia. Advised Power Systems and Controls about needing time off to go to Court. Power Systems required I take Vacation time.

Richmond City Courts

Court was held at 9:30 a.m. The Judge in the Civil Court a male; heard testimony from Beulah and Virginia. Then Bonnie and me. The Judge did not believe Beulah and Virginia's evidence or story. Gave them a fine for their actions of $150 each with no jail time. "It would be more. Neither of you look like you could pay it. Mr. Hinson, you are dismissed of any charges."

"Thank you, Your Honor." Mr. B. was very pleased with the verdict but warned that the next Court may turn out very different. "Because of your child; this Court will be a lot tougher." My infant son Richard Dwayne Hinson, now three months old. [Little Man in Head: *"You got this, Harold."*]

In the afternoon we are all in the second Court Building. A different male Judge comes in. Looking around and there is another person in the Court Room. I do not know who he is. Suga Pie's husband is there. The trial begins with the Judge asking the Bailiff to call the first witness to the stand. "What do you have to say on this matter."

Virginia produces a hand full of Polaroid Photos. "Look at what that woman did to me. That person Man-handled me, causing a lot of pain." The Bailiff calls for Beulah Hinson. "What do you have to say, Mrs. Hinson?" Beulah also hands the Judge a handful of photos. The Judge looks through them as Beulah is explaining how bad she was bruised and cut up by that woman. How I threw her to the pavement and beat her head on it. "Harold also hit me multiple times." The Judge asks for the next witness. The Bailiff calls for Mr. Watson. The gentleman that I did not know. "Mr. Watson. Where do you work?"

"I work at the Gulf Service Station on the corner of German School Road and Midlothian Turnpike."

"Were you working on the night of this event?"

"Yes, Your Honor. I am the person that called the Richmond Police."

"What do you have to add about this matter." "Well Judge. Mr. Hinson did not lay a hand on Mrs. Hinson. All that Mr. Hinson did was put that woman [pointing at Beulah] on the ground. Sit on her. Held her head down. Judge. If it had of been me, I would have killed her." Wow.

The Bailiff calls for Mr. Harold Hinson. "Mr. Hinson, were you in Civil Court this morning?"

"Yes, I was."

"On what charge were you there for?"

"Judge it was for Assault and Battery."

"How was that case decided, Mr. Hinson?"

"Charges against me were dismissed your honor."

"Mr. Hinson, what do you have to say on this matter?"

"Your Honor, I had to leave my hometown of Warsaw, Virginia. I had a very good paying job at the Telephone Company for the better part of seven years. It was my first civilian job after serving four years in the United States Air Force. We became separated when I felt that I could not go on any longer. She was abusive. Threatened me with a loaded weapon. She also threatened to cut my throat while I was sleeping. That was it for me. The Richmond County Court Judge would not grant me a divorce until the child was born. Put me on support payments. I did not believe or even knew that she was pregnant. Beulah attacked my car one night. Cursing and trying to rip the windshield wipers off. There were other Telephone Operators getting off work who witnessed what was happening. Reported to Telephone Company management the next day. The Company ask me to move to Manassas and go to work for Contel. I did not like being told where to work or where to move. Beulah had me summoned to the Richmond Count Court for Show Cause Non-Support twice. Two different Judges have found no failure to pay on both occasions. Judge, I moved to Richmond to start my life over again. Make my own way. On my own terms. I am attending Virginia Commonwealth University on the GI Bill, four nights a week. Seeking a degree in Electrical Engineering Technology. I have a full-time job. A crew of four people report to me."

"Mr. Hinson; you may step down." Then the Judge turned his attention to the sisters. "I find you guilty of filing a false report of Assault and Battery and fine you $250 each. I will not give any jail at this time."

"Mr. Hinson, what would you like me to do with Beulah Hinson?"

"Your Honor. I just want to be left alone to go on with my life. Complete my degree. Be able one day to get back on my feet. Have some peace and quiet."

"Mr. Hinson, I will see to it that happens. If your phone rings and you think that Beulah Hinson did it, call this court. We will take care of it." "I am putting you two on a Peace Bond for a year. If you break it. You will go to jail. Mr. Hinson; you are dismissed of this charge."

"Thank you, Your Honor."

Third Show Cause

Letter from Richmond County Court. Appear in the Richmond County General Court. I call Attorney Dan B. "Will you go to Richmond County? I do not want to go into that Courthouse again without a good lawyer."

"To save you money, how about you drive." I pick Mr. B. up at his office and was glad to see him wearing his overcoat. My TR-6 does not have a lot of heating. Convertible top. Very drafty. We arrive in Warsaw at the General Court House. "Harold, have a seat. Going to see the Judge. I am a stranger in this Court." Beulah comes into the Courthouse with her lawyer Mr. Joe S. My attorney returns and goes over to Mr. S., introduces himself. We wait for the hearing to begin.

The Judge comes into the Court. It is the same Judge as first time I was summoned to show cause. Beulah tells the Judge that she is not receiving the support check as ordered. "Mr. Hinson you have been summoned to appear in this Court for non-support. You do realize that if you are found guilty today, you will be arrested by the Bailiff and taken directly for detention at Camp 17? Do you have any proof that you are not in contempt of non-support payments as ordered by this Court?"

"Yes, I do Judge." I hand over the now-famous Cigar Box. It took the Judge a little longer to go through the checks this time. We all wait in silence.

"Mr. Hinson. I do not find anything wrong."

"You will not find anything wrong, Your Honor."

"Mr. Hinson, have you been in this Court before?"

"Yes I have, Judge. Two other times."

"For what was your summons to this Court?"

"Show cause non-support, Your Honor."

The look on Judge's face as he turned his attention to Beulah. "Miss, I know what you are up to. How dare you put this man through this. You will not do this again in this Court." Then he turns to me. "Mr. Hinson. Can you afford to write a support check for two weeks in advance today?"

"Yes, I can Judge."

"From this time forward; I want you to mail the support check to the Clerk of Richmond County Court. Mrs. Rosa F. will give you the mailing address and instructions before you leave the Court. Mr. Hinson; you are free to leave. I do not believe that we will see you in this Court again for Show Cause."

On the drive back to Richmond I ask the question. "Mr. B., when you went to introduce yourself to the Judge, did you tell the Judge about my arrest for assault and battery in Richmond?"

"You know I did." I thought the world of Mr. Dan B. He later ran for the Virginia House of Delegates. Did not win that election. State of Virginia's loss. He was a good man that came into my life when needed the most. God Bless him.

Two weeks later I receive a letter from Attorney J. S. asking to set a date to meet in his office in Tappahannock to take depositions. "We need to get this divorce completed. You also need to send me a payment for $300." I was prepared to get this over with. Sign the document. In my haste should have read it more carefully. When reading it again. "Accused of Desertion." Real reason should have been for the preservation of my life. [Little Man in Head: *"Glad that it is over, Harold."*] It is not.

Want to Talk with You

I traveled to my mother's home on a Saturday. My day to see Thomas. An old friend Wayne L not seen in years standing in the driveway. "I need to talk to you about Beulah. Can we talk for a bit?"

"What is on your mind?"

"I have been taking Beulah to see a Physiologist in Richmond. He would like to talk to her first husband. Will you go with me?"

"Yeah, just make it on an afternoon. I get off work at four."

"I will let you know."

At the Physiologist's. He requests to talk with me without Wayne. I "relived" my whole story with Beulah. Threats with knives and weapons. All of it. The Physiologist called Wayne back in. "One of you guys are going to have to put her away."

"Wayne, you are married to her."

Since the Richmond Court decision, Beulah has refused; made excuses whenever I wanted to have time with my son Ricky. Months passed. I tried to do that. Ricky was three. Wayne had called; said that Beulah was not treating Ricky right. He gave her address. A trailer park off Jeff Davies Turnpike. I was unaware that Beulah had moved to Richmond. Called the Social Services of Richmond and explained my concern with the treatment of my son, by a mother who might not be fit to care for him. In a few weeks the Social Service person calls me at work. "Mr. Hinson, we went to the address you gave us and spoke with a Beulah L. We did not see anything that would warrant any further action."

"Sir; did you announce that you were coming?"

"Yes. We have to let the person know that we would like to visit."

"What did you expect to find? Why do not you go around 9:00–10:00 p.m.? See what is going on without prior notification?"

"Cannot do that. Thank you, Mr. Hinson. Let us know if we can be of further help." [Little Man in Head: "*Help, you got to be kidding me.*"]

I took a day of vacation and drove to the Social Services Office in Warsaw. They did not provide any help either. Treated me like a criminal. That is the way I felt. I am torn between "better to" or "not take" this further? I spoke with Maston D. about the situation. I had to decide. Drag my young son through this. Fathers were not given rights. Being a single father even less. Money and attorneys. Time off work. I could not see a way to do it.

Many nights before classes students would sit at Shaffer's Court. Other students playing a game throwing a Frisbee. Never understood all the rules. One evening a tall gal with long black hair, books under her arm, came over and sat beside me. She started the conversation. Her name was Gretchen. She had transferred to VCU from the University of Maine. Studying for her Double Masters Degree in Physical Therapy and Math. Was from Waterville, Maine. Her parents have a Summer Cottage in Friendship, Maine. Looking at her. She had the features found of an American Indian. We part to get to our classes. [Little Man in Head: "*A natural beauty with brains.*"] The next week I am at the Union Jack on a Thursday Night. There is Gretchen with some of her gal friends. This time she will not go away without me getting her phone number. We have a few dates and it begins to get more serious. I was not looking for this to happen. A long-time relationship. During the Winter Gretchen invited me to go with a group to Massanutten Ski Lodge. Gretchen fitted me with the longest skis available. "Helps you stay up." I did not get further than the "Kiddy Area." She was a beautiful site to see on skis. Coming down the main run with the rest of the experts. A fun night and no broken bones. *Life is good.*

Job Change in My Future

PS&C Shop Intercom system. "Harold, you have a call on Line 2." John J. was a former engineer at Power Systems. "I am down the street at H.P. Foley Electrical Contractors. They have just been awarded a large contact with Philip Morris, USA. Construction of walk in Custom Instrument Panels. They do not have people here that can do the work required. The Manager asked me if I knew of anyone who can do this type of work. Told him I knew of one guy. Are you willing to change jobs?"

"Willing to talk to them. Always open for a job change, if there is more money and benefits. Interview will have to be after four."

"Will let Jim know that you are interested." The meeting was arranged for the following day at the Union Jack on the Boulevard. Had a few beers while we talked about my work experiences. Jim S. cuts to the chase. "How much do you want to be paid, Harold?"

"I am working fifty plus hours a week, six days a week. I want to make that amount of money in a forty-hour week with full benefits, Medical, Vision, Dental, paid Vacation and Holidays."

"That will be no problem." Done. Shake hands. "If you are as good as J.J. told me, you will receive a raise in six weeks. Come to the Main Foley office. Report to Robert T., the Shop Foreman."

"I will see you in two weeks. Must give Power Systems proper notice." I gave notice to Bill the next morning. Posted a letter addressed to the shop on bulletin board. The shop put together a going away party. All the well wishes cards and blender I still have. This is when "Hard Nosed" knew how much people cared and would miss me. During a night class at VCU during Lab I told Ron and Jack I was changing jobs. Looking for an apartment. "Going to work at H.P. Foley in the Panel Shop."

"Hey, that is where I work."

"Getting a divorce and looking for someone to share an apartment with."

Ronnie became my best friend. Jack and I signed a lease on a new apartment off Patterson Avenue. Jack's girlfriend also had an apartment in Faircroft. Most times I see Jack is when we are at college or he stops at apartment to write the check for rent and utilities. Basically, I have the whole apartment to myself.

Howard P. Foley
Custom Controls Shop

My first day at Main Office Building located one block over from Power Systems on Westwood Avenue. Shop located in a small room with a roll-up door. The room is only large enough for benches/stools/materials and employees building small control panels. My first week task was to read and get familiar with the Philip Morris Engineering Standards Manual. "Specifications must be followed."

Second week in the shop I changed the radio station from Country to Rock. Mr. H. arrives to work. "Who the hell changed the Radio Station?" I raised my hand. "That a problem?" Harvey goes to find Robert with his complaint.

H.P. Foley Custom Controls Crew

Robert calls a shop meeting. "This is how we will deal with the Shop Radio. First person in the shop in the morning picks the Radio Station. [Little Man in Head: *"Got it."*] The rest of the week I am in the shop first. Robert calls another meeting. "First person in the shop gets to pick the Radio Station. Station will be changed after Lunch." Seems that I was the only man in the shop with "balls" enough to ever touch that Radio.

For the next two weeks, management had me doing control panel sheet metal modifications. Punching holes. Laying out subpanels with wireway, relays, controllers. Mounting materials on the doors. I preassembled the control panels making them ready for the shop to wire. Four more weeks passed. I have not connected the first wire. Pay Day was every Wednesday, just before morning break. Six weeks I opened pay envelope. Per hour pay was the same dollar amount. This morning I was getting a snack from the vending machines. J.S. came to do the same.

"Hey Jim. Just looked at my paycheck. The hourly rate has not changed. You remember at my interview? If I was as good as you were told, you would give a raise in six weeks. Am I doing what you expect from me, Jim?"

"I will take it under advisement." Next Wednesday my hourly rate went up $1.00. Following week, the small shop space was delivered a twenty-foot enclosure. A custom-built sheet metal enclosure, with a door on either end. Five feet deep and seven feet high. The front of the enclosure has rectangle cutouts and round holes. Tom and Jim watch as the panel is delivered. "Harold, this is why we hired you. It is your Enclosure to assemble and wire. First for Foley Custom Controls. We need to demonstrate to Philip Morris, what we can do. There will be more Instrumentation Enclosures soon, if Foley per- forms. Show them what you and Foley can do." Now I know why Foley hired someone like me. I will earn my raise. Six months later a Philip Morris engineer, Ben S., came to inspect the Instrumentation Controls. I worked with Ben on the checkout. It took two weeks.

On the second Friday Ben told me he was going to get Jim. They come back into the shop. "Jim, I do not know if you realize this. In my years of inspecting Instrumentation Controls, it normally would take me three weeks to do one like this. This is the first time that I have inspected one that had zero mistakes in 10,000 terminations. Do not know what you are paying Harold. He should get a raise for work like this." Then Ben shakes my hand. "Was good to work with you, Harold. Looking forward to more in the future." Word got around at Philip Morris Engineering. Contact Foley for top-notch work done to PM Specifications. [Little Man in Head: *"You did it, Harold."*] There was not a project that could not be taken on. Growth. The "little Panel Shop" has moved to a large warehouse building. Shop personnel grew to sixteen from four. The original Panel Shop space was converted to an Engineering Department. The Company branched out adding the Instrumentation and Controls Division. Projects came from consulting engineers as far away as Washington State. The Hampton Roads Tunnel. The Super Dome in LA. Philip Morris expanded manufacturing to Charlotte, North Carolina, Louisville, Kentucky. I received another raise. Life is good.

With the raise I had enough money to save for some furniture. My existing bed is one that Harvey and wife Brenda let me use. Brenda's mother was born in that spindle bed. I started out slow on the furniture. A full bedroom set will have to wait until I have a home of my own.

Philip Morris Manufacturing. Infilco [water treatment] Plants. Robertshaw. Dupont Can Division. Wastewater Treatment. City of Richmond Water. Hempstead New York Recycling Plant. The work was pouring in at H.P. Foley. The Panel Shop had to go on six days a week to keep up with the schedule. No problem. [Little Man in Head: *"Overtime dollars, Harold."*] Time and a half on Saturday. Double time on Sunday. Triple time if a holiday. Remember one holiday that the Panel Shop worked for twelve hours to get a project done on time. Thirty-six hours in paycheck for that one day. Jim showed up at the Shop with Pizza and a Cooler of Ice down Beer. "Thanks guys." I also continued my VCU night classes. Four nights a week during the normal school year. Only had to take a Summer Class once. That was Calculus. There was enough of us night students to make this class possible. [Little Man in Head: *"The kid getting Ds at Warsaw HS."*]

Thomas and Dad at Mama's, 1979

Fairlawn Townhouses

The year lease was coming up on the apartment. Jack told me about a new townhouse development being built over in Highland Springs. I went and looked, liked it. Signed a contract one being built on Cosby Street. A very happy man after all the years of struggle. I finally have been rewarded with a home of my own. Used the GI Bill for the mortgage, $130 a month. Jack with his girlfriend in a townhouse on another street. Harvey Lee and Brenda had purchased a house one development over off Hanover Road. Hinson Twins now living very close to each other again. Driving to softball games together. Spending time together. Family time for birthdays and holidays. Memories with the kids. Harvey Lee had a very nice garden and shared the rewards. I could not have a full garden. Association rules.

Thomas and Brian came after the school year was over. Spent a month in the summer with me. They enjoyed going to the pool. Playing with the girls living at Fairlawn. I would set up the Crockpot in the morning, before going to work. Pork Chops. Chicken. Chili. Different meats cooked with Sweet Onions, a Can of Mushroom Soup.

260Z Parked at 1917 Cosby Street Fairlawn Townhouses Home

Something new for each day. Pot ready when I got home from work. Fix some Mashed Potatoes and Bisquick drop Biscuits. Pot of Butter Beans with a piece of Ham. Took the boys over to Richmond Airfield off Airport Road in Sandston on nights I did not have a softball game. We would park at the fence at the end of the runway. The planes took off right overhead. An added treat when the Air Guard was flying those military jets.

Twins in Uniform for Mama, 1970

**Daddy, Ma and Twin Sister Martha
Front of Hinson's Lunch**

Summer Break Vacation

First real one for me in years. During that summer break from VCU, Gretchen invites me to go to Maine with her. Meet her parents and go to the summer cottage on the Bay of Fundy. I agreed to drive up. Asked Foley for a second week of vacation. We decided to camp in National Parks on the two-week trip. Gretchen set it all up. Where and how many days we would stay at each. At the Memco store off Broad Street, we purchased a Two-man mountain tent, sleeping bags, and other camping gear, split the cost. She was experienced with camping. Packed up the TR-6. The luggage rack over the 'boot' came in handy. We traveled up Route 1 most of the time, keeping near the coastline. The scenery was fantastic. Made the drive longer. We were not in a hurry. Camped the first night in Maryland. The next morning set out for the Seashore Park in Maine. What a beautiful place. We decided to stay there for three days. Gretchen introduced me to a Lobster Pound. Never eaten a Lobster. Gretchen explained how it worked. The "shack" was built over the salt water. The staff opened a trap door in the floor, with a long-handled pole net, scoop up some Lobsters. "Which one would you like?" You pick the one you want and go sit at the picnic tables. They bring the cooked lobster to you. Those fried full-body Clams. What a treat those were. All we had growing up was frozen Clam Strips. The New England Clam Chowder was like none I had ever had before. Been deprived all these years. This woman, Gretchen, is showing me another world.

    We arrived at Friendship, Maine, coast three days later than expected. I had never seen anything like this. Not sandy beaches. The coast is all rocks. Big rocks line the shore. On the other side of the Fundy Bay is Canada. The tide here changes sixty feet between high and low.

Gretchen introduces her parents. They were old folks. How did they have a daughter now twenty-three? Gretchen explains later. She and her brother were adopted when they were very young. I now know why she has a lot of Indian features. Her adopted parents were retired professors from the University of Maine.

    A day on the low tide. "Mother wants us to go dig some clams." We change into swimsuits. Put on rubber boots. Take a five-gallon bucket. Two clam rakes. Walk out into the bay to a dark sand area. Gretchen gives a lesson on how it is done. "These are Soft Shell Clams that are buried in the black mud only accessible on low tide. When you walk on the mud, you see a squirt of water. You must be gentle with the clam rack so not to break the shells." Clams are everywhere. We filled half a bucket in less than two hours. Back at the cottage the Clams are put into a homemade Clam Hock. A box constructed from wood slates about one foot square with a curved top that opens. "Put seaweed in the bottom of the box. Add the Clams. Put more seaweed on the top of the Clams. The hock is attached to a sixty-foot rope. Throw the Clam Hock out on the Bay on outgoing tide. It floats on the tide for two days. The Clams clean them-selves spitting out all the black sand on the tide changes." Dinner is Clams that have been steamed in sea water. You end up with a large pile of empty shells in front of your plate.

    Gretchen's seventy-two-year-plus mother swims in the Bay of Fundy every day. "Helps the blood circulation." Gretchen joins her. I can only stand it up to my knees. Legs turn blue in short time. Her mother picked fresh Raspberries growing near the cottage. Cooks them down into a Raspberry Sauce. Serves the sauce over Vanilla Ice Cream. One day a pickup enters the driveway driven by their "Lobster Man." The parents had ordered Lobsters for our next dinner. "Would you like to go out on the Lobster Boat with him?"

    "Yes, I would."

Lobster Man

Gretchen took me the next morning before sunrise to the dock in Friendship. The woman can drive a four-speed floor shift. The first time we had a chance to kiss in days. "Not in front of my parents." The Lobster Man was waiting at his boat. "This is going to be a working trip. Call me George." The Lobster Boat a local-built wooden craft, some forty feet long, ten feet wide. A small, enclosed cabin with wheel and controls. Second mounted outside. A wrench on the Starboard Gunnel. Inboard diesel power. Sturdy boat. Reminded of our fathers Deadrise. Dock crew loaded boxes of bait. Did not think of the fact that I could not swim. George fired up the Diesel. We set out from the dock into the dark. A thick morning fog. Could not see beyond the boat. The fog was so thick. Fog and the sound of the Diesel. Dock is gone in a minute.

George gave a lesson on what to do when we get into the lobster. "These here wooden pegs. You put one into each claw on the bottom in the hinge. Make sure that you are wearing rubber groves." I was having a hard time understanding George. "After 'pegging' drop the lobster in this drum." He puts his hand on one of the fifty-gallon drums. Has pumps running sea water into them. There are drains at the bottom. Water runs on the boat deck, overboard through the opening in the Gunnels." George maneuvers the boat to a painted wooden float bobbing in the saltwater. Everything is in slow motion. "Each lobsterman has his own colors on his floats." George reaches down with a hook pole. Secures the float line. Feeds the line over the running wrench wheel. Within seconds, up comes the lobster trap. Trap is a wood slate box two feet square by four feet long. Has a curved top. Nothing like the crab pots we use in the Northern Neck. In the trap are lobsters and crabs. Crab is different than Blue Crab on the Chesapeake. "We do not keep the Crabs." George takes out one lobster at a time. Carefully measures the lobster with a metal tool from one eye socket to the back of the lobster hard shell. "Just where the tail is snapping." Throws Lobster back into the sea.

"Why did you do that, George?"

"Lobster must be at least to this edge and not bigger than this edge. That Lobster was too big." A waterman concerned for the next crop. George measures the eight Lobsters in the trap. Only keeps one. Hands the Lobster to me. Do my thing. Drop the Lobster in the drum. We did this for hours before the fog lifted. A bay appears slick as glass. A wonderful site. We have been within twenty-five feet of the rocky shoreline all this time. I took time between Lobster traps to look at this place. [Little Man in Head: *"A place you will remember."*]

The next pot has a Lobster with a growth on it. At least that is what it looks like. I had seen eggs attached to the Blue Crab. A female Lobster with eggs more of a gray color. George took her out of the trap and lowered her over the side carefully. Gently into the sea. "Next crop." George had a big smile. Not time for taking pictures, must wait until we break for lunch. Gretchen and her mother packed us some sandwiches, chips, and drinks. What is it about being on salt water and this hunger thing. I ate lunch quickly. Brought out my camera.

George motors the Lobster Boat closer to the shoreline. "Heading back to the dock." The man does not talk much. Guess that George is used to being out here on the Bay by himself. On the way to the dock George asks me if I want any of the Lobster. "If you do. Have to tell me before we dock."

"Four of the largest ones."

"Lobsters are going for $1.25 per pound today." The sea pumps are shut off. Water has drained out of the drums.

"Throw the lines." A dock hand lashed lines to the dock just as the boat comes aside. The dock hand swings over a crane with a large metal basket. George and I start unloading the Lobsters from the drums.

George put the largest lobsters in a bucket as he pulled them out of the drums. He knew which ones to look for. The basket is swung back over the dock and lowered onto a scale. One hundred seventy-five pounds. Then they weigh my Lobsters and tell George, "12.25 lbs." George drives me back to Gretchen's family cottage.

On the drive back, I started the conversation. Told you the man does not talk much. "How do you get paid?"

George explained the system. "The dock records how much Bait, Fuel, and Lobster weight. At the end of the month, they write me a check for the difference. Honor system has worked up here for many a year." We arrive back at the cottage and George tells me what is owed him for the Lobsters. $15.63. Thanked that old Lobster Man for a day always remembered.

Friendship Sloop Fishing in the Bay of Fundy

On first weekend a family day on the parents' Friendship Sloop. These boats were built in Friendship, Maine. The boat craftmanship in Mahogany and Teak a site to see. Mast, Helm and Sails were impressive. Mr. Moore let me have the wheel for a while under close supervision.

During the week Gretchen took me fishing. I learned something else about this lady. She handled the small skiff like a seasoned sailor. Pulled the rope on the motor. Tiller in hand. Off we went around the shore. I rigged two fishing rods with "Red Devil" spoons. There was another fisherman in the area in a small boat. After he put his baits in the water, starting rowing as fast as he could. Fishing Rod between his legs. Bang. Rod got a hit. Stopped rowing and reeled in a Mackerel. Gretchen put our boat in gear. We started a slow troll. Immediately catching Spanish Mackerel. Each catch followed by Sharks trying to feast. "What was that?"

"Sand Sharks," the man hollers. Chopping off the fish before we could get them on the skiff. The sea was so clear you could see them circling the caught fish.

Man in other boat hollers over. "Catch those damn Sharks and kill them." I rigged up a rod with a No. 8 saltwater hook baited with the remaining fish head. Cast over the side. The hook up was sudden. The fight on and fun. The caught shark starting to give birth in the water. Each baby shark eaten by other sharks. It was a frenzy. Caught another shark. Landed it in the boat. Instantly popping out babies. I had to try. Put a baby shark on the hook. Lost count of how many more were caught. The guy in the boat hollowed over again. "Hey, these sharks are ruining the Mackerel fishing. Take to the shore and throw up on the rocks. The sea gulls will eat them. Thank you." I fillet the Mackerel in the bottom of the skiff. Mrs. M. broiled them for our shore lunch. Nothing better than fresh-caught fish. At dinner that night Gretchen's mother handed over a wrapped package. I opened the package to find a Trader Vic's Bartender's Guide. Gretchen told her what to get for my birthday.

Gretchen's mother was preparing to cook the Lobster. Called me over to watch how it is done. I had asked. She sent us with a large pot down to the shoreline. "Fill it three quarter full with sea water." Brought the pot to a full boil. Lowered each Lobster into the pot head first. "That way you do not hear them scream." She was smiling.

At each place setting was a small bowl. We were instructed to put the Tamale in it. The Tamale to be served with crackers next evening as an appetizer. "It is better once it is cold." Gretchen wanted to show me some other places in Maine. We put the top down on the TR-6 and drove to Camden, Maine. A ride in a sports car on those winding roads. I found out what was possible in that TR-6. "Ease up Harold." Camden, a college town, and artist haven. Artistic with the architecture. Veterans Park. Monuments. There is a river that runs under the main street. Over the rocks; waterfall; past the park up on the hill. Many artists selling their paintings. Photos. I fell in love with Maine. Even more in love with the lady. This summer for two weeks. The best summer in my life. I purchased eight more Lobsters to take back to Virginia. Mrs. M. stayed near when I cooked them. Packed them in the cooler with ice packs for the trip home. Strapped the ice cooler on the luggage rack. We did not stop to camp. Drove straight to Virginia on fastest route.

Henrico County Court

A day on the way to get some parts at Import Auto. I was going the wrong direction on the Boulevard. Turned onto Robbin Hood Road. Just do a U-turn. A Henrico Police Officer lights flashing. "ID and Registration. Mr. Hinson, Warsaw Virginia. Do you know why I stopped you?"

"No sir."

"Going to issue a ticket for making an illegal U-turn. Did you see the sign?"

"Did not see any sign, Officer."

"Mr. Hinson. Suggest that you appear in court on the date and time shown. Do not pay this ticket out of court."

"Thank you."

I appeared at Henrico Court Building. Noticed the Commonwealth Attorney gave me a nod. Do not know why. The morning Court is held. A break for lunch. We are back for the afternoon Court. Did not think this was going to take most of the day. Maybe should have paid the ticket out of court. Bailiff calls, "Mr. Hinson." I approached the Judge and the Commonwealth Attorney.

"Judge, you recognize Mr. Hinson. He has been working with Henrico County to change those U-turn signs that are the size of a dollar bill." The Judge looks toward the Henrico Officer who had just confirmed the sign. "If people cannot see it, why did you issue a ticket? Case dismissed, Mr. Hinson. You are free to go. Thank you for your work on this sign issue." [Little Man in Head: *"Harold not Harvey Lee."*] Commonwealth Attorney. They are good friends. Won the election for governor.

ASA Softball

After I moved to Richmond, I began playing on Harvey's team, Smith Mayflower. I was the twelfth member under contract of the team. The regular ten players had been together for several years. The mid-June date for breaking a team contract was coming up. Manager Wilmer was approached one night after the game. The first-year team, J.A. Walders coach. "We would like to have Harold play outfield for us, if you will release him." It would not be fair to continue with Smith Mayflower when there is a chance to play with another team. Wilmer released me to play full time for another team. I signed the new contract that night. We are playing against each other. Gretchen loved to watch and kept a

Champs in Rocky Mount, NC 1971

scorebook of every game. When I was chosen for the Richmond ASA All Star Team. She had me buy a new pair of white cleats. "You need to look your best." She even took a picture of those shoes. We have become very close. I am having less "women trust issues." [Little Man in Head: *"Different this time, Harold."*] J. Granger from NBC Channel 12 in Richmond was at the ballpark almost every game. He videoed the games and showed them on his 11 p.m. evening Sports Show.

The Walder Team made up by a bunch of younger guys. Half of the team were related. Larry C. was the pitcher. A good one. Jim's brother. The Shortstop Bubba C. was just seventeen. Left & Right Fielders, Ervin, Tommy eighteen. The twenty-year-old First Baseman, Jessie H. was a slick glove. The Second Baseman Calvin, Third Baseman Butch; Catcher Earl, Pitcher, and me. The only members that were fathers. It was a Class B Team, only two power hitters capable to hit home runs. One of the best teams in the area. Those young guys were fast. Speed is a winner in Slow Pitch Softball. Jim C. entered the team in every Class A Tournament he could get us in. A Class A Team is made up of mostly Home Run Power Hitters. If we met those "boomers" on an open field, we beat them with singles and doubles. When we had a game on an open field, just a fly ball. We won some Class A Tournaments. Many times, came in the top three. Getting seasoned against better teams. Well known when we took the field. Won the Class B League Championship that first year.

The following year we are entered in the Memorial Day Tournament for the first time. It is the largest softball Tournament in the United States. Organized by the ASA Commissioner F. Taylor. There are teams entered from all over the country. Every softball field in the area was used. Sometimes when it rained, and it almost always rained on Memorial Day weekend, teams may be playing a game at 1 a.m. Each team is guaranteed seven games. After seven games are played, the teams with the best records from each bracket continue to the elimination brackets. Four teams remaining continue to play on Memorial Day for the Championship. Quality Meats and Walder were last Richmond teams left in the Tournament. Walder being the only B Class Team. The other two, NC Furniture and Fredericksburg Cable Vision. J. Granger was there with his video camera. The Byrd Field

Annex is packed with spectators. Walder has the first game against Fredericksburg Cable Vision. In the fourth inning Calvin when sliding into second base got sand in his eyes. Calvin was carried to the hospital. I came in from the outfield to play second base. Cable Vision had a player from Colonial Beach in the Northern Neck. We grew up playing against Jake. Very fast left-hand hitter. That evening on the Channel 12 Sportscast J. Granger kept showing the play repeatedly. "Bottom of the fifth inning with game tied. The last inning because of 50-minute time limit. This was the way Walder lost the game. Second Baseman Harold Hinson fielded the ball in the "hole" and threw to Jessie at First Base. First baseman does a 'hot dog' stretch. Ball glances off his glove. Jake under full speed, rounds first and slides into second. Safe. No outs. Next batter for Cable Vision hits a fly ball to Right Field. Jake tags up and goes to third. Next batter hits a long fly ball to right field. Jake tags up and scores. The game over."

The following year Smith Mayflower did not sponsor a team. Harvey Lee signed a contract with the Walder Team. We are back together again, playing on the same team. Harvey, one of the top outfielders in the City of Richmond, Virginia. Many a player was cut down by that arm. The last time the Walder Team played was in the qualifying tournament for the World Series. Only one team from Richmond, Virginia, can go each year. The game we were beat in was what could have been a bad call. We were playing the Class A Siegel's Supper Market on an open field. They kept "booming." Our outfield caught the fly balls. Then Siegels got smart. Walder was winning in the last inning for the championship. Siegels started hitting singles and doubles. A game-ending play at home plate with E. Campbell, Walder catcher fielding the throw, sitting on the runner's back. Umpire call. Safe. Siegels took two allowed players to the Worlds. Walder Shortstop B. Crosic and D. Chrisum from Fredericksburg Cable Vision. Won the World Series. First time a team from Richmond had won the World Series.

Harvey Lee and I decided, why don't we put together our own team? Dumbarton Square Crabbers. Team was good and more laid back. On two occasions Harvey and I went back to Warsaw to play in softball tournaments at the Jaycee Ballpark. Each time we were greeted by the hometown folks. "Good to see you boys still playing ball together." We also played for Richmond County Old Timers in the Annual Fourth of July Event against Tappahannock. The games were played in Warsaw one year and in Tappahannock the next. Those ballparks were always packed. Families and friends remember how important "balling" was.

Life-Changing Decision

The evening I got a call from Thomas, a very upset ten-year-old. "Mama is going to take me to Maryland. I do not want to go."

What? "Is your mother there?"

Betty comes to the phone. "What is this all about?"

"I am moving to Maryland and going to take Thomas with me."

"No, you are not. Thomas does not want to go. I will do all that I can to keep you from doing this. Put Thomas back on the phone."

"Son, how about you coming to live with me?"

"I want to stay in Warsaw."

"Okay, let me talk to your grandmother."

"Margaret, what can we do."

"Tom is happy here with Rudy and me. We would love for him to stay with us. If that is okay with you. Just help us out."

"Would you rather stay with your Grandparents?"

"Yes."

"Betty. From now on the support check will go to their address."

I began sending Thomas his own check of $10.00 a week in the same envelope.

If I was going to get married again, likely going to be with Gretchen. All my family loved her. We were compatible in all things and had been together for two years. One Christmas we made a second trip to Waterville, Maine where Gretchen and her brother grew up. We stayed at the family home. One day we made a day trip to the cottage in Friendship. Her parents wanted to see the progress on new construction having a basement dug, new foundation so cottage could be moved further back on the property. We were in Maine for five days. Gretchen most likely thinking I was going to talk with her parents. Ask for their permission. I did not. I had a decision to make. Do it quick. I could not.

Gretchen was ready. Had even asked, "Marry Me." I was not sure. Too many trust issues are jammed in my head. Gretchen's parents continue putting pressure about moving back to Maine. One day Gretchen told me what was being said. "You either get married in Virginia or move back to Maine." Gretchen has graduated from VCU. A Math teacher and Girls Basketball coach at a private school in Powhatan County. South. I live in the East End of Henrico County. More than sixty miles apart and without the Expressway(s). With my job and night classes. We saw as much of each other as time allowed. Sometimes Gretchen would come to Highland Springs. Most of the time working on school papers. We talked about her moving in. Will not work. "I have too much going on at the school, practice, games, math class. Cannot make that drive every day."

She leased an apartment off Huguenot Road. We saw less and less of each other. Months go by. I drove to the school to watch the basketball games, whenever I could. When she was speaking at a school awards dinner, she invited me. I was there. We were seeing each other but things are not the same. One evening Gretchen calls me. "I am engaged to Robert, a teacher at school." [Little Man in Head: *"What did you expect, Harold."*] Gut punch. "Going to leave your things I have, the photo memories in the apartment office. Told them you are going to pick things up. I am so sorry, Harold. You know why this is happening." I knew. The man with a failed pass was hard to explain. I never went to pick up my things. Did Gretchen leave a goodbye letter? Will never know what could have been. Harvey Lee and sister-in-law Brenda were invited to the wedding. Brenda was Gretchen's Maid of Honor. Harvey told me that Gretchen's parents talked with him. "We really liked Harold, but for some reason he would not let us get close." How do you explain to parents. In love with your daughter. Am a very good guy. Asking your permission to marry her. Two failed marriages. Two kids. I was not prepared to share a whole lot with anyone. Timing is not in favor. Life was my shame. Next two years I regretted letting a good one get away.

College Graduation

I gave myself one night a week to go out. Local establishments where there was a live band. Dancing. Beer. Cocktails. Women. My last class for the week was on Thursday evening; at the Bars by 9:45 p.m. The rest of the weekend was for studies, taking twelve credits. I was in the world that I wanted to be. It has been a struggle to pull out of the bottom I ended up in. In the past but not forgotten. My poor life decisions were not going to keep me on the bottom. Howard P. Foley Company was like a family. We all knew each other. Families. Kids. Wives. Girlfriend's. Hunting and fishing. Parties. We were like brothers and sisters.

In 1968 RPI became VCU. It was 1971 when I received a call from Mr. Ankeny, Head of Engineering. Ankeny was at RPI when Harvey Lee attended. Mr. A. offered me a chance to complete the degree at VCU in June 1972. "Before the change is made to the Community College." I would have to attend classes during the day. He would set up the curriculum to make it happen. I had to decline! "Do not know how I can do it." Could not pull the trigger that quick. My situation was what it was. My doing, on his own, ask no favors. In 1972 VCU dropped the engineering curriculum and became a liberal arts College. The engineering teaching staff and students were moved to the New J. Sargent Reynolds Community College. Added years to my dream.

June 1976. It has taken me ten years, mostly in night classes, four nights a week, while working a full-time job. This was how it had to be. Work, responsibilities, obligations, money to live. Maybe a time in my life that I should have given the offer more thought. Commonwealth of Virginia State Board for Community College J. Sargent Reynolds Community College.

This is to certify that Harold Thomas Hinson has satisfactorily completed the Electrical Electronic Technology curriculum and upon recommendation of the faculty is awarded the Associate Degree in Applied Science together with all the rights and privileges thereto: Given at Richmond, Virginia, this month of June, Nineteen Hundred and Seventy-Six.

H.P Foley Engineering

My advanced plan after graduation was to meet with Jim S. during a lunch break. It is the Monday after graduation.

"Going up the street to see the Boss Man."

This always gets the Shop Foreman apprehensive. "What are you up too, Harold?"

"Going to have a talk about my future." Billy is at his desk just outside of Jim's office. "Is Jim in?"

"Yes, just knock on the door."

"What is on your mind, Harold?" Looks like the shop foreman has called ahead of me.

"As you are aware I finished my degree? Just wanted to let you know that it is my intention to get an engineering job. Do not intend to crawl around the Panel Shop much longer. I want to give you the opportunity before moving on. Want to thank you for allowing me to go to day classes when needed. Allowing me to work after hours. Not lose any Pay."

"Will take it under advisement." If this sounds cocky, so be it. It is really about a proud man who has seen the bottom and dug his way out.

That afternoon shop foreman Robert's voice over the intercom. "Harold, up the street is on Line 3 for you." I had not told the guys in the shop what I was planning to do. Foley Panel Shop now included Bill, my former manager, Howard the painter and Lyn from Power System and Controls. All had called me about the possibility of coming to Foley.

"Hello, Jim."

"Have thought about what we talked about. I want you to report to the main office next Monday morning. Robert knows where you will be. Want to see what you can do in engineering."

"Thanks Jim." [Little Man in Head: *"Need to tell the Shop guys."*]

Monday morning, I am working in the Foley Engineering Department for Tom F., an Electrical Engineer Graduate of South Carolina University. My first job was to estimate a Project from Reynolds Can Engineering Documentation. When is the expected delivery? Contact the vendors for material price and delivery. I knew what was required to punch a hole in sheet metal. Time and material required. Mount a relay, terminal blocks, cut a length of wire, put a wire number on each end of the wire, etc. I used my experience from doing control panel assembly over the years. I could see it as I wrote down the numbers. I was able to come up with an accurate estimate. Estimates were not a guess. Foley will never lose money on projects that I estimated.

The job duties went from estimating to drafting and design. Consulting Engineering Documentation contained a description of what was needed. Fabrication documentation drawings. Just a sketch of what was required, a brief description. [Little Man in Head: *"A pretty picture."*] I taught myself how to draw, never been on a Drafting Board. The days of pencil on Drafting Paper/Mylar. Make a mistake, a change, erase it. Do it again. No delete buttons. Typewriters were the norm.

When a copy of the drawing was required, a blueprint was made. Hope that everything worked like it was suppose too. If not, the original document could be destroyed.

How I Met Shannon

I had been in the Engineering Department for less than six months when it happened. "I want to introduce you to our new receptionist." The existing receptionist, Happy, was introducing her to office personnel. "This is Shannon." Shannon smiled. Our eyes met. I was stricken at first sight. I would see Shannon in the office every day. At the breakroom, copier, and when she brought me "You Missed a Call" pink notes, we exchanged small talk. Word got around the office that Shannon and her husband have split up. This time it is for good. Then that day etched in my memory the message written on a pink note: "Mr. Edwards called. 804-555-5108. OVER." On back of the pink note she wrote: "Would you like to go for a drink after work?'

[Little Man in Head: *"Sweet Jesus."*]

We decided to meet at the Holiday Inn Bar on Robin Hood Road. Talked and laughed a lot. Had two drinks. Hugged. "See you tomorrow." Have dated many women over the years. Told myself it had to be someone real special to get me hooked again. Thirty-four years young. Do not screw this up. [Little Man in Head: *"Hooked, Harold."*]

Janie G. worked in the Engineering Department calling on vendors for prices and delivery. One day while talking, "Going to meet some friends after work at the Skiligalley. Would you like to come?"

"Sounds good to me." I arrived and looked around. Saw Janie and Shannon sitting at a table booth. Janie waves me over. I slide into the empty side of the booth. Thirty minutes later, Janie looks at her watch. "Have to go. Babysitter is leaving in a half hour." Now Shannon and I are facing each other across the table. We talk while dropping coins into the slot of the record selection station. We like the same music. All time lost with just the two of us. Talking, laughing, playing music. Then the lights came on. Chairs had been turned over on top of the tables. The waitress is sweeping the floor. "You must leave. We are closing." That was the first that we realized the time. It was one in the morning. I escorted Shannon to her Duster. "Goodnight." Shannon pulled out of the parking lot on her way home. I drove to Highland Springs in the opposite direction. *Life is good.*

We started dating. Movies. Dinner. Concerts. We left after work and drove to the Norfolk Scope where Billy Joel was in Concert, then back to Highland Springs.

First Dating Time

Moving HP Foley PU

Shannon's Parents

We would see each other most every weekend. Shannon coming to Highland Springs. One weekend Saturday she called, "Will you come to Stonehenge today?" Shannon lived with her parents, Rosalie and Erwin H. This was the first time that I would meet them. Shannon's father had a standing Tee Time, 9 a.m. every weekend. The parents moved into a custom-built home in the Spring of 1977. The home up on a hill overlooking the 16th Hole. Tee to Green. Back deck overlooking from Green up to the Tee. A golfers dream.

I arrived at noon. What a home this place is. Parked the Z in front of the right-side garage door on the lower level of the home. Shannon was looking for me. Waved from the deck. She appeared in the doorway leading to what turns out to be her room. Her mother Rosie was waiting in the kitchen. Shannon introduces this lovely Southern lady. Rosie was born and grew up in North Carolina. She graduated in Chemistry from Wake Forrest. "Can I get you anything, Harold? Cold beer; drink?"

"I will take a cold beer, thank you."

We are talking when a horn starts blowing. "Oh no. You are parked in front of Daddy's garage door." We hurry down to the lower level. Shannon opens the garage door. I exit the door. A wave to her dad and moved the Z to front of another garage door. We all meet again in the kitchen. Shannon gives me a proper introduction to her dad. Erwin H. is a handsome gentleman of six foot two. Trim with a small pot belly. Mid 40s-to-50s in age. Dressed in plaid golf pants with a golf shirt color coordinated to the pants. White penny loafers. About 175 lbs. Erwin has a firm handshake. I was taught to always give a firm handshake.

Erwin gets a beer and motions me to the family room. Shannon and Rosie disappear, leaving us to talk. We are telling each other about our lives. Growing up with a single parent in a small town with our mothers. He was born and grew up in Marietta, Georgia. Not having a whole lot when they were young. Has a brother. Military veterans. Attended college on the G.I. Bill. Erwin graduated from Georgia Tech. Mechanical Engineering. Working our way to where we are today. Not looking for a handout. Just a hand up. Erwin worked for two years. "Did not like Engineering." He had a friend that worked with Crawford and Company, Atlanta, Georgia. Erwin left Engineering. Went to work with Crawford. Erwin and Rosie got married. First daughter Shannon was born. Takes over as Manager of a failing Crawford Office in Corpus Christy, Texas. That is where the second daughter Melinda is born. Erwin gets transferred to Richmond as manager of the new Crawford Office. They purchased this property and are founding members of Stonehenge Golf and Country Club. This was the first time that I met a parent that I felt comfortable telling about my past. Erwin heard the story of the failures and success.

Shannon and Rosie come back about the time I was getting ready to leave. After the goodbyes, Shannon walks me back to the Z. "I hope your dad liked what I had to say." I leave Stonehenge and head back to Highland Springs. Southside to the East End, a two-hour drive. *Life is good.* Shannon called me soon after I got home. "When you left honey, I asked Daddy what he thought of you." He said, "You have finally found a man that can take care of your ass."

Datsun 260Z with Me in Driveway of Shannon's Parents' Home

Engagement Ring

My new life has begun with Shannon and her Collie Wendy. She divorced her husband. "He was not good for me." We loved being with each other. I had never known a more everyday fun-loving-life woman. Shannon put up a Christmas Tree in her room. On the tree I hung a Koala Bear, holding a ring box. I waited as long as I could, before asking Shannon over to the tree and pointed. She started crying as she opens the box. I had already asked Rosie and Erwin if they were okay with me asking to marry their daughter. They were overjoyed. From that time the Koala Bear was hung on every Christmas tree. In the Fall and Spring every chance we would go to Nags Head. Shannon would find us a place for long weekends that did not cost an arm and leg. The favorite place was the new Islander Motel. Small and the room rent was reasonable. No pool but right on the beach at Milepost 16. This is where we decided to have our Honeymoon.

Shannon and Harold, 1979

Two months before the Wedding, we went to see Pat M. Foley Fleet Vehicle Purchase Agent. "We want you to order us a Chevy Van from Hechler Chevrolet in Highland Springs?"

"Can do it on a purchase order. You go to the bank and get the loan. Pay Foley for the Van when it comes in."

"We want it built on a special order."

"Suggest that you purchase the Van like done with Foley Vehicles, Transmission Cooler, Heavy Duty, V8, Automatic Transmission, Size increase in the tires, Towing package."

"We want no windows in the Van Body, a Radio Delete, High Back Captain Seats, Tinted Glass, Gray Color exterior, Burgundy Interior."

"Should be here in a month."

Van by September, wedding in October. I went to the Audio Exchange Store on Broad Street and purchased a Sony Cassette Stereo Radio with Separate Amplifier. Must have our music.

The Wedding

Shannon moved to Highland Springs. We started fixing up the Townhouse. She putting her women's touch on the place. We worked well together, most of the time. We had strong ideas on how it should be done. Most of the time I was not the strong one. Shannon started making the wedding plans. To save cost we decided to have the wedding at her parent's home at Stonehenge. The family would make most of the food. Shannon and Rosie coming up with a menu. She found a two-piece band. Sister-in-law Melinda and her roommate in college are going to sing a song. Harvey and Brenda's pastor Ken agreed to marry us. We would provide the booze for the party. You know we had to have a party. All our co-workers, family and friends invited. Jerry J., Mike H. and Rick R. asked to do wedding pictures. Howard H. furnished two iced down kegs of beer. My best friend Ronnie M. agreed to be my Best Man. Susie O. was Shannon's Mistress of Honor. I told Harvey Lee that he was Best Man twice. Not this time. They set the date in the Fall on a Saturday. Was same date that Erwin and Rosie were married.

Could not have ordered a more perfect weather day. Fall and all its splendor. The trees were still full with multi-colored leaves. The sun was shining. Temperature in the high fifties. The humidity was low, a blue bird day. Shannon's family; Aunts; Uncles and all the children have arrived at 12000 Bromwich Drive. The wedding ceremony will be held on the front steps. Chairs are arranged on the lawn for the older folks. Standing room for others. I got to the house around noon. "Shannon has gone to get her hair done. She wants to look special for you, Harold."

"Where do you want me to go get dressed, Rosie?"

"Come with me to the Master Bedroom." Erwin leads the way. I had showered before leaving home in Highland Springs, knowing that it was going to be a mad house. It was. Cousins, Sister, Children all trying to get ready at the same time. Lucile. The wonderful black lady that has helped Rosie at home for many years with the care of the family Matriarch Zell Kearney. Mother of Rosie, Molly, Annie, Martha and brother Ike. He was not here. Zell. When their father passed, started making homemade potato chips. There were four siblings to feed. After they are all grown, Zell is still young and begins to travel. The first trip was to Italy and a visit with her daughter Martha and husband Charles B. Uncle Charlie is in the Foreign Service. They have four children, Barbara, Charlie, Becky, and Nan. All the children were born oversees. Zell liked it so much that she took a job at the Embassy. Manage the Commissary. "Just for a little while." Zell stayed for ten years. Quite a lady, even knew Frank Sinatra. Lucile is craving a Smithfield Ham. I walk in the kitchen from the bedroom. Lucile begins shaking the butcher knife. "You better be good to my Shannon." I walked over to Lucile and gave her a big hug and kiss on the creek. "Don't you worry about that darling." [Little Man in Head: *Sweet lady, Harold."*]

The guests start showing up. Early. The circle driveway is left clear for now. Wexwood Road is filling up on the edges with wedding party vehicles. We have a lot of friends and family. Shannon is not back yet from the hairdresser. She is late. "Big E" opens the bar. Shannon would have said, "That was a good move, Dad. Help yourself, please."

Jim S., "Now this is my kind of wedding." Jim pours himself a Scotch on the rocks. Erwin is next. The band has shown up. Shannon has not. I directed the band where to set up in the lower level. Brenda was busy finishing the Wedding Cake baked like I requested. Devil's Food with Fudge Icing. Shannon returns from the hairdresser. "Not happy with how my hair turned out." I loved her hair.

The preacher is waiting on the front steps with the others when we came walking down the sidewalk. People start smiling and pointing. We did not know, but walking four feet behind was Wendy. Glad that picture was taken. Wendy was not going to be left out. Went to Rosie's side. Laid down. It was a long ceremony. Pastor Ken did a fabulous job.

The Wedding

After the Wedding. Pictures. Cutting the cake. Toast. Opening the Wedding gifts. The Wedding party is directed to go down to the lower level where the party is going to be. Tables are set up for finger food. Mama and Warfield, our Father H.A. with his wife Retta are here. A table with booze and Howard's two kegs of beer on tap out on the Patio. When the band took a break, Shannon, Bob B. Eugene M. and I sang an old song. The statement made by most when leaving: "When are you two getting married again? This is the most fun I have had in years." We spent the night there.

The next morning everyone up for breakfast. The family members that went to hotels have come back to the house. After breakfast everyone starts cleaning up from the wedding. After we help get everything straight, we leave for the honeymoon. The family have all gathered outside to see us off. [Little Man in Head: *"Have not seen you this happy for a long time, Harold."*] We leave Wendy with Rosie and set out for Nags Head Islander Motel. The weather was great for the entire week. There are not many places to eat out in October 1979 Nags Head, but this Fall a new restaurant is opening, Tail of the Whale, and we were there. Tale of the Whale is owned by a young couple. Bring your brown bag, purchase the setups. They have a roving musician that found us on a honeymoon. Came to our table and played. It was magic. The seafood was out of this world. We went back three more times that week. Fall fishing season in the Outer Banks with lots of fisherman in the area. We played Gin Rummy and Yahtzee. While playing on a chilly day and looking out of the picture window overlooking the ocean, "What is that?" It was Bluefish swimming through the surf. I put on some warm clothes and grabbed my fishing pole. Ran down to the beach. Could not have taken me more than five minutes. The surf fishermen started showing up from everywhere. Word travels fast when the Bluefish Blitz is on. Did not need cut bait, just throw a hook in the surf. Did not matter what. Instant hook-up. Reel that one in, take Bluefish off the hook, back in for another. This went on for fifteen minutes. Then gone. Nothing. The surf fishermen take off in their trucks up the beach. Chasing. I go back to Shannon after giving all but one fish to a young fisherman. "On my Honeymoon. No time to fool with more than one." I cleaned the Bluefish and cooked it on the Gas Grill. We took many pictures. There was a small kitchen in the room with just a counter, cabinets, and small refrigerator. Shannon made us lunch sandwiches. Sometimes she put together a meat, olives, pickles and cheese platter with crackers. We went out for dinner. It was a wonderful time. Waking up every day with my beautiful wife. Shopping what was there back then. Sea Shell place and Craftsman Shops. There were no large shopping centers. The Honeymoon was over too soon. We would be back many times.

Wendy Following the Newly Weds

Shannon and Harold Oct 20, 1979

Shannon on Our Honeymoon 1979

Thanksgiving 1979

A four-day weekend. We drive to work together in our Chevy Van. Have been married a month. On the way to the townhouse, we stop at the ABC Store, Eastgate Mall. The parking lot is jam packed. We are waiting with the van running for someone to leave a space. "Hey, is that the ABC Store manager fighting with that guy?" I look. There are two men pulling on each other's coats. "Can you do something to help the manager?"

"I will." Just then the guy comes out of his leather coat. Booze bottles start hitting and breaking on the sidewalk. He starts running into the parking lot on my side of the van. The manager chasing. I put my left hand on the door handle. Pull up while holding the door closed. My left foot on the door bottom. As the guy gets to the van fender, I pushed the door open with my foot. He slams right into the door frame edge. Falls to the pavement. Face first. I jumped out of the van and sit on him. The store manager comes running. Stomps on the man's head. Out cold.

"You ain't going anywhere." Two Henrico Police Officers show up. I am still sitting on the man.

"Who are you, Sir?"

The store manager tells the officer. "This man stopped this piece of shit from getting away." "You can get off of him now." "Give me your name and address." The second officer was handcuffing the guy. I recognized that face. It was Margaret M. that I dated some years before Shannon. All the way home, Shannon kept saying, "Her Hero."

We spent Thanksgiving Day with Rosie, Erwin and the extended family. Erwin and I played nine holes at Stonehenge Golf Club with a pair of Erwin's golfing buddies that morning. Shannon helped with the large Thanksgiving meal. It is always a good time when this Irish family gets together. Aunt Molly; Uncle Jeff and daughter Leslie. Sister Melinda home from James Madison U. Bellies and cheeks are hurting from food and laughing. Great food prepared by wonderful cooks and plenty to drink with Irish music on the turntable. Every holiday we spent with her family. Chevy Chase. Virginia. Maryland. Nags Head. The family setting that I loved. So many years not having this in my life.

Phillip Morris Employment
First Try, Second Try

Been at H. P. Foley Controls Division Engineering for four years. Married for a year in the Fall of 1980. We talked and agree we want more for our future. Will require me to find an Engineering Job with better benefits. During a WESCO Bull Roast I see some guys that I had done projects for. Some also worked at Power Systems and Controls before move to Philip Morris, USA. Philip Morris is expanding. Hiring the best engineering talent for the Operation Center located on the property next to the Manufacturing Center. "Heard PM looking for people in Engineering."

"My Group Leader Andy S. is right over there. "Harold is interested in coming on at PM."

"I know of you. Give me your home address. I will get HR to send you the required paperwork." That is the way it worked. The person had to approach PM about the job. Philip Morris had heard from Phil E. Commonwealth Controls Corp that I was the first engineer using all the Modicon 284 Programmable Logic Controller functions. In a single program. A project I engineered for Burlington Fibers in Clarksburg, Virginia.

The Philip Morris Human Resources paperwork came in the mail. Shannon and I worked on the papers. Sent them back. A few days later we got a phone call. "My name is Joe F. I am the Manager of the Group you are applying to join. On your paperwork you show that you have a two-year technical degree. You want a salary of $25,500."

"That is correct Mr. F. Five hundred more than I am now making."

"A man with only a two-year degree making $25,000 a year. I suggest you stay right where you are. Philip Morris requires four-year degrees for engineering."

It has been two months when Shannon answered the phone. "Yes, he is here." Hands phone to me.

"My name is Joe F. Do you remember me?"

"Yes."

"We want to take a closer look at you. Are you still interested in working at Philip Morris?"

"Yes, I am."

"You will not need to redo the paperwork. The Human Resources contact, Mr. Jim K., will send you a letter containing all the details. Should be in the mail tomorrow." Our life is about to change for the good. I take a vacation day. Meet Jim K. at the P.M. Human Resources Building.

My engineering interview is with Steve C. Also at the Interview is Bill S. "Joe usually does all the interviews. Joe is out of town." Steve starts the interview with question of background experience. Moves to reading an elementary drawing. I have been reading elementary drawings since Air Force Tech School. "What is this device?" I named the Symbol. Steve said it was known by another name.

That is when Bill gets involved. "Dam Steve, you know Harold knows. Cut out the crap." I have been doing projects for Bill and Steve over the past ten years in the Panel Shop and Foley Engineering.

Steve says, "Harold, I talked with my Uncle Fredrick K. at Burlington Fibers. He spoke fondly of you. It is always a good thing when using a reference to contact that person. You did." The German engineer I worked with on the conversion of German language elementaries to English. Used a Modicon PLC to replace the Punch Card Selection Switches. The program using every function.

"Did not know he was your uncle, Steve."

"Where would you like to go to lunch, Harold?"

"How about the Red Lobster?"

"Knew we were going to like you. Joe always took us to McDonalds." I gave Foley two weeks notice.

July 16, 1981. My first day at Philip Morris Engineering. Shannon was promoted to be Jim S.'s Secretary. Four Foley Engineers went to Philip Morris the same month. Jim called Philip Morris. "Stop taking my people." After the October Performance Appraisal, I received a 9.9% salary increase. Profit Sharing was 14.99%. Shares Philip Morris Stock. I drive the Datsun 260Z to Philip Morris and Shannon drives the Chevy Van to Foley. [Little Man in Head: *"Miss being with Shannon at work."*]

We decide to start our own family. Shannon not happy doing that in the townhouse. "It would be like living in an apartment." I agreed and we start looking for a home. The Real Estate Broker Peg J. calls. She has found the perfect place in the West End, Henrico County on a street that has little through traffic. We meet at the house that has not been lived in for over a year. Needs a lot of TLC. The price reflects that. We sign the contract and apply for a loan. The mortgage loan was 14%; Jimmy Carter is the President. We sell the townhouse to a lady that wants it as rental property. Things are going to be tight. Still learning how to manage money as a married couple.

Driveway at 9020 Sparrow Drive

Sparrow Drive

All the streets in this West End development are named after Birds. Sparrow, Blue Jay, Starling. The homes were built in the 1950s. Ours on Sparrow Drive built in 1955. The previous owners both died in the home.

Before the move. Sparrow Drive needs a lot of work. Money is tight. It is a three Bedroom; one Bathroom; Living Room; Dining Room, Utility Room. A screened side porch and front and back stoops. On a half-acre fenced lot. There are three apple trees and a big Sweet Gum shade tree. A great side yard space for the garden. A tool shed that can be redone with some siding and a new roof. We decided to refinish the Knotty Pine Cabinets in the Kitchen. I found out how much new hardware cost and remembered using Pax Powered Hand Soap in boiling hot water on KP. It took the dried egg yolk off silverware. I decided to strip existing hardware and repaint. Shannon wanted a pot rack and an island in the kitchen like we built in the townhouse. Pantry shelves in the Utility Room. We redid the Bathroom with a new vanity and fixtures. Shannon also wanted a clothesline in the back yard. Every room painted, then new carpet. Torn out old shrubbery. Planted shrubbery moved from the townhouse. Home was not perfect, but a good start. The next year we added a deck off the back stoop around the Apple Trees. Enclosed the screen porch with patio doors to make a Sun Room. Moved the TV and stereo equipment there. Shannon helped me put in a great garden, using the Crockett Victory Garden method. A lot of plants in a small area. Shannon loved to can the bounty. She put up a lot of food. There were so many Apples to share with the neighbors. We had family and friends over all the time. One Winterday we get home to find hanging on the front door handle a Yellow Tag from the City of

Richmond Gas: "Your Gas is cut off. We took a reading on the Meter. Call 555-5555. Do Not Turn the Gas Back On."

"What are we going to do?" For five months I had been contacting Richmond Gas to come out and read the meter. "We do not read the meter each month. The gas usage is estimated with the records on file."

The house had little insulation in the attic. Crawl space had none. We had the insulation fixed. I knew how to read the gas meter. "What we are being billed for is more than has been used. I am going to turn the gas back on. Light the pilots."

A month passed before I called Richmond Gas. "You did what? I am transferring this call to my supervisor." Finally. I get to talk to the person in charge.

"Mr. Hinson, I understand that you turned your gas back on."

"That is correct. A month and a half ago."

"Why did you do that?"

"Cold. No Heat. No Hot Water. And our pet parrot. I had tried to inform Richmond Gas about the overcharge. Your tag left on our door said that Richmond Gas read the meter when it was shut off."

"We do. let me find that information. It says that the meter reading was 1234560."

"Now Mam, look at the last bill that we received."

"Oh, Mr. Hinson, I see what you mean. Richmond Gas owes you a credit of $535.00. I guess turning the gas on has not caused an issue."

We loved living in the West End. So convenient to everywhere. Regency Mall was a block away. Most Saturday mornings would find me in Sears Roebuck Tool Department. Our favorite Italian Restaurant, La 'Talia, just up Patterson Ave, before you cross the James River into Goochland County. Family-owned with fresh-made meals. My favorite dish White Clam Sauce with Pasta. Shannon liked the Veal Picata. Do not be in a hurry. Cooked fresh when you ordered it. Sunday morning, we went to Otto's Bakery and Coffee Shop. Carried the Sunday paper. A couple of pastries and coffee. Stayed there for an hour. Seconds on the coffee. Life was so happy and carefree. Shannon often finished a sentence before I did. Was like we had the same brain. Two people could not love each other more. Love the same things. Love-making. Music. Food. We were meant to be together. Then life begins to change.

Our World Changes

Shannon's GYN, Dr. Henry B. has her on hormones for a couple months. Increase the chance for the pregnancy. She starts having female problems. "Please get a second opinion." This is where a husband has zero control. I knew when to butt out. Shannon must have an operation to confirm what is wrong. Doctor brings the petri dish into the waiting room with a large cyst the size of a tennis ball. Looked like it was living. Veins. "I think that this is the problem. Only took half of this Ovary. She still has one whole Ovary left." I did not like the arrogant doctor. Shannon takes months to recover. Settled back in our home. Wonderful life will start again.

Collie Wendy begins to limp. Take her to Broad Street Vet Hospital. She has cancer in her left leg. Dr. Neil R. operated and removed the leg. "Wendy will walk after time. She will learn how. Believe it or not you will be amazed. She will be okay." Having a half-acre fenced back yard was great. Wendy loved that yard. She stayed outside during the day while we were at work. Always greeted us at the gate when we drove into the driveway. Three months have passed on a day Wendy did not greet. I found her laying in the hole going to the foundation crawl space door. She could not get up on her own. After the call from Vet, we knew we had to put her down. The cancer had come back in the stomach area. No operation this time will save her. We loved on Wendy all weekend. Fixed her a Steak on Sunday. Monday morning back to Broad Street Vet Hospital. I carried her inside. Shannon said she could not be with her. We had her cremated. Two weeks have passed when I came home from work. Shannon had taken a day of vacation. Sitting on the front steps were Shannon and a ball of fur. She went that day and purchased a female Sable and white Shetland Sheepdog. Full papers from a well-known breeder in Blackstone, Virginia. Named her Donacales Tess. The loss of a pet better if you get another. We have a ball of energy with us now.

Shannon with Sheltie

Shannon is beginning to have more female problems. Seeing a different GYN. "Need to go to the Hospital." Shannon is not a person that complains. I have learned that when Shannon says she needs help, she does. Constant abnormal pain. Our dream of starting a family was over. We discussed adoption. Did not happen.

May 1983. Memorial Day, four-day holiday. I was rear-ended while driving our van on the way to Westbury Pharmacy. We purchased a Toyota Celica GT. Need two dependable vehicles with our work in different locations. I decided to see what was wrong with the 260Z. Removed the spark plugs from the L26 engine. Shannon helped with cranking the starter. "Going to do a Compression Test." I have the Compression Gage 'pressed' in the number six Spark Plug Hole. Blew the Compression Gage out of my hand. Water started coming out of the Spark Plug Hole. "Found the problem. Blown Head Gasket. That is why the engine bucks and shuts off when trying to start."

"How about helping me this weekend to pull the Head on the Z Car?" Cary L. came early Saturday morning. Shannon had the Toyota to go to Rosie's and shopping. Off to Boulevard Datsun Service for the parts. I gave the parts counter person the list of parts. He provided other parts also needed. I see another box. "Are those 240Z Carbs?"

"Yes, but I cannot sell them if you are going to put them on your 260Z." Datsun 260Zs had a known problem since 1974 with Vapor Lock. Federal Emissions prevented problem to be fixed because it would require dealerships to change the carburetors to earlier Datsun 240Z type. I had been researching the problem and knew what was required. "Are you going to do that?"

"Of course not." Parts guy sold me the Round Top Carbs. "Will also need the Phenolic Carb Spacers and the Throttle linkage."

We started taking the 2600CC Straight Six Motor apart. I had ordered a Factory Datsun Service Manual and had researched what was required. I also purchased the Full Gasket Kit, new Timing Chain and Water Pump. Might as well do other parts that may fail soon. We had the motor back together by late afternoon. Only one problem when trying to start. A big backfire. "Damn it." Put the Distributor in 180 degrees out. Reset the Distributor. Started right up. No leaks. Made a test drive down Parham Road. All is good.

Sunday morning, I started pulling the Intake Manifold with Stock Flat Top Carburetors. By early afternoon the new Round Tops Carbs were installed. Primed with oil. Changed the Stock Carburetor Air Filter Assembly to same Air Filter Assemblies used on the Triumph TR-6. The Z started right up; adjusted the idle, took the Z for a road test. This 260Z has now been turned loose. She is very good. I again started driving the Z to work.

Thomas Summer Job
United States Navy/Air Force

Shannon talked with Billy P. at Foley about getting Thomas a summer job. A 'Go For' working with the field electricians. Thomas will learn a lot about life with those guys. He turned seventeen in May. Son and Father will get to know each other better. Most nights the two go to the 7-Eleven, for a half-gallon of ice cream. Cut the carton in half. Two dinner plates and eat. Jimmy Mac Foley Electrician. "What is up with that boy of yours? It does not matter how much we mess with Tom. He never says a word."

"You are not going to get that country boy upset. Give up."

Next year summer job with Foley was the same. Thomas has turned eighteen. One afternoon he brings two beers to me sitting on the front steps. "Dad, have heard Mama's story. Now I want to know the story in your words."

"Son, you know me well enough. If you ask, I will tell you. Are you sure that you want to know the whole story?"

"Yes, Dad. I want to know." I told Thomas what happened. "Thought I was not being told the whole story."

Couple of afternoons later. "Thomas you are eighteen now. We are going out together. Dad is buying you a beer." There were many laughs and hugs. Thomas did not have many beers. I did. Thomas took the car keys. Drove us back to Sparrow Drive. Father/son bonding overdue for years.

One evening I receive a call from Thomas. "Dad, I need your advice. Just failed the swimming test to become a Flight Rescue Seaman." *What?* "I am in Basic Training with the Navy. The requirement to become a Rescuer has a final test in the pool with weights strapped to your body. Test must be done without touching the side of the pool. Was going to drown. I must tell the Navy what I want to do?"

"Let me ask you something. First place. Did not know that you had joined the Navy. You did not call me before you joined. Now you want me to tell you what to do? Think about that for a moment. You have always been fascinated with airplanes. Navy–boats, at sea for months. Air Force– airplanes. Both feet on the ground most of the time. What is the Navy offering you?"

"Can get an Honorable Discharge with a clean record."

"I would take the Discharge. Come home. Get your head out of your ass. Enlist in the Air Force, if that is what you want to do." One of my peeves with Thomas was his lack of talking with me. All the years growing up with his mother and her parents. Rappahannock High School Baseball Team pitcher. "Call me, Son. Let me know when and where the games are being played. Will get off work and come." I never got that phone call. Harvey Lee's friend set up a meeting for Thomas with the Air Force Recruiter. Thomas got it together.

Harold and Tom
Dumbarton Square Team

Erwin

We are at Rosie and Erwin's home in Stonehenge. Celebrating Shannon's Birthday. This family taught me how to do birthdays. Person having a birthday got to pick what food. Never remembered having it that way. Being born on the fourth of July was pretty much the same thing. Hamburgers. Hot Dogs. Potato Salad. Mac Salad. Watermelon. Ice Cream. Shannon celebrates hers for a solid week. She loved birthdays. Shannon has opened her gifts. We are sitting in the dining room to a special dinner Shannon requested. "Big E" stands up and gives a toast to his oldest daughter. Erwin goes to sit back in the chair. Misses the chair. Sits in the floor. Erwin looks dazed. I gave him a moment. When he did not try to get up, I leaned over. "You okay. Erwin? You want me to help you get up?"

"That would be good Harold." Shannon's big birthday present was a check to buy a Microwave for our fixed-up kitchen. The island I built will be the right place for it. The next day after work we go directly to Sears Roebuck. Look at Microwaves and get something to eat at Obrianstein's while at the mall. Back home. The phone answer machine is flashing. A message from Melinda. "Come to Henrico Doctors Hospital. Dad was brought here late this afternoon." We find Rosie and Melinda in the Emergency Room.

"What is going on, Mom."

"They think that Erwin had a mild Stroke. He was able to reach the call button on his office phone. They found him sitting on the floor."

"Just like last night, Mom?"

"Yes."

It is now near midnight when a doctor comes to see us. Introduces himself. My specialty is Cancer. "Mrs. Hayes, your husband has Brain Cancer. It is inoperable. Mr. Hayes has three months to live. Take him home and let him enjoy the Masters. It will be the last one he sees." Shannon breaks down. Rosie comes home with us to Sparrow Drive. Shannon takes the next day off and spends it with Rosie. The family starts making plans for Erwin coming home from the hospital. Treatment options. Two days later, Erwin is discharged, like his old self. Plays Golf with his buddies. We do things together. Erwin's best friend has a cottage at Duck, North Carolina. "Take it for the week." The whole family goes on vacation like we have done many times before. Harold has spent more time with Shannon's family than his own. Life. The thing that Shannon and Harold enjoyed, going on vacation to Nags Head. Most of the time Erwin and Rosie would join them. After breakfast Erwin and I played a round of Golf at Seashore Golf Links. Shannon, Melinda and Mom Rosie spent the day shopping. Planning food for next meal. Sitting on the beach. Erwin spent rest of his day reading a book. I took gear to the beach and surf fished, catching enough for dinner, Puppy Drum cooked on the BBQ grill. We also went out to eat at our favorite restaurant, George's. The week was wonderful. Sad. Knowing this will be the last one together. No one brought it up. You could see it on the faces.

Shannon and Harold at Nags Head

Erwin's health takes a turn when he starts the chemo treatments. Golf is not for him any longer. Riding on the golf cart to be with his long-time buddies will do. Erwin gets to that place where he cannot say or explain what he wants. Shannon and Melinda take leaves of absence from their jobs. Move back home to help their mother. I visit only when told it is okay. Shannon, Melinda, and Rosie cut their hair short. Erwin has lost his. He does not want to see anyone else. A ramp built to get Erwin in and out of the house. He is now confined to a wheelchair. The girls transport him to and from the hospital. The time comes. A hospital bed is set up in the Great Room looking out of the Patio Doors towards the Sixteenth Hole.

Shannon purchased a Blue Front Parrot for him. Erwin loved to tell jokes. Most of them had a Parrot in it. Shannon thinking "Quito" would give her dad some joy. After a while Erwin got tired. Blunt. "When are you going to take that God-damn Parrot home?

June 27th. Shannon calls me. "You better come now. Daddy is not doing well!" Before I can travel to Stonehenge, Erwin has passed. It has been three months to the day, just as told to the family that early morning in the emergency room. When the Chesterfield Police came, Shannon goes into hysterics. "We have to see the body to make sure there was not any foul play."

"Why?" I take Shannon out of the house.

Erwin's service was held at the home in Stonehenge. Family; all of Rosie and Erwin's many friends; employees. Lots of Toasts just as he would have done. Later that night the family held our goodbyes to "Big E" around the 16th Hole at Stonehenge Golf and Country Club. Each of us took some of his ashes and spread them there. Shannon, Melinda and I spent that night with Rosie. The next day was different. We now prepare for a life without "the main man." This will take time. Erwin was here, gone in three months. Too soon. Life is forever changed.

Rosie wants to stay in the home. We visit often. She has closed most of the big house. Living mostly in the end of house with the Kitchen;

Great Room; Half Bath. Sleeping on the couch. Lived this way for almost a year. One day Rosie called Shannon. "Would you and Harold think about moving here with me? I am in this big house by myself. You can bring all your furniture. Take the Master Bedroom and Bath. Will move my bedroom furniture to the Guest Room. All the other furniture that is here can move to the lower level." Rosie has been thinking about this for quite a while. We talked. Have only been living at Sparrow Drive for just over two years. Just finished fixing the place the way we wanted it.

"Do you want to do this Shannon?"

"Only if you do."

"I think it will be good for Rosie and we can save for that place at the river."

"Mom, we will move." A whole new life for us.

Shannon and Rosie at Bromwich Drive

Sparrow Drive Sold
Bromwich Drive

The call to Peg J. Real Estate Broker that found us the house. We met with her on Wednesday. She loved all the improvements that were done. "This house will sell quickly." The contract written for $25,000 more than we had paid for it. "Planning to hold an open house this weekend. If that is okay with you? Keep it neat. The open house will start at 1 p.m. on Sunday." Peg left a lockbox on the front door. Sunday morning. Made sure that the house was neat. Went to Rosie's taking Tessie and Quito with us. Back home at 6:30 that afternoon. Sitting on the coffee table was a signed contract for the asking price, if the perspective buyer can take procession in thirty days. "We did not ask enough, Shannon." Go into panic mode. Lucky, we work good together. Going to miss this place. We learned a lot about each other in this home. The gain from selling the house ended up at $23,000 after expenses for moving. Put that money in the savings account. Ten percent interest each month.

One street from Farnham Drive, on the corner of Wexwood. From the West End to South Side. Rosie and Shannon together again in the same house. They are quite a pair. Tessie is missing that big fenced-in yard. She runs from one window to another. School Bus. Trash Truck. Mail Man. Delivery. Quito is happy back in the same corner where Shannon first brought him to this house. I now have garage space to keep the Datsun 260Z. But no space to have that wonderful garden. I take up the golf game again. Playing in the PM R&D League each week and another two golf afternoons. Sometimes on a weekend. Many times, breaking 85. I had learned a lot playing with Erwin. "Key to golf is playing more. When you hit the ball in trouble, look for the best way to get the ball back in the fairway." Watching "Big E" play was a lesson. Shannon got a set of clubs. Starts taking lessons with Rosie. Rosie plays in the Ladies League at Stonehenge. Never lived in a house this nice. Four full bathrooms. No need to pee outdoors.

I set up my drafting board in the lower level. We start discussing about finding a place on the water. Back to the Northern Neck. Find open land without a house. We plan to build our home. Shannon starts ordering building plan books. When we could not find a plan that we both liked, "Why don't you do our house plans, Honey?" Shannon was my rock. "That way we will get what we want." Found the book, *Carpentry and Building Construction*. "How did you know how to do house plans?" "Read the book."

Shannon suggested that they go to Warsaw on Saturday. Barbara's for her Mother's Day. Be back to Stonehenge for Rosie's Mother's Day. That way we would see both mothers on the weekend. We are having lunch with Barbara and Pop. Mention about looking to buy some land on the water and build a house. Mama and Warfield are so happy for us. Mama suggested that I call old school friend Marion. Marion and his wife Carolyn have the Rice-Packett Real Estate Firm in Warsaw. "That is a great idea." Mama looks up the phone number and hands me the phone.

Waterfront Search
1984 Closing

"Rice/Packett—Marion." "Hey Marion. This is Harold Hinson."

"Harold you are the first person that has called me on my new Bag Phone. I am out here in the garden."

"Looking to buy some waterfront land, at least a half-acre for my wife Shannon and me."

"How much do you want to spend?"

"Thinking nine-to-twelve thousand."

Marion laughs. "Have a six-tenths acre on the water. The owner wants $25,000. I get 10% commission for waterfront. That is out of your price range; but you should see this place to get an idea what $25K buys."

Simonson Penninsula
Richmond County, Virginia, Page 40, Rod Coggin. Morattico Creek is a small estuary a mile and a half long. Upstream from the mouth of Lancaster Creek. Named for Marraughtacual villages, located where they join the Rappahannock River

"Okay."

"Meet me at the Rice-Packett Building at 2 p.m."

This is the first time that Shannon has seen the man. Marion is hard to understand. When he speaks it is like his mouth is full of marbles. When he sings, he has a wonderful voice. "Marion, this is my wife, Shannon." We travel fourteen miles from Warsaw to Simonson.[8] A place I remember growing up. This is where our daddy H. A. kept his Deadrise. We went fishing from here. The land is right in front of the parking lot for the boat ramp. Marion drove them up the driveway overlooking a creek. Stopped under the Willow Tree. The wide water view looked like a river. I was sold.

Getting out of the car, Shannon has that look. "Do not like it. That boat ramp is going to be a problem."

"I do not think so. It is a perfect day in May and there is not a soul here but us."

"How are we going to pay for it? Still build a house?"

Marion overhears Shannon. "The owner wants to hold the paper. Charge 10% interest for ten years. All you will need at closing is $5,000. Another good part of the deal. There is a 400-foot Artesian Well and a three-bedroom septic system already in place. That will save you about $4000."

We walk down the driveway to discuss it. Look at the property from all sides. The land is on a narrow strip. State Highway Route 606 is on the boat ramp side. A wide creek that flows out to the Rappahannock River. At the end of the State Road is an island. Beyond that is the Rappahannock River. This place is surrounded by water with views all around. "Consider how much it would cost us to put in the well and septic."

"Okay Harold, let's do it." With that Shannon smile.

---

[8] Richmond County Virginia, Page 62, 'Simonson. A locality at the Southwest corner of the county on the narrow peninsula between the mouths of Morattico and Lancaster Creeks. Watermen of the Simonson Family operated there in the latter part of the Nineteenth Century including Isaac and John H Simonson.'

"Marion, we will take it."

"The place belongs to Clifton Douglas. They live on a farm up by the Farnham Post Office where Bland is the Post Mistress. Clifton crabs in the Summer from here. He would like to sell that boat and the 17-foot travel trailer. They would be separate from the cost of the land."

"Not interested in the boat, but would like to talk to Clifton about the Trailer."

"Let's go back to my office and fill out the paperwork." We return to Mama and Warfield's. They are so happy.

We talked about the land all the way back to Midlothian. "We can sell the Toyota. That will make the land payment." We were so excited we loaded Tessie and Rosie in the van. I grab my camera and we drive back to Simonson. Started taking pictures. Shannon and Rosie looked at the travel trailer in more detail, making a list of things she wants to do to it. New curtains, need to redo the cushion material. I check where the sun is, where is South. The driveway bank is overgrown, I can work on that this Summer. Meet with Clifton to close on the trailer next week, will call Marion on Monday. Rosie likes it too. We stay for over an hour taking pictures and walking all around the land. Tessie is having a ball. A place to run again.

Monday morning, I tell co-workers about what Shannon and I did over the weekend. "You paid what for that little bit of land?"

Marion contacted Clifton. He was waiting at the trailer. A man about sixty-five years, 5'8", beer gut.

Simonson Trailer

Has the farmers/crabber's tan. We sat at the table in the trailer, hashed old times when Clifton knew Harvey Lee and me growing up. Clifton trying to give me a good deal on the Center Console boat. "Cannot handle a boat right now. Must keep my mind on building our home. What are you asking for this trailer?"

Waterfront Lot

"Fair price is $2000." I take out my checkbook.

"No need to write me a check now. We will take care of that at closing." Clifton holds out his hand to shake. The way things happen here in the Country. "Memorial Day weekend is coming up in a couple weeks. Not going to use the place. Billy M. has used the place in the past. He is not this year. Here is the key, bring your family to the creek."

"Thank you. That is mighty generous."

Thursday afternoon Memorial Day weekend. Shannon has the food; drinks; sheets; blankets; pillows; cooking gear; dishes; cups; glasses packed in the van ready to go with Rosie and Tessie. The trip from

Midlothian to the river took two hours. First thing Shannon and Rosie got done was cleaning that trailer, then we unloaded the van. Shannon and Rosie measure for the materials needed to do curtains and cushion covers. Took me a while to figure out how to set up the beds. I took notes and measured the land for possible house layout. Found the septic tank location. There are two entry pipes in place for the septic. The trailer is sitting in the middle of the lot where the house will be built. The second septic entry is on the driveway side. "Going to move the trailer to the driveway side next Spring before the foundation work can be started." The pump for the artesian well located in a well cubing with concrete lid cover. Clifton had the pump working for us with garden hose connected to the Trailer. All I had to do was turn the pump switch on. There are two propane bottles for the Gas Stove, Heater and Hot Water Tank and a Window Air Conditioner. Tight quarters, but workable. Shannon fixed a simple dinner. After dinner we took a walk towards the river. The Sunset seen for the first time. Unbelievable. We played Yahtzee for a couple of hours and arranged the Dining Table for Rosie's bed. What a sound sleep. Only sounds. Nature, peaceful. Waking up at Sunrise. Alarm clock not needed. Greeted with that first Sunrise on Lancaster Creek. A site we never forgot and talked about often. [Little Man in Head: *"Dream came true, Harold."*]

Next day the neighbors came over for introductions. Facing Lancaster Creek on the left are Sam and Elenore Hull. Both retired sixty-plus-something. They tell us the history. Their Cinder Block Ranch Style home was built in 1955 by Mr. Mangus, a builder from Northern Virginia. He also owned the land that we are purchasing from Clifton. Sam very willing to be sure I knew where the property line markings were located. The property to the left of the Hulls also owned by Mangus. Mr. Lurtheral now living in. He was going to build his 'forever home' on this vacant lot but developed health problems. Lost his wife. Sold the land to Clifton in 1972. The neighbors on our driveway side see us all in the yard and come over. Leonard and Carol Jean Burton. "My brother Earl was going to buy this land." The house that the

Burtons purchased in April 1984 is a two-story residence. The original building, four rooms with a chimney built in 1929 for a fishing lodge.

We purchased the land from a deed with full description of the property boundary. Had the location of "Slave Quarters." The property has never been surveyed. Every weekend we went to "Simonson on Lancaster Creek." Holidays, vacation days.

Clifton became a close friend. "Have you got some crabs we can purchase?" Clifton is pulling his crab pots right in front of the land in Lancaster Creek. All I had to do was call out to him.

"How many dozen do you want, Harold?" Clifton heading home from the crabbing pier he had on Pierson's Island pulled up in the driveway. "Here are the crabs. Will pick the basket up later."

"What do I owe you?"

"We will settle up later." Clifton never settled. When Shannon went for groceries, she picked up a case of Clifton's favorite beer. Pabst Blue Ribbon and a bag of ice. I iced the beer down in a large cooler. While Clifton in the creek pulling crab pots, we put the cooler in his pickup. "Found this cooler in my truck. Do not know where it came from. That beer was mighty good on this hot July day." Winks. Leaves cooler in the driveway. Clifton also supplied me with Peelers. The best bait for fishing. Then on a Sunday afternoon, I started packing to go back to Midlothian. "Why are you not helping?"

"I want to stay here for the week. Is that okay?"

"Just wish I could stay." We had Shannon's Grumman 17-foot aluminum canoe at the creek. Decided to purchase a small boat. Shannon came back to Midlothian the following week. She needed to sew the curtains and cushion covers. "Need some more things at the river." Shannon purchased a journal and renamed the little green book, "Favorite River Recipes." Captured many stories in the green book. Never known. Until I read the journal. This is our story.

Shannon's River Journal

Simonson Rt. 606 Box 391-C1, Richmond County, Farnham, Va. When we bought this land, I had no idea of all the beauty that existed here.[9] Several mornings, we are awakened to find wild Canadian Geese on the beach of our front yard. Seagulls, Ducks, Mockingbirds, Martins, Cardinals, Brown Trasher, Hummingbirds, Shorebirds, and many other birds enjoy the abundance of creepy, crawly things, the knats and mosquitoes, and the many types of fish in the creek. Crabs are easily caught with a string and a raw chicken back, or any type of food that will stay on the string. Crabs peel several times during the Summer. They gorge themselves, then swim to shore to hide in the grasses until they gain the strength to survive in the water. July 4th, Harold's Birthday, he picked up a dozen Soft Shell Crabs on the shoreline. Fried them for breakfast. We fish and crab off the pier in the Burtons' yard. Catch huge Catfish, Stiff-backs, Perch and Bluefish. Tess loves to watch the families of Rabbits feeding on grass and weeds. You can get within 12 inches of the Rabbits without them moving. They are almost tame. Our neighbors are super. We are very fortunate. Bob and Julie Baughman in the quaint white house next to the corn field; Leonard & Carol Burton in the large white house with the great screened porch; and Sam & Eleanor Hull in the green Rancher with the beautiful interior, re-done with pride, themselves. The Langhorne's own the old Simonson Home, a majestic old home that they are renovating to the original beauty. Being on the water without a boat is usually frustrating, but our

---

[9] *Close Ties,* Richmond County Intermediate School, Indian Banks, Page 19.
Richmond County, Virginia 1776-1976, "Indian Banks," by Virginia D.M. Pearson, Page 98, Northern Neck Historical Society Magazine, December 1972.

friends across the river always made sure we were included in the River and Creek Trips; swimming, skiing, and all-around good times. Mack and Mary Brown usually pick us up since they put in at Garrett's Marina, across the river and closest to us.

After pouring over several issues of the Trading Post, we found a boat within our price range. That sounded promising; driving way out in Chesterfield County to check it out. The boat was owned by a couple with five children and the boat looked like all five had been living on the boat. We were very disappointed. On the way back home, I noticed a green and beige Wellcraft sitting in someone's front yard on Courthouse Road. We turned around and proceeded to check the boat out from port to stern. He could not believe the great shape it was in. The boat was a 1967 14-foot Wellcraft that had been completely re-done, with a 1975 50HP Mercury Motor, all on a newly painted homemade trailer. We decided on the spot to buy the boat. After the motor was run. Call the boat a birthday gift and river must-have. We have never owned a motorboat before.

Looking forward to our Mini Vacation. Five days next week. But things do not seem to be working our way. Friday, we put the boat in the water, but it will not start. (Forgot to open the vent on gas cap.) We run the battery down. Sam loaned us his battery charger and the boat was finally running by Sunday. Time to go home.

What a disaster. We put the Wellcraft overboard at the boat ramp. Was a Friday morning. Making sure that there would not be a problem, I ran the motor in the yard. Made sure the drain plug is in the boat. Fishing rods; tackle box; bait; gas tank full; PFD's; cooler for fish; drink cooler; snacks. At the ramp gives Shannon a tow line from the boat. "Do not let the boat pull you off of the ramp deck." Unhook the boat wench. Back the van down the ramp. Hit the brakes. Boat comes off trailer the way it is suppose too. Take the van and trailer back to our yard. Shannon gets in and off we go to the river. As we leave Morattico Creek, the motor starts sounding an alarm. Steam is coming from the lower unit. The previous owner had a homemade water collar that is hooked to a garden hose. It required a wrench to remove. I forgot to take this off. The motor is not getting enough water for cooling. We see Clifton and wave him over. "Can you tow us back to the ramp? The motor has overheated."

"Throw me a line." We get the boat back in the yard. Sam and Leonard come over with advice. Some good. Some not. Trusting Sam more, we remove the lower unit. A call to the June Parker Marina in Tappahannock. "We have the parts." Had the new water pump installed by the late afternoon. Clifton in the creek. I motor up to him to get some Peelers. Leaving under full power. The steering went out on the boat – full circle - and crashed head-on with Clifton. The owner refurbed the boat. Did not tighten the steering wheel nut. These old boats are steered with a stainless steel cable system using pulleys. I was showing off how well the motor was running.

"You don't know much about boats, do you Son."

Tessie and Harold
First Tree Planted on Simonson Property

Christmas Day 1984

Our House Plans

Spent the following Winter looking through House Plan Books. Not a one that we wanted. Decided to do our own plans on my drafting board. Thomas is home on leave from Mountain Home Air Base, Idaho, for Christmas. On a weekend we took him to Simonson. Show him the land. It was a cold day in January. Lancaster Creek is frozen. Wind is blowing. Getting a good idea what it will be like living here in the Wintertime. Still so beautiful. On another weekend we rented a room at the Whispering Pines Motel in White Stone, Virginia. A get-away to be by ourselves. A visit to Simonson to check on things. A date night out dining at the Seafood Restaurant located in the Eagle's Nest Country Club. On the way back to Midlothian we stopped again in Simonson. Cannot wait till Spring to get back here.

    We arrived a little late Friday night. I stopped to talk to a man about the foundation for the house. I tackled the task of hooking up the water, normally a five-minute job. Eleanor & Sam, enjoying their cocktail hour. Mentioned that they wondered if the kids were coming. After priming, the pump finally came on, would not cut off. I decided to wait until the light of Saturday morning. Got the Pump started, but we had no water; no wait, we had water, but it was all over the floor. Checked the pipes and found two that had burst. After a phone call to the Browns, we were on our way to Center Cross with two split pipes in hand. Mack and Mary's neighbor, Dick, is a plumber and had our pipes in working order in no time. Charged $2.00. We spent a lovely evening with the Browns. Even got to take a shower Sunday morning before returning to Simonson. We found the Burtons had left to return to Richmond. They had come Saturday and found burst pipes, and after cutting a hole in the Utility Room floor, had gone home. New pipes installed. Check for leaks. I went outside to turn the pump on and water began to gush out of the hot water heater. We then decided to call a plumber. Mack and Jimmy S. used Mack's jeep, moved the trailer to the new location over where the second septic down drop is. The phone line has been installed. I finished the installation.

Arrived in Simonson 7:00 Friday night after traveling in the worst storm ever. Very high winds, hail and heavy rains. Sleeping was great with the windows open. In the morning I went next door in hopes of helping Leonard find some broken pipes At least we have cold water. Leonard just crawled out from under his house with the kitchen pipes in his hand. He said that now he will call a plumber. The weather has turned cold and gray, and the wind is damp. Saturday evening. Sunday morning early, Lancaster Creek was full of Ducks, fishing for breakfast. Breakfast consisted of BLT Sandwiches & fresh Strawberries. I dropped the Eggs Friday night.

Arrived in Simonson at 5:30. Eleanor called and invited us for dinner. We got both heaters fired up for Quito & Tessie. Went to the Hull's at 6:00. Dinner was delicious: Beef Bourguignon, Carrots, Spinach Salad & homemade Rolls; Chocolate Ice Cream w/ Cherries and Eleanor's homemade Lemon Cookies for dessert. After dinner we enjoyed Coffee & Brandy while looking at slides from the Hull's two trips to St. Thomas. 6:00 a.m. Start to work on replacing the hot water heater while waiting for the Foundation and Mason Contractors to show. Mary B. called and we decided to get together for "Dogs & Cards." Exhausted. Asleep before my head hit the pillow. Up at the crack of dawn, refreshed and ready to face another challenging day of "River De-Winterization." I went to help Warfield put a battery on his riding mower. Applied for credit at Tappahannock Building Supply. Purchased various plumbing supplies for the hot water heater. Back home around Lunchtime. After a sandwich, spent the rest of the afternoon hooking up the hot water heater.

We went to Mack and Mary's for a cookout. A much-needed shower. The River Crew was there. Good to see everyone. After helping

Sam fix the starter on his mower, I was going to relax. Watch Basketball and Golf. Promptly fell asleep. A storm blew up. We left about Mid-Day. Get ready to leave for Florida in the morning. The Engineering Team are designing, fabricating, testing the Production Laser Perforator in Clearwater, Fla.

Stopped, talked with Thomas B. on the way down. Bob hollowed, invited us to dinner. Sam and Eleanor were there. We feasted on Venison baked with Vegetables. Slaw and Mexican Cornbread. Eleanor and Shannon cleaned up the dishes. The men sat around the table discussing attributes of fast cars. Last week Sam introduced me to Tex, who lives on Lancaster Creek. Tex and Irene purchased the waterfront in 1929. Depression. I told Tex who my father was. "Have known H.A. for many years. He never told me that he had any sons." The Burton's arrived with their lawn tractor. Carol-Jean proceeded to cut the grass. Leonard began burning dead limbs and branches, testing the Fire Department and Sheriff's Department. Was before 4:00 p.m. Gale warnings had been broadcasted on the weather radio. Consequently, the yard began to burn. Leonard said "Ah, leave it alone; it ain't going nowhere."

Hinson Family First Cousins and Sister Linda 1997

Ma with Daughters on Birthday

Meet Joe Monk

Saturday morning. Barbara and Warfield came by with the ten Red Tops. We spend the remainder of the day working in the yard. Made it to the hospitable Brown's for our "Shower Appointment" before joining the Savages for the Aylett Country Day School Oyster Roast. I brought the house plans to talk with Joe Monk about hiring him to be the Master Carpenter.

Tess and I took a walk. Discovered wild Asparagus growing on the side of the road. Most stalks had gone to seed. I did find one tender stark. Will have it in our salad Friday night. Thomas B. and family arrived at 7:00 to square up the house foundation. They left in the dark. Clifton came by after Crabbing. Sold me half bushel of Crabs for $10.00. Tommy Beasley came by at 4:00. Finished putting up the batting boards. Tommy Beasley showed up with Clifton. Clifton showed Tommy exactly where the septic system is. Tommy started digging.

Clifton sold me another half bushel of Crabs. Hopefully, the Browns and Savages will come tomorrow. Help us eat them. Saturday morning. Clifton came by, gave us another half bushel of Crabs. The Savages and Browns came over Saturday night. We ate lots of Crabs. Toasted the foundation with Pink Champale. I ordered the cinder blocks from Tappahannock Building Supply per Mr. Thrift, the

The Foundation is Finished!

block layer. Friday, it rained almost all day. Saturday, Sam, and I put up the Martin House Rosie had made for my birthday. Clifton came by with another half bushel of fat Crabs. Sunday, we spent the day working in the yard and got a lot done. The foundation is finished. Looks great. I sent the house plans to get prices on materials to four supply houses. We have decided to go with Lillian Lumber out of Burgess, Virginia, for most of the materials. They will not charge for delivery. Will deliver only what I need each week. Delivered by the day before needed. The first delivery will be a big one. The house construction will begin next week. Memorable Day. Four-day holiday weekend and vacation. Joe and I will work at least ten hours per day. Ten days. Hope that it does not rain.

Ready for Joe tomorrow morning at 7:00. We awoke Saturday morning at 5:00. Pouring rain. Strong winds. The building materials are under cover, staged where I marked the area. Joe M. arrived at 6:45. The sun began slowly to shine. Shannon will take pictures at every step on the construction. We are working well together. By Sunday, the first-floor decking was on. After Joe leaves each day, I spend the rest of daylight, adding nails to the plywood decking. Every six inches apart. Roll water proofing on the plywood in case we get any rain. Completely exhausted each day. Call in at sundown. Feed dinner. Take a shower. Hit the bed. Asleep in minutes. Monday, end of the workday, there are three exterior walls standing. It is amazing. We've been here for a year but have not met that many people. Since we started the house, lots of neighbors, fishermen and watermen have come by to look and talk. We met Mr. Leslie Gaskins. He owns the Fishing Party Deadrise anchored in Morattico Creek. He is 82 and just about completely deaf. What an interesting black old fellow. My Gaskins had driven in our driveway and would not get out of his pickup until I ask him. "Captain Leslie, come on over here and sit for a while with me." We talked about Simonson. What use to be here.

"Would like to take a picture of you with Shannon. If you let me." Mr. Gaskins broke out in a big smile. I took the picture, standing side by side. Captain Leslie towering over her. Monday evening, Jim S., Jim S., Tom B., Bruce K. and Dave P. stopped by on their way home from a fishing trip. Visit and see how the house construction is going.

We started the second floor. The end of the second week, have the second-floor joist and plywood flooring down. All the wall framing completed. Nails with claw hammers. The third week we start preparing the construction for the roof. Begin on the Morattico Creek end of the house. Its long, hard work. End of the day on Sunday we had thirteen roof rafters constructed. Must stop there until next week. All this house

Shannon and Leslie Gaskins, 1985

construction was done in ten days. Saturday, we finished putting up the roof rafters. Joe had an architect look at the house plans. All of it was good except the roof. The architect suggested adding more construction. Addition bracing within the roof rafters in the Great Room with a Cathedral Ceiling. Sunday, work went slow. Working from the ground up. Joe handing up sheets of plywood to me on the second level. We were able to lay three rows on the steep pitch.

Saturday, Cary L. came to help work on the steepest pitch of the roof. "Man, you really do live in the sticks. I looked all the way here from Greys Point for a 7-Eleven."

"I have a Pepsi for you." By evening they had finished one side of the roof.

"Building me a mighty nice house." I started building the house before we had paid off the land. "No worry, Clifton." I constructed the end wall in the Craft Room. Working alone with Joe on vacation. There will be an opening from the Craft Room to look out into the Family Room. We may add a window to the east house wall so that a view will also be out to Lancaster Creek. Saturday evening, we got all gussied up. Mom and Pop took us to dinner at Lowery's in Tappahannock. Sam came over with some Perch and Croakers. Sam, Leonard, and Bob had been fishing with Charlie Langhorne. I have not been fishing since starting the house construction. Work on the house every day from sunrise to sunset.

Sunday, I worked on the roof rafter bracing and the attic loft. The Savages, Chinns and Wilsons made a boat trip from Garretts Marina. Essex side of the Rappahannock to Simonson. We ate some Crabs and drank a few beers. They admired the house. Back to Richmond. Shared Fried Fish and the first Tomatoes from our river vines with Rosie and Lenny.

The Hummingbirds have been coming to the feeder all evening. Eleanor said she thought they liked our feeder best since they have not seen any Hummingbirds since we put our feeder up. The skylights were delivered on Thursday. Not the Velux that I wanted. Delivered are a "piece of crap." Going to have to think what to do. The roofers are coming soon. We started Saturday morning correcting the plywood on the roof. We are going to have to use the "crap skylights." The fireworks and my Birthday celebration on the Savages' beach. We came home and fell in bed. Soon, serenaded by neighbors singing "Happy Birthday." Melinda and Chip came to spend the day. Wish me a Happy Birthday.

Forty-Third Birthday Picnic

Thursday. Our forty-third Birthday. I gave Joe the day off and worked until the family arrived for the picnic. Thomas and Chris got into Richmond on Tuesday night. We have planned whole family party in Simonson. Harvey Lee helped me put in the last house window, lower level overlooking the porch. First time that he has helped me on this house. I did not work on the house the rest of the day. Enjoy the party with the family. The first time that the family have all been together, other than a funeral, in many years.

I set up the sawhorses in the future Family Room area with sheets of plywood. Shannon and Rosie put white sheets over the plywood, making a table for the food. The river crew came by boat from the Dunnsville side. Were sweet to take Chris water skiing. Barbara asks, "Where is Chris?" She had not met her yet. Brandy Chinn introduced herself to Barbara as Thomas' wife. It is obvious Brady is very much with child. A lot of laughs. Was corrected right away. I made Thomas and Chris a "Honeymoon Suite" in my office room with sleeping bags, pillows, and blankets on the plywood floor. Nine months later. First grandchild, Brynn.

Friday. We worked on the house energy shield. Decking for the screen porch. Friday evening, we had "the neighborhood" in for Happy Hour. In the house. Eleanor was the first to tap dance on our screen porch floor. I used tongue and grove 2 x 6 pressure-treated lumber, twelve foot long. Flooring runs from the house out to the end of the porch. No butted flooring. Started the cedar siding on the north side of the house. The screen porch is going to be 12 feet wide by 35 feet long. Sam is taking a hard look at it. His porch is six feet by 12 feet.

Shannon's first week back at work. Labor Day week the house is complete with all siding except where the Garage will be constructed next year. I paid Joe his last check for this year. Joe is going back to Sweet Briar College where he is a professor. Will be back May 1986. The house construction started the third week in May. A "dry in" house by the first week in September. Not bad for a guy who was told. "You can't do that." Put building materials, tools, inside the house. Locked the doors and windows. Going to start on the house wiring over the Fall and Winter, as weather allows.

We have used most of our savings. Joe was paid each week and Building Supply Houses were paid each month. We have some lumber; hardware for later construction. I am getting prices for house wiring, fixtures, heat, and plumbing. Looking into getting our construction loan to complete a live-in house. Loan rates have gone down. We feel this is the right time.

I am making some changes on the second-floor hallway. I went to the trailer, holding my face in my hands. Blood and mustache hairs are running down my wrist. "What happened?"

"I was removing a stud with the 20-oz framing hammer. My elbow hit the wall stud. The 'claw' hit me in the mouth."

"Let us go in the bathroom and wash it. See the damage." The 'claw' had cut through the top lip. Cut the mustache with a clean gash to the top gum. Missed the teeth. "Let's go to the Hospital."

"No, I will be fine. Pour me a glass of Mr. Beam over ice. Taking the rest of the day off."

Getting ready to do the electrical and plumbing. The house looks finished from the outside. We were lucky during the last tropical storm. Suffered minor Willow Tree damage, boat cover ripping, TV antenna broken and some Tyvec ripped on the north side. The Potomac River residents were not as fortunate; nor were the people on the south side of the Rappahannock River. The Northern Neck is only twenty miles wide between the two rivers. Storms are known to go down one river and back up the other. We spent Thanksgiving and Christmas with family.

December and January. I drove to the house most weekends. Started drilling holes and installing the outlet, ceiling, and switch boxes. mounted the electrical circuit breaker panel in the Utility Room. Work I can do without any help. Will need some help pulling the Romex on long runs. Shannon is helping where she can. Called Robert C. and Jimmy S. to come over on a weekend.

Drove down on Friday afternoon after work. Should have picked up some take-out, but am always in a hurry to get to Simonson. Got the heat turned on in the trailer and the water pump going. Jimmy and Robert arrived just after dark. Robert said he would sleep in his car. "My snoring will keep you guys awake." We spent the next day drilling holes for wiring.

I started the process of obtaining a construction loan that can be turned into a mortgage when we complete the home. Started with hometown Northern Neck State Bank. "We cannot and will not give you the loan." Was turned down two more times at other local banks.

"What makes you think that you can finish building your home? You are not a Building Contractor."

"I am the General Contractor. Licensed Electrician." I went to Kilmarnock and met with Signet Bank.

"We will get back to you." Signet calls. "We do not see why you need any money. Was at your property yesterday and the house looks finished to me."

"Mam, did you look inside of the house?"

"No, I did not, Mr. Hinson."

"If you go back and look inside, you will see that the interior is only stud walls."

House Construction, Both Floors

Future Garage

Porch Facing Lancaster Creek

Construction Loan

The letter from Signet Bank came the following week. Your loan has been approved for $65,000. With these conditions: "The entire house will have to be completed. That includes the second level that you were planning to do after you move in. The house will have to be completed in ninety (90) days. You will also have to pay off the land agreement that you have with Clifton D." We went to Signet Bank and signed the loan. "Will need the first draft to be $40,000." Clifton D. $20,000. Electrical, Plumbing Supply Invoices; Plumber Ogle F. Have been sending them $300.00 each month out of my paycheck.

I have been working on the electrical during the Winter. Been waiting for warmer weather to continue. Mama and Warfield came by and visited for a while. We are now using the Porch, not screened in yet, but good for sitting. The Hinsons arrived in Simonson at dusk. Proceeded to get settled. The trailer was a bit disorganized. I was here alone for Easter weekend. In the cabinet I found a can of Lucks Pinto Beans. Did not check the expired date. Opened the can and heated the contents in a small pan. Crackers and Beans. What could go wrong? The crew of Robert and Jimmy arrive. "Do not think I am going to be able to work today. Was up all night with major de-rah-rah and belly cramps."

"Show us where you want some holes drilled, Harold. At least we can do that for you." I went back to bed.

We have a three-day weekend this week. It is Kentucky Derby on Saturday. Philip Morris has a manufacturing plant in Louisville, Kentucky. All Philip Morris employees get a three-day weekend no matter where they are located. Two weeks ago, we ate our first Steamed Crabs of 1986, courtesy of Clifton. The Martins have found their home. So have the Hummingbirds found the feeders. We worked in the yard.

Planted 11 Better Boys, 4 Sweet Tomatoes, 2 Cayenne and 2 Jalapeno Pepper Plants for Quito.

I was down last weekend alone, since it was Mother's Day. Cary L. came to help with wiring. The glass in the front door got broken somehow. Clifton came by. "All of the Crabs are white and paper shells." We got a cup of Java. Took a walk-in search of the first Soft Shells. Met up with Keith H. He has Soft Shell floating cages off the Langhorne's dock. "The Cranes ate all of my Soft Shells." We went on down the road to Pierson's Island, Fidler Oyster Company. Joey has a Soft Shell operation on the shoreline. We left Joey a note. We took Quito out to the screen porch. Not sure if she liked it. Had to give her a spray bottle shower to cool her off. 90 degrees today. The Martins are here in full force. Seven pairs. The Hummingbirds have disappeared. I went under the house to staple Romex. At least it is cool there. Planted a few more Tomato plants. Chives, Dill, Parsley, and Basil.

Memorial Day, four-day Holiday. Year two. I took some vacation with the four-day holiday. Whole family made it to Simonson for our "vacation." Working on the house. Joe came for his first day of construction in 1986. We framed the Garage walls. Ready for the roof trusses. This is the only part of the house using trusses. We do not believe that we need additional space above the Garage. The house is already bigger than the first plans that I drew up. A single-level house with a clear-story glass wall facing to the South. Now it is a story and a half with a Craft Room, Guest Bedroom, Full Bathroom and my Office on the second level. We were advised that the Waterfront value will warrant a bigger house. We headed out early for Center Cross. Even with all the work it has taken to build our house, we still take time to be with our friends. There will be a beach party at the Savages sand beach on the Rappahannock, complete with a Keg. Mack and Mary Kay Birthday Barbeque at the Brown's.

Ogle, our plumber and his helper are hard at work. Jim S., Robert C., Mack, Tom helped me and Joe put up the roof trusses in the Garage. We followed a terrible storm to Simonson. In Tappahannock, a tree had fallen on a car blocking Rt. 17. Roads were flooded and cars stalled. When we finally arrived at Rt. 606, we found a tree had fallen across the road. Two trees had fallen on Al's house. Bob and Julie lost their Locust Tree. Electricity was out. Back on by 8:30. Ogle finally showed up on Friday. Ogle started digging trenches everywhere. "Trying to find the well." Determined it was too deep to be detected by a metal detector.

We worked on replacing the tar paper on the Garage Roof. The storm on Wednesday ripped it off. Continued with putting on the cedar siding; trim boards. Miscellaneous work inside the house. I am under a lot of pressure. It is hot – 98 degrees. The humidity is unbearable. At least there is a strong wind. Ogle finished what he could do. Lilian picked up the order that was delivered last week. Delivered miscellaneous material that I ordered. We plan to work on the Garage this weekend. The weather forecast is for more hot and humid days.

We had the Northern Neck Electric meter box installed and the power line to the house. Ogle Forrest made the connections to the house and circuit breaker panel. We now have power and water to the house. I moved our mattress off the bed in Midlothian to Simonson. We are sleeping on the plywood floor. A big thing over that bed in the trailer. We also moved our refrigerator and electric cooking stove that we stored at Rosie's from our home on Sparrow Drive. We do not have a kitchen sink. The one delivered from Ferguson came damaged. I sent it back. "Not interested in knocking out the dent. Get me another one." Shannon uses the utility sink when washing dishes. We gave our washing machine and dryer to Rosie when we moved in with her. There will be new ones. We also brought our couch. We are eating at the bar. Shannon found some bar stools for a good price. We have six months to get the house finished and will not be able to put the fireplace in now. There is a framed area for it later, after I get the bank off my ass. I am doing all the wood trim. Purchased a chop saw for this work. Beats the heck out of that meter box and trim saw. We designed custom kitchen cabinets. They are birch with early American stain. I also designed a pantry cabinet. All the cabinets have roll-out trays. We met with Beasley

Cabinets in Kilmarnock for a price. "Not sure of that Pantry and how you want the cabinets that deep over the refrigerator. Never seen cabinets done like that."

A month later Mr. Beasley called. "I want to thank you for that Pantry and Cabinet Design. I have sold three more kitchens like yours once customers have seen it." Our old River friends, Jim and Mary Kay, have moved to Springfield. H.P. Foley is no more in Richmond.

I am working alone. Joe is back at Sweetbriar College. We are spending most of the time in Simonson with me commuting to work every day. One hour, twenty minutes each way. Leave at 5:45 and return home around 5:00. Home. Change clothes. Work on the trim. We went to Richmond. Going to stay a couple days. Started a habit; if we are going to be away, turning off the water pump and hot water heater circuit breakers. In Midlothian overnight was a foot of snow. Simonson got seven. Not going anywhere. Then there are ten more inches in Richmond. Simonson ended up getting twenty. We made it back home the following week. I turned on the water pump circuit breaker. Pump started running. "That should not be on. We have a leak." Found it in the outdoor shower. Water was spraying out of the pipe, running up the side of the house. Pipe froze and busted. I went under the house and checked if the steamer valve was closed. Call to Ogle. When his helper soldered the copper pipe to the valve, the heat damaged the washer. The valve leaked into the shower piping. "Fixed now, Harold." Most of the trim work is complete. Still have a few more interior doors to hang. A few more to stain.

Saturday the wind is unreal. several limbs have broken on the 'disputed' Cedar tree between us and the Burton's. We have been feeding the birds. Have enjoyed watching the Geese and Ducks this Fall and Winter. Never got to see them before. Not living here in the Winter. The creeks are partially frozen. Clifton pulled up in the driveway one day. "Harold; what are you going to do with the trailer, now that your house is in move-in shape?"

"Going to sell it. You interested?"

"You probably want a lot more than you paid me for it. All that work Shannon did and the new hot water heater."

"No; I will let you have it for the same thing we paid you. $2000." Clifton turns his pickup around. I help him hitch the trailer to his truck. "Will bring you a check." Clifton goes out of our driveway, turns left. Takes our temporary first home to Pierson's Island. His land. That afternoon Clifton brings me a check. The day after Clifton moved the trailer there was a flood tide. Clifton was sucking a cool one and heard strange noises. He opened the trailer door to find the water lapping at the steps. Next day Shannon saw him airing the trailer out. Shannon was looking in the *Northern Neck News*. Rice-Packett has listed for a receptionist. Decided to go back to work.

The house is really coming along. Just a few odds and ends to tie up. The carpet was installed. Looks great except for the seams downstairs. I called Phil, Scott Flooring and Tile. "Mr. Hinson, no one thinks about the flooring when designing a house. Carpet comes in twelve-foot width. The seams cannot be changed." That is that. The Ducks are still here in full force. Most of the Geese have flown North. We are looking forward to the third Annual Totuskey Creek Yacht Club [TCYC] reunion in Sand Bridge. The family met at Lowery's in Tappahannock to celebrate Ma's Birthday, 87 years old.

The weather had turned cold and windy. Not much work was done on the deck. We plan to be totally in the house by early Spring.

My job at Philip Morris had gotten even more intense. The Team has been working on a Project, Code name "Ringtipper." The Mechanical Engineer Steve S. is not having success with the gluing to bring the emboss strip and tipping paper together, without sticking the whole bobbin together with glue. All the known gluing methods have been attempted over the last three months. During the weekend I remembered the time I was building Shannon's Pantry on Sparrow Drive. I used Elmers Glue on the board ends, before nailing together with 6d finish nails. Too much glue and it oozed out. Made a mess. If I touched the tip of the glue bottle to the wood and pulled it away, a "spider web" glue line was created. [Little Man in Head: *Too much glue; problem solved."*]

Monday morning at the Operation Center Philip Morris I could not wait to share this with Steve. In the Cage where Engineers are allowed to work with tools, I fabricated a "Glue Applicator" made with fourteen inches of Poly Tubing, Shim stock to form a funnel, Swaglock brass fitting with mashed barb to create a small opening. Screwed the tubing into the fitting and attached it all together with duck tape. Steve was running the Rewinder machine. "Steve, where is the glue?"

"Over there in that bucket. Do not bother me, Harold. I must get this Rewinder working before Wednesday. Report progress to management." I poured some glue in a styrofoam coffee cup then into the funnel. Gave the glue time to travel down the tubing to the fitting. At the running machine, pushed Steve aside. Held my glue applicator above the tipping paper. A minute, drip of glue touches the paper. A "spider web" of glue was pulled out of the orifice by the moving tipping paper. Steve with a do- not-believe-this look. Stopped the Rewinder and unwound a strip of the tipping paper off the bobbin. first time the tipping paper was not stuck together. "You SOB, you have done it!" Brings back another fond memory with Steve. One of the great Mechanical Engineers on the Team and a friend. "What do you do around here anyway, Harold?" I pressed the Emergency Stop button, went to the wall-mounted electrical breaker box. Pulled the Handle to OFF, disconnected the 480vac power plug. Tossed the plug on the floor. "That is what I do. Now run your machine." We are a close team of engineers and have worked together for six years on many special projects. The six team members were awarded this in their name:

> United States Patent 4,666,550 Granted on May 19, 1987
> Apparatus For Producing A Strip of Laminated Sheet Material Harold T. Hinson Inventor

My First Patent at Philip Morris, USA., son Ricky's birth date, May 19. He will come into our lives soon.

House Is Ours!

Time at the river now for Shannon and me enjoying the outdoors. The house is ours. Built. Mortgage payments. No more worries of finishing in the ninety days. I began looking at the shoreline for a longer pier for boat mooring, Crabbing and Fishing. I constructed a roller ramp off the side of the short pier. The pier only twelve feet long. Enough to keep our feet dry when fishing off the end. I dug in a post, added a winch at the end of the roller ramp. The Wellcraft boat fits well on the ramp. To keep the weather out of the boat I constructed a roof with tin corrugated sheet. One day Shannon called me at work. "We are having a real high tide. It looks like the boat is under water." *What?* When I got home that afternoon, it was true. Under water. Battery was connected to the outboard. Salt water. Electroless. We learned a lot with that first motorboat and these waters. Sam helped me get the boat up on the shoreline and back on the homemade trailer. Pulled the rig over to Whelan's Marina located just before Hales Point.

We fished out of that little boat when the waters were clam, staying close to the shores. Learning the waters of Lancaster Creek. Where the best places were. Shannon is quite a fisherwoman. One occasion we were up Lancaster Creek where the "Boat Graveyard" is located. Great fishing spot. We were fishing with cut Squid strips. "Something is fooling with my bait."

"A Crab, Shannon." She reels the line in. "Yep, a Crab." Shakes the rod to drop off the Crab. At that instant a very large Rockfish broke out of the water. Grabs the Crab and the hook. Shannon screams while fighting the Rockfish. Brings the fish beside the boat.

"Have to turn it loose, Honey. Not season yet. That would taste good for dinner." I worked the hook out without pulling the Rockfish on the boat. Shannon gives me that look. "Rockfish are off limits." We caught White Perch and Catfish most of the time. Occasionally we would catch a Spot, Bluefish or Trout. Shannon did not like any of those fish to eat. I scaled, head off and gutted the Perch. Fileted the Catfish. Cut the Catfish into nuggets. House Autry Seafood Dressing, Butter, and Peanut Oil in a cast iron pan. Good eating with Hush Puppies and French Fries.

We were fishing in the river area coming into Lancaster Creek. More than one wave broke over the stern of that 14-foot Wellcraft. I started bailing. There is not a bilge pump installed on the boat. Not much free board either. That is when we knew it had to go. Was a good learning boat. Traded the Wellcraft at Whelan's Marina, located by the water just as you leave Morattico Creek, Rappahannock River. Johnny is the owner with son Keith. Has been in business since the 1970s. Purchased the property

Harold and Tessie, Summer

from Mr. Sichol. "Will be honest with you. I need to sell one more Mercury Outboard before the end of the year. Mercury will give me a large bonus. If you purchase this Sportcraft 16ft Center Console boat. Outfitted with a 75-HP Mercury Outboard, on a galvanized trailer. I will make you a deal you will not be able to refuse. Getting close to the year-end." Johnny was correct. Fixed the outboard on the Wellcraft. State Farm paid for the repairs. Johnny gave us more than we paid for the Wellcraft, and we purchased the Sportcraft Center Console. When we looked at the figures. "Got something for free." We figure it is the boat. Sportcraft was out of business in two years.

Ricky

September 1988. Friday Evening. I have just answered our home phone. It is a call from someone that I have not talked to in many years. "You remember me? I am Beulah's sister Elsie."

"I remember you well."

"Ricky is staying with my mother Gertie in Dunnsville. He says he is not going back to Plainville, Georgia. Working at Food Lion in Tappahannock, putting up stock after school. His grades are failing at Essex High School. Can you help him?" Have not seen my son; ten years.

"I can help him. Will go over there tomorrow." Saturday morning, Shannon and I travel to Dunnsville. On the way we continued our discussion about Ricky. What we could do for him. We agreed we want him to come live with us. Only if he wants too.

Ricky, 17 Years Old

At Gertie's home place off Rt. 17, South from Tappahannock. I knocked on the door. Gertie answered. She knew who I was. Gerty had nicknamed me years ago. "Hairy Ass Hinson." It was the night I slammed Beulah's half-brother "Terp" against the wall. He had hit his mother. "You do not, will not hit your mother."

Gertie pointed to the house trailer set up on the property. "Ricky is over there." I knocked on that door. A red-headed lady answered the door. Must be Earnest's daughter. She has grown up.

"Is Ricky here?" A skinny long-haired boy bounds off the couch and to the door. "I am your father."

He grabs me in a bear hug. "I know who you are." We had not seen each other since his mother last married and moved to Georgia when Ricky was six.

"We are going to Aylett Country Day School Oyster Roast. Why don't you come with us?" Shannon gets out of the van to greet him. On the way to Aylett, Shannon starts a conversation. First thing we notice is Ricky does not have much to say. We spent the day introducing Ricky to all our friends. He was very shy. You could tell he was not at ease being in a bunch of people. "Would you like to go home with us? Shannon will make us dinner. She makes a fantastic Angel Hair Pasta and Meat Balls. We can talk and get to know each other better."

"Would like that."

Shannon started making dinner. I took Ricky through the house, showing him what we had built with Joe, seen at the Oyster Roast. The guy cooking the Brunswick Stew. I took Ricky outside and walked around the property. "Come in guys; dinner is ready." At dinner Ricky starts to talk more, scooping up the Spigets and Meat Balls like he has not had a good meal in a long time. Noticed the way he held the fork. Hand is wrapped over the top of the folk. Used like a shovel. Ricky complimented Shannon. "The best I have ever eaten." After dinner I invited him out on the front deck. We begin a serious talk. The first time between a father and the son.

"You do not know who I am. Or me you. Have shown you your room, if you decide to come and live here. That will be your choice. We will learn together. Who we are. One thing you will have to promise me. You treat Shannon with total respect. What you become is what you want to be. We cannot do it for you. Shannon and I will support that effort." Ricky looked at me. A father talking to a son not seen for more than ten years. We went in the house. Ricky thanked Shannon for the dinner again. Gave her a hug. "Goodbye." I carried Ricky back to Dunnsville. Wrote a note with our address and phone number. "Call us when you know what you want to do, Son." Drove back to Simonson wondering what the future may be.

"Ricky is not going to come here after the way you talked to him."

"There are things that Ricky needs to understand. We do not know anything about him. Making sure that Ricky knows what we are expecting. We need to keep an open mind."

October 20. Wedding Anniversary. Every year we have gone to Nags Head for that week on vacation. Stay at the Islander Motel. I tried not to think about Ricky. But could not. Miserable! Not knowing what his decision will be. I know Shannon wants to be there for him. I constantly think about the lost years. Home answering machine is checked constantly.

Wednesday morning. "Let us go home, Harold. We are not having a good time." Discussed what was going on with Islander owners. They understood and gave us a refund for the remaining week.

No call from Ricky came through the weekend. We return to work. Do not remember what day it was. Ricky called one evening. "Is your offer still good?"

"Of course it is, Son."

"I have my own car and some affairs to deal with here. Will be at your home this Saturday morning."

He came carrying two paper grocery bags containing his clothes and belongings. A .22 rifle and fishing rod. Shannon helped him unpack his clothes. That afternoon she took him to J.T. Harris in Warsaw. They outfitted him with a whole new wardrobe. Top to bottom. When Ricky and Shannon returned to his new home, he asks for a trash bag and went immediately up the staircase to his bedroom. Threw away almost all the clothes he brought to Simonson.

"Help me put the boat in. The family is going fishing."

That Sunday was the first of many more days that the new family went fishing together. Ricky had never fished in salt water before. In Georgia he only fished in ponds with his grandfather. I showed him what was needed to set up saltwater tackle. He was a quick learner. Was wonderful to see that smile on his face. Excitement. Peace.

Nov. 22, 1988. Juvenile and Domestic Relations District Court. There are legal things that must happen. Date before the Richmond County Court. The same court years ago that denied me a "father's rights." Going to be different this time, Judge Walter Fidler. "I hereby order that the temporary custody of Richard D. Hinson be awarded to his father Harold T. Hinson Sr." There are not enough words to describe this day. Ricky has been living with us since September 1988. Commonwealth of Virginia Department of Social Services Child Support Department. Beulah Bailey files for non-support. Mandatory withholding of earnings ordered by the State of Virginia. The Philip Morris Payroll Department is obligated to follow the court order. *You have got to be kidding me.* It took months of lost pay to get this corrected. Beulah did not return the money. Ricky decided to transfer for the remainder of his senior year from Essex High School to Rappahannock High School.

Late Fall finds Ricky and me Squirrel hunting for the first time. Still have the memory of the first Squirrel we saw. Ricky was beading down on the squirrel with his .22 rifle. I hand him my Winchester Model 61. "Try this." He made a perfect head shot dropping the Squirrel from 75 feet. "Dad." That Christmas we gave Ricky a Marlin .22 Lever Action. Same as done for Thomas on his sixteenth birthday. Shannon treated Ricky as her son. Special breakfast of Link Sausage and Scrambled Eggs. That is what he wanted before he left for school. Shannon left for work. She promised him if he made the A Honor Roll the next quarter, "We will let you drive the Datsun 260Z to school." He did it. Can still see that boy's smile. Ricky would get dressed to go out for a school function. When he came down from his room, "What are you all going to do tonight?"

"There is a good movie coming on HBO."

"Think I would rather stay here with you and watch a movie." Ricky changes into his sweats, grabs a blanket, and rolls up with a pillow on the floor.

**Dad and Two Sons
Together After Ten Years**

Thanksgiving Rock Fishing

There were many fishing trips for the three of us. That first Thanksgiving was one to remember. Just Ricky and his dad fishing. He had never been Rock Fishing before. This will be a 'teaching day. "We are going Rock Fishing before sunrise in the morning, Shannon."

"Count me out." We fill travel mugs Shannon had given us with coffee. Leave the dock in a heavy morning fog. Visibility about 10 feet off the bow. I know this creek. Where to go and the way to get there. Thanks to "old timer" Peyton Fidler. Peyton in his Deadrise came by our dock one fall day motoring slowly back to his boathouse.

"If I were you, I'd go up Lancaster Creek."

"Going slowly to Peyton's Hole, Son."

I found the area Peyton described and cut off the outboard motor. Sit back. Quiet. Sipping coffee. Talking softly.

"Rockfish get spooked with noise, Son."

Wait. The sun just breaking above the tree line. The creek explodes.

"Feeding Rock Fish. Get on the front of the boat, Son."

Father and son start casting 2-oz silver with blue back rattle trap hard baits.

Ricky is excited. I am enjoying watching him. The SPORTS CRAFT nears the 10-foot hole, just twelve feet from the bank.

"Cast to the shore, short of the grasses."

We hook up at the same time. The Rockfish start running around the boat. What fighters they are. "These boys are hungry this morning." Two "keepers" go in the cooler. The Rock have 'chased the bait fish up against the bank. Outgoing tide is running strong. Start the outboard, ease boat in closer to shore.

"Cast towards the bank. Let the bait drop in the hole. Flick the rod tip. Start reeling."

The Rattle Trap Bait nears the surface with Rockfish chasing the shiny bait. A flash in the clear water attacks the enticing wiggle. Starts running sideways.

"Keep the rod tip raised. Reel in line when you are able against the reel drag and strong pull."

"Rip it, Dad." Ricky smiling. Hold on. Two more keepers caught. A four-fish daily limit in less than ten minutes.

Thanksgiving morning was a day still remembered. A dad watching his son. Forgetting the lost years. Bonding.

My rule. Catch the limit. Stop fishing. Do not want to ruin fishing the next day. Catching Rock to turn loose makes their mouths sore. Rock Fish remember and will not bite. Also stresses the fish. May kill them.

"Let us go home, Son. Get some of Shannon's breakfast." We slowly motor back to the familiar dock. Still very foggy, but lifting. Quietly enter the house.

Shannon hears us. Gets up. "Tried to be quiet, Honey."

"Thought you were going Rock Fishing?"

"We did. Caught our limit. Now we are back to have breakfast with you." Shannon gives us that smile.

"Need to start the weber grill charcoal, Honey." Shannon wants me to smoke the Turkey this year. Leaves Kitchen oven free for the side dishes. This Thanksgiving Ricky will enjoy Shannon's wonderful holiday feast.

Harold with Rockfish

Pop Pop with Rockfish   **Ricky with Rockfish**

My message to wives long overdue. If you chose to punish, keeping sons/daughters from fathers for no legal reason. Take it from a father who knows. Been there. Lived it. If you are that mother, stop it. For me. A decision made was a hard one. A fight in the court system? Put my sons' thought that? I made a choice not to do that. One day my sons will find out the truth.

Fall 1988. After 17 long years I have both of my sons together as adults with me. Thomas was home on leave from Mountain Home Air Force Base and Ricky chose not to return to Georgia, come live with Shannon and his dad. He often told us that he did not know where he would have been, had we not given him the chance to come "home." Thomas and wife Chris have two daughters, now living in New Mexico. He is stationed with the Air Force Special Ops – PAVE LOW. Living his dream. Flying. Since he was old enough to look up whenever he heard something. Tech Sargent Flight Engineer flying on the MH53 Helicopters. Thomas has earned his Masters Degree in Computer Science.

Proud Dad with Sons

We start discussing life goals with Ricky. "What are your plans for the future?"

"Thinking of going to Automobile Mechanics School. I like working on cars. Not sure yet."

"Was in the same place when I finished High School, Son. Have you given any thought about going in the military?" We realized that Ricky did not have a lot of support from Georgia. "If you do not mind me giving some advice, consider what your brother Thomas and I did. Go in the Air Force. Get some training for a skill level. See some of the world. Then go to college. That will mean more to you."

"I'll think about it, Dad." The next week Ricky tells us he is going in the Air Force.

Another father/son talk occurred. We are getting to know each other better over these months. Trying not to control his direction. Give some dad advice. "What are you planning on doing with the money earned while in the Service?"

"What's on your mind, Dad?"

"In the service will be given housing, clothing, and three-square meals. Think about the purchase of some land that will be paid for by the time you get back home."

"That sounds like a good idea."

"Call Savage, see if he can help." There was an acre of property just off Simonson Road on Lanier Road. Ricky purchased the land. Owner financed. Ricky got home after four years. Land paid for. We spent the holidays together with all the family. The second week of January Ricky meets the Recruiter in Tappahannock. Trip to Richmond for physical. Air Force induction. Ricky comes home on leave after Basic Training. A grown man. *Life is good.*

Rockfish Back in the Day

Croaker Fishing in the Summer

Help Honey - Broken Leg

Laying on the floor watching the last day of a Golf Tournament on Sunday. Shannon and Rosie were sitting on the screen porch. It started. A sharp pain in my right side radiating down to my groin. Pain kept getting worse. Not letting up. Last week I went to a new family doctor in Richmond for Prostate exam and physical. "You have a mushy Prostate, Mr. Hinson." [Little Man in Head: *"What is he talking about?"*] Hands me a prescription. "Get this filled. Call me if you have any problems." This new doctor. Not sure for how long. Shannon called the doctor exchange.

"Get him to sit in a tub of warm water. If he does not get better in half hour. Go to the Hospital."

Now bent over from the pain. Shannon helps me get upstairs to the tub. Sitting in the warm water. Shannon keeping time. A gut-wrenching pain hits me like non other ever had. I projectile vomited on the wall at the other end of the tub.

"Mom!"

Shannon helps me out of the tub. Spark buck naked, we go down the stairs. I lay on the floor. Shannon is wiping me down with a towel. Rosie calling 911. The Rescue Squad takes me to Rappahannock General Hospital. Nurse starts an IV. Doctor ordered a Kidney Ureter Bladder [KUB] Xray.

"You have a kidney stone, Mr. Hinson. We are going to admit you." The first of many stones.

I was tying up the Ivy Shannon had planted in front of the Trellis to hide the old tool shed next door. The ladder starting tipping to the left. Jumped off. No problem. Except I landed the right foot ball on a landscape timber. Heard and felt the leg snap. Reached down while keeping my balance and grabbed the leg above and below the ankle.

Rolled on my back holding leg. Rested the leg on my left knee. Have been lying there for a while. Tonight's occasion was going to dinner with Jim and Mary Kay Savage. Shannon opens the front door. She was taking a shower and wondered where I was. "What are you doing lying on the ground?"

"Call the Rescue Squad. Have broken my leg." Shannon has never been good with things like this. After she calms down, calls 911. Sam and Eleanor arrive.

Hulls want to fashion a splint. "Just leave it alone."

The Rescue Squad Unit arrives with two members. Apologizes for taking so long. "Had to go to the Firehouse. Get the unit. Find out where we are going." I have been lying on the ground for forty-five minutes. Holding the leg together. My tube sock was helping. "Are you in any pain?"

"Compared to a kidney stone, Mam, doing okay." Squad puts an air cast on the leg. Everyone helps to get me on a gurney. Rescue Squad heads down Rt. 3 for Rappahannock General in Kilmarnock. Shannon and Rosie following. The female Squad member taking my vitals. "You know that at Rappahannock General, you do not know who the doctor will be? Tappahannock has a wonderful bone doctor."

"Mam, I know you do not like to do this. Can you take me to Tappahannock?"

She calls up front to the driver. "Mr. Hinson wants to go to Tappahannock." The Squad Unit makes a U-Turn at Little Sue in Robley. Shannon and Rosie think that something has gone very wrong. "Why would they turn around?"

At the Tappahannock Emergency Room. Nurse removes air cast. Foot flops to the right. "Oh yea. Sure that leg is broke. Maybe the Fib and the Tib. Dr. S. has been called. He is out on his sailboat. Said to get the X Rays done. Start the IV. Do not give any pain meds. He may have to operate. Will be at the hospital in an hour and a half." Now my leg is starting to hurt. Let us cut to the chase. Bone doctor. "Mr. Hinson, you did a good job of not letting the bones break the skin. If that happened

Help Honey

we would definably operate. Put plates and screws in. It will be much better if we do not have to cut. You are a young man. I believe we can set this without operating."

The nurse reminds the doctor. "Mr. Hinson is fifty."

"Well, it may take a little longer. We are going to set the leg now" Doctor has the nurse help me sit up. Swing legs over the side of the table. Doctor is looking into my eyes as he is injecting two syringes into the IV. "There we are." [Little Man in Head: *"OH CRAP guess that means pain will not be bad."*] Doctor grabs the right leg with both hands. Pulls down as he twists. *Wrong about the pain.* Rest a minute. Pulls down again. And again. Twist. Pull. Twist. Did not pass out.

"Think that is the best that we are going to be able to do. Your bones are shattered."

Puts his two hands together with the fingers passing each other. [Little Man in Head: *"Oh shit."*] The first cast of many. This one all the way to the hip. "You will be non-weight-bearing for many months. At least six. And you are going to have to learn how to walk again. Admit you to the hospital. The night nurse has instructions to give you pain meds when you ask for it."

I asked for a shot soon after in the room. Well. Must have pissed someone off. Could not sleep from the screaming coming from hallway. Had to ask the nurse again. "Pain meds please. What is that screaming about?"

"We have patients that will not stay in their bed. We are short staffed at night. So we tie them in a chair outside of their rooms, where we can see them." [Little Man in Head: *"You got to be kidding me, best behave, Harold."*] Finally, a different nurse shows up holding a syringe. "Roll over." Pulls up garment. Jammed so deep, hit my hip bone.

"Get me the hell out of here." First thing I said to Shannon the next morning. Will be four days before that happened.

Shannon ordered a Lazy Boy recliner delivered before I came home. After getting settled at home, I called Gary A. my Group Leader. Been in his group for six years. "Gary, the doctor says I will be out of work for at least six months. Leg is badly broken. Brain is still working. If you bring me a computer and hook up a network, I will finish that Project Documentation."

"No one asks to continue working when on short team disability."

"I am."

"Damn, Harold. Let me call Barry C., Director Human Resources to see what he says. Will get back to you."

Short time later, Gary is on the phone. "I do not believe this. Barry says if you are willing to work, I should get you what you need."

"Thanks, Gary, for helping me keep my sanity."

"Brian G. will be coming to see you with the equipment."

"Have Brian bring my Project Documentation Book when he comes." Brian set it all up. Every two weeks a young Engineer working with me comes to Simonson. Brings my mail. I provide him the Magnetic Files completed to load in the archives at Philip Morris. I finished that project from my Lazy Boy.

Shannon and Harold

President's Award

That November I received a letter from Philip Morris. Invited to attend the President Awards Banquet, December 1993. "You have been chosen to receive the President's Award for 1993 given to the Dual Hopper Max Project Team." What an honor that was. I called Gary to tell him probably could not make the banquet. Traveling with broken leg would be difficult on Shannon. A call came back. The Director of Engineering Mr. Lou T. has directed that a Limo be sent to Simonson for you. "Harold Hinson is to be here whatever it takes." Shannon and I figured out a way to get into her van's back seat. She drove us to Rosie's. Martin G. drove her van to the banquet. He was also one of the engineers honored.

Lou presented me the framed wall hanging Presidents Award. "Will never forget this guy."

**Philip Morris,
USA President's Award**

As he handed me a check. "Do not give this check to Shannon to buy groceries. Use it to purchase something you will remember."

Spring when the doctor took off the last hard leg cast. The first time that I tried to take a step, foot would not go to the floor.

"Warned you." He fitted the right leg with a walking boot cast. "Never try to walk without this boot on. You can remove the boot when you go to bed." Shannon and Rosie are gone for a three-week trip to Scotland. I am holding down the Home Front. Have not returned to work full-time yet. Three-hour days to satisfy Short-term Disability. Stayed at Rosie's house with Tessie and returned to Simonson on Fridays.

First Patent

Harvey Lee, Mama and Harold, 2014

Screaming Animal

Sunday afternoon I took my cane and a five-gallon bucket. With Tessie we go for a walk along Lancaster Creek shoreline. There was a Northwest wind overnight. Tide is very low. Tessie was having a good time exploring the shoreline. Low tides are times to pick up broken glass and other stuff. Back in the old days people had burning barrels for the house trash. The barrel bottoms rotted out. Creek was where the things that were not burned ended up. Tessie and I returned home with a full bucket. I went inside to the bathroom. Left Tessie on the front deck. I heard her barking and stomping her front paws on the deck. She did that when excited about something in her yard. She never left our yard unless we were with her. I went out on the front deck. Tessie was not in sight. The animal-in-destress sounds were coming from Simonson Road. I called for Tessie. Then realized that the sound must be her. I forgot about broken leg or a cane. Must get to her. Tessie was being attacked in the middle of the road by two Sharpies. One had her by the back of her neck and the other by her hind leg. Pulling Tessie apart. I tried to pry open the jaws of dog on her neck. The dog only clamped down harder. Tessie screaming in pain. I started beating the dog in its side with my fist. It turned loose. Tessie lay motionless on the road looking up at me. I picked her up, embraced her in my arms. She is bleeding profusely. I scaled the bank in front of Sam and Eleanor's. Up their front steps and kicked on the bottom of the front door. Sam opened the door. "Have to get Tessie to a vet." Eleanor was already on the phone calling the Tappahannock Vet. Me and Tessie covered in blood. Eleanor brought a bunch of towels and helped me wrap around her. "Come on. We are going in the New Yorker." Sam had the keys in his hand.

The vet was waiting for us. "Come with me, Harold. Put her here on this stainless steel table. She is skinned alive. See all these punctures." Vet is using forceps picking up Tessie's skin loose from her body. "Infection will set in from all the punctures. Leave her here till Monday Morning. I do not know how much more that can do done."

Sam and Eleanor take me back home. Monday morning 7 a.m., I was at the vet in Tappahannock. "Take Tessie home and put her on a plastic sheet. There is nothing else that can be done."

"No way I'm going to do that." I had brought Tessie's crate with fresh towels in it fearing the worst. We loaded Tessie in. "Heading for Broad Street Vet Hospital in Richmond." I put the crate on the passenger seat. Want to be able to talk to Tessie on the way.

I left Tessie with the vet staff at Broad Street. "We will do all we can." Continued to Rosie's house. Shannon and Rosie are coming home this afternoon from three-week trip to Scotland. Not looking forward to telling her. Lots of crying. Broad Street vet called. Shannon and I went to see Tessie every day after work. Then two weeks later, "We thought that Tessie was going to be okay, but she cannot on her own stand. We have done X-rays after the swelling went down. Her back is broken, in two places." Devastated, had to make "that decision" again. What is best for our girl. I made a resting place with cinder block and concrete. Tessie's ashes were buried with Wendy in the Pet Graveyard at Simonson, overlooking Lancaster Creek. I can see Tessie running down to the pier chasing the Ducks and waiting for Clifton to bring some Crabs.

The vet bills came to $1500.00. With bill in hand, I walked to Tony and Betty R.'s house two doors from us. While I was recouping from my broken leg, Tony's daughter and husband had moved to Simonson from Puerto Rico. Brought their Chinese Fighting Dogs with them. Had them penned up in the back yard. The daughter and husband went on vacation. Instructed two local teenagers to walk the dogs. We never were able to find out if the teenagers were told how dangerous these dogs are. How they attach any animal that barks at them.

Screaming Animal

"We are not going to pay those bills."

"This should be covered under your Homeowners Policy. Call your Agent and get back to me."

"My name is Mr. P, Tony's Homeowner Agent. We are willing to pay half of the bills. We feel that would be the correct thing to do."

"Here is what we are willing to do. Take your Company and Tony to court. When we do, will be asking for far more than the $1500.00 dollars. How does that sound to you?"

"Provide your address. We will issue a check for the full amount."

Days later our cousin, Richmond County Animal Agent Mr. Grayson, came to Simonson. "Want to let you know Harold, have researched those dogs. We do not want them in this County. I want you to come to the Board of Supervisors Meeting on this Thursday morning. Have you talk. Explain what your family went through with those dogs."

At the Board meeting, Chairman Barry G., "Harold, come up here and sit at the table with us. Tell us what happened to your family's pet. What would you like us to do about it?" Grayson gives his report. "Have never seen dogs like these. They have one purpose. Fight in dog pits. I researched and found this information with pictures." Hands a copy to the board.

The County Administrator Steve asked Commonwealth Attorney Bill K. to issue a Vicious Dog Law for the County. "Cannot do that. Richmond County is not populated enough."

Steve jumped up out of his chair. Bangs his fist on the conference table. "Bill, I want it done today."

Mr. K. directed that a Petition with no less than five signatures will have to be completed.

"I can write one today when I get home."

"No. My office will provide that to you, Mr. Hinson. When you get the signatures, bring the Petition back to my office. My office will direct Grayson to pick those dogs up."

"When will I have the Petition?"

"You need to give me time to draft it up. May be Friday afternoon. However, you feel, Mr. Hinson, do not kill those dogs."

Shannon received the call from the attorney's office Friday afternoon. "This is Karen at Mr. K.'s office. Tell Harold. I rushed to get the Petition done today. Going to put the Petition in your mailbox on my way home. Otherwise, you would not get it until middle of next week if I mail it. Sorry, that you and Harold had to go through this." Petition was in the mailbox that afternoon. Early Saturday morning I had twenty signatures in less than an hour. Clifton was the first to sign. He loved Tessie as much as we did. On the way to work Monday morning, I delivered the Petition to Attorney's Office. Put it in the drop box. Someone tipped Tony and family off with what was going to happen. Attorney K. was their good friend. Actions took place over the weekend. The daughter and son-in-law rented a U-Haul Trailer. Left Richmond County, taking the dogs with them.

I found the property survey and marked off the lines. Spent that Spring with a post hole digger. Supply of split rail, fence post. Rolls of wire mesh. Fenced in the yard. Shannon wants to get another Shetland Sheepdog. "We need a fenced-in yard before we do that."

She called the breeder in Blackstone where she got Tessie. "You called at the right time. We will have puppies in eight weeks."

"That is good timing. My husband will have the fence done by then." Welcome home our Cassie girl.

Shannon with Puppy Cassie

Leonard told me that Whelan's Marina had a new 15-foot with V Hull fiberglass boat. Made by CHAWK out of NC. I purchased the CHAWK boat with the money received from the President's Award. Shannon surprised me on July 4th

Cassie Coming Home

birthday with a 15 HP Mercury Outboard. I had purchased a 4 HP Evinrude from Bob. Motor was not enough for the fiberglass boat. Traded the Evinrude to Johnny towards a galvanized trailer. We spent many hot days fishing in Lancaster Creek up in the shady areas. Living the dream of Harvey Lee and my youth. [Little Man in Head: *"Life is good, Harold."*] Not for long.

Family: Dad, Son Ricky, Mama Barbara, Father Warfield, Son Thomas

Shannon's 50th Birthday
Luncheon, The Inn at Montross

Melinda, Rosie and Shannon
50th Birthday

Toasting Shannon's 50th

Admitted to MCV and Boot Hill

Shannon took the call from our Mother Barbara. "Where was he taken, Barr."

"Richmond MCV. Warfield stood up to sing a hymn this morning and fell between the pews. They think that he had a stroke."

"Harold is coming right now, Barr." Pop is setting up in the bed laughing. Telling one of his jokes. Good to see him. We left the hospital late that evening. Pop is smiling. Assured us that he was going to be okay.

Harvey Lee and I met back in MCV on Monday morning. Pop could not talk. "What happened here?"

"Your Dad got up in the middle of the night to go to the bathroom. Had another stroke. We found him on the floor." The strong man a father to us. Has been crippled. Pop has lost the use of his left arm and leg. A stroke would have taken many a man down. Not our Pop Warfield. A strong Christian. Continued to do things with only his right arm and leg. Did not get depressed. Did not blame. Thing he told us, "Take good care of yourselves. You do not want to have a stroke." He started us at the age of twelve to think about a coin collection hobby. "You will have a lot of change to look through from collections on your paper routes." He gave us an assortment of coins to start with. A Red Book to record what we were able to find. Wish we had been able to keep all the Silver Coins from our paper route. One week-end Warfield asks us to come "home" together. That day he divided his coin collection with us. It was a sad day. We had watched him many nights working on his collection. Warfield had a desk/office in one corner of our small bedroom on St. John's Street. He knew a lot about coins. Many books and wonderful stories. We knew what Warfield must be thinking. Not going to be around much longer. Our "Little Sargent." Those coins are special.

Spring 1996. "Mama, are you okay? I will be on the way as soon as I get out of this meeting." I am at the Philip Morris Operation Center just off Interstate 95. Less than one hour from Tappahannock. When I arrive at the hospital emergency room, do not see my mother.

"Can I help you, sir?"

"I am looking for Mr. Warfield Sirles."

"Oh, he died." *What?* The Nurse saw the look on my face. "Did you know him?"

"Warfield is my father."

Warfield's service was held at the family's Cobham Park Baptist Church. Pinned to his coat was his forty-year Sunday School Pin. Never missed a day until he got sick. He looked like the man we have known since we were twelve. Peace on his face. We spoke about the man that was a father to us. All those funny stories growing up. The time Warfield had us "till up" the small front yard of the house on Bell Ville Lane with a Graphing Hoe. Then he planted lots of grass seed. "Water this yard every day." Grass was growing very good. Nice, thick, and green. He came one day with a new push style lawn mower. Not one with a motor.

"Cut this grass every three days."

We did not do as told. Argued a lot as we tended to do. Whose turn was it? "Not mine." Days went by. The grass got taller. Thicker. Warfield watches the grass grow. Does not say a word. Then.

"Now you boys cut this grass as I asked you to do." Big lesson learned. Very hard to push that mower.

Your Father Passed This Morning

A Sunday afternoon Shannon answered the door. I looked to see our father H.A. standing in the doorway. He came inside holding his hat in his hands.

"I just wanted to stop by and talk with you. I have been diagnosed with Colon Cancer."

Shannon was fixing dinner and asked Daddy to stay with us. Daddy and I talked while walking down to the dock and came back to the house when Shannon called us.

Fall 1996. Where has the time gone. Missing all life. Daddy spent the next months in and out of the Hospital. No hope. Too far advanced. He was never a man to go to the doctors. We will never know what or where his cancer started. Only where it ended up. We are both survivors of Prostate Cancer. The time comes and our father needs a place to die. One evening I got a call from the Administrator for McGuire Veterans Hospital. "The Board has met to discuss H.A. Hinson's request to be in Hospice. We are calling to inform you and your brother that we are not going to allow your father in this hospital." *What?* "We have had too many families that do not attend to their family. The Board has been informed about your relationship with your father."

"Ms. A., our relationship with our father over the years has nothing to do with what he needs now. How dare someone tell you anything about our life. We will be there for him." They granted him a hospice room. I have fond memories of the lunch times with my daddy. Many times, he would be sleeping. Had him on a morphine pump. I just sit looking at him. Studying his face. The next day he would be awake. "Have not seen you for days."

"Was here yesterday. You were sleeping. Did not want to disturb you."

"Always wake me up, Son." One day when Harvey Lee was not there. "You are not like Harvey, are you?"

"No Daddy. We are not the same."

The first time I remembered my father telling me, "I love you." Sometimes we would be there together. Our father looked at us fondly. "I am so proud of you and what you have done with your life. I knew it was a good thing being in General George Patton's Army. Look at this private room they have me in." He did not realize he was in the Hospice Unit. We would clean him up. "Had an accident, boys." Cousin Bobby called. Daddy forgave all his sins. Sister Linda with her husband Douglas and kids, stepmother Evelyn. All of us are there. Family was told it was not going to be much longer. We divided time with him that day and through the night. I remember rubbing his hairy left arm where he has a tattoo heart with an arrow done during WWII. The word "MOTHER." We left at sunrise the next morning after being told that we should leave.

The call was from McGuire Veterans Hospital in Richmond, Virginia. It is our father Harvey Alexander Hinson. H.A. Hinson's funeral was one of the largest in the Town of Warsaw. Hinson's Lunch, a beloved place, will never be forgotten. Daddy was buried at the Cobham Park Baptist Church Graveyard. Founded by members of the Hinson family in the early 1800s.

I named her when she called one-night months after Daddy died. "I have decided to give you and Harvey Lee the farm place. I think that is what H.A. would want me to do."

"That would be what our father wanted, Rita." I find out that Rita had Daddy's will rewritten while he was in McGuire Hospice. She brought people in his room to witness. Had him sign the "New Will" written to leave everything to her. She died a few years after that. Her kids ended up with everything. Daddy promised us the guns that were handed down to him from his father and grandfather. That did not happen!

Son's War, Ricky Home

I took a vacation day to be with them in Virginia Beach. Thomas and Ricky are both going overseas. Thomas to Kuwait and Ricky to Turkey. Pave Low forces were training with the Navy. We had pictures taken. Harold Thomas wearing his dad's Air Force work shirt from 1961 to 1965, Vietnam War Era Veteran. They wanted to hear the stories of when we were growing up. With a few beers I told the stories of the summer times in Marion and Seven Mile Ford Virginia, with our Grandmother Ma, Granddad Ervin, and Aunt Sauce, Uncle 'B.' Sleeping in the attic of Ma's home on that feather mattress. Me, Harvey Lee, Bobby sinking in that mattress. Out of sight. Grandfather Ervin Blevins. "Those things falling off that tree are poison. Do not touch them."

Ricky and Tom Going to War

One day we caught Ervin sitting on a stump peeling one of the "poison things" with his pocketknife. We found out it was fruit. Good eating. He also had a 25-pound bag of Brown Sugar kept in the Attic. Caught him one day with a fist full of it. Catching Craw Dads in the Brook that ran behind the house. Ma's big garden, those fresh vegetables. The Tobacco plant seeding bed near the garden. The Tobacco Plants growing on the hill sides. Ervin taking us up the hill in a horse-drawn trailer. "You boys pick off these Tobacco leaves, pointing to that leaf. Throw them on the ground. I will be back later to pick you up for lunch."

I understand why we got so light-headed. The pig pen. Slop bucket from the house fed to the Pigs each morning. Ma's chicken coup. Her gathering Eggs each morning in her apron. Amazed how she never broke one. Her grabbing a Rooster by his legs as she proclaims.

"You got to go." Taking the "yard bird" to the chopping block. Picking up the axe with one blow.

"Off with his head." Then turned the Rooster loose. He ran all over the barnyard. Not sure where he was going. Spraying blood everywhere. Then he dropped. Quivered. Died.

Cutting the Sugar Cane growing on the hill sides. The men feeding the Cane through a press. Catching the juice in a large pot set over a log fire. Watching intently as juices cook down to make Molasses.

Following Ma milking the cow twice a day. "You try it boys." She showed us how. "Don't let the cow kick the bucket." Getting slapped in the face with the "shitty" tail.

Watching Ma churn the milk fat into butter. That breakfast fixed every morning. Plate of Fried Eggs. Home-made Sausage. Bacon, from the Hog slaughtered last fall. Home-made Biscuits. Butter. Molasses. Sausage gravy. Fresh milk, still warm from the morning milking. Had to get used to the warm milk. Everything came from the "little farm." Nothing from the Piggly Wiggly. Except the coffee.

Ervin showed us how to mix the butter and molasses together. "Put that on the biscuits, boys." He with his large saucer and coffee cup. He poured the coffee from the cup into the saucer. Drank from the saucer. Ervin finished his meal, taking out his false teeth at the table. Picking them clean with his pocketknife. Eating the pickings.

The cold storage house built into the hillside. An earthen cave with a wooden door. Shelves for Ma's canned goods. Whole hams hanging. The "outhouse" with the Sears Roebuck Catalog. No toilet paper here. Those sounds at night. The trains running over the tracks. Through the mountains. Steel wheels on the rails. Clack, clack. The Steam Whistle blowing. Tin roofs on the house with gutter downspout into the top of the well. Bird shit and leaves, into the well. Hand pump at the kitchen sink. Running water. Kitchen wood stove fire kept going all day.

One day I tripped in the tool shed while following Ma. Struck an oil can snout into my left arm. She pulled the can out. Ervin poured kerosene into the puncture hole.

"You will be okay, darling." [Little Man in Head: "N*o stiches."*] Carry the scar today. She was right. Did not get an infection. Ma's, "Oh Lordy B."

Aunt Sauce and Uncle B's little house "up in the hollow." Running down the hill trying to beat Harvey Lee to the bottom. Hitting the clothesline under my arm pit, throwing me up in the air. Hard hit to the ground and rocks. Unconscious. Dizzy for days. Could not see without a blur. Headaches. Haziness. No doctor seen. Loved those sweet Aunt Sauce's hugs. Aunt Sauce's cooking. To have those meals again. We ate till bursting.

Uncle B grabbing our arm. Then the electric fence. Mr. H.B.R., Sr. using a pocketknife to drill a hole in my finger when I hit it with a hammer.

"Let me get the blood out, Son. It will quit throbbing." He was right. The times Uncle B or his brothers Howard, Buddy would grab our arms. Fold it. Rub the hair at the elbow. Created this ball of twisted hairs. Not any fun to open the arm up.

Taking us to the Drive-in movies on Saturday nights. Giving us whatever we wanted to eat. Learning to drive the Pickup Truck while sitting on Uncle B's Lap.

"You steer and shift when I tell you." Harvey Lee almost steering us off the side of a mountain. The road trips to Saltville, Chilhowie, White Top Mountain. "You can see four States from here. The little town of Marion. The cool nights with open windows. Fresh mountain air. No humidity. Air conditioner not required. Walks on the winding narrow road to the Grist Mill with that waterfall and wheel. Natural brook from the mountains. Down the opposite way on that narrow road to the Country Store and Post Office. [Little Man in Head: *"Wonder how life would have been here."*] On many occasions Mama commented. "We are going to move to Marion." [Little Man in Head: *"Fork in road not taken."*]

Ricky has completed four years in the Air Force and set his future in motion attending the same Community College that I did. Staying with Rosie in the lower level where Shannon was. "Why not find a job doing what you are majoring in college. Call some of the control panel shops in the area."

The call from Ricky. "Just got a Summer job with Dallas Electric Controls." My old friend from H.P. Foley, Donald G. company. Was not long before I got another call.

"This is Donald. Had this kid in here today looking for a job. Hired him. Did not tell me who his father was. Looks just like you."

"Thanks, Donald. Teach him the nuts and bolts."

May 11, 1996. Ricky graduated from J. Sargeant Reynolds Community College Engineering, Associate in Science, Summa Cum Laude. Continued to Virginia Tech where he graduated in Electrical Engineering. While attending VT, Ricky worked at Philip Morris in their Co-op Program for three years. There is no way to make up for all those lost years. Forever grateful for what is given. Will not look back. While in college at Virginia Tech, Ricky met future wife Elsie B.

Volunteer Separation Will You Do Project?

Another *Fork in the Road.* The Attorney-drafted letter was "cut and drive." Gave me two choices. Continue my seventeen-year career with Philip Morris, USA. Take the separation offer. Decision with Human Resources must be completed not later than April 12, 1998. 3:00 p.m. Five years added on age and service. Pension based on those numbers. A pension and health care. No management to be allowed in the decision. I can find a job to supplement the cash flow. There was no way to make those dollar numbers work. I accepted the offer at 2:30 p.m. on April 12. Management was waiting for me at my cubical. "What did you decide?"

"Took the package. What would you have done?"

"Was hoping that you would not. Probably would have done the same."

June 1, 1998. Retired. I had business cards made Hinson Design Build. Applied for Class B contractor license. Volunteered for Richmond County Habitat for Humanities and Richmond County YMCA boards. Shannon had been nine years without any medical problems and became involved with Susan McF., Carolyn P., Sheila W., Vivian M., and Mary Jane A. in the startup for a YMCA in Richmond County. The Y needed to raise $35,000 dollars 'faith' money before the Peninsula YMCA would be involved. Shannon chaired the Dinner Auction Events and provided lucrative items each year. Uniqueness and fun for the auction-goers. Helped to raise nearly $300,000 for the Y. She used fake names on most of the items. Did not want people to know that she was providing those. A special fantastic lady and loved being a part of this place.

Mid-August 1998. The phone call from Electrical Engineer in the Manufacturing Technical Services Group at Philip Morris. I was a member of this group before retirement. "Management has asked me to contact you."

"Has management forgotten about the letter I signed stating cannot work for Philip Morris for one year?"

"We have learned that that would only apply if you were in any facility."

"We want you to work from home. If you accept the offer, you will be working through S. Design Services."

"Will do it." "Thank you, Harold."

"We are sending you the required paperwork and Lab Core Drug Test. Can you be ready in two weeks?"

"Sure." The opportunity with Philip Morris went from this project to others, requiring me to be at a Philip Morris Facility. Commuting again to Richmond. This contract will be based on a four-day work week. Time to spend with Shannon.

****Second U.S. Patent. United States Patent Granted on October 12, 1999. Harold T. Hinson Inventor 5,966,218 Bobbin Optical Inspection System. ****

Second Patent

Shannon's Health

Shannon wrote these memories in her Gratitude Journal.

Thankful for the quick sale. Brenda, Bobby, and Lowery P. Front Street, Sharps, Virginia.

After my fall, burnout and getting ready for the holidays. Great to lie back, relax and look at life. Barbara, Ricky, and Elsie visited today. We enjoyed a mid-afternoon lunch. We gave Ricky and Elsie four dining chairs we brought at the Realtor Auction (will go with the table we gave them). Life's full of surprises – good and bad; but the bad ones need to make us stronger; rather than weaker with no control. Thoughts need to be positive and each day taken one at a time. I have gotten thru today, and tomorrow will be better. Real Estate of the Northern Neck, chosen to be their next President. Had to decline.

Free Vascularized Fibular Bone Graft on Left Hip. The 75th person in the United States to have this type hip surgery. "May help someone else in the future." Non-weight bearing. Confined to hospital bed for eight months. Moved the furniture from the Great Room to our Bedroom. Mom comes and stays with me. I found out that the Richmond County YMCA was not going to have their Annual Auction Dinner. No one willing. "I will do it from this bed." Some may have forgotten. Some may have never known.

Been a tough year. Right and left hip. Lenny, Lauren, and Andrew are coming to visit next Saturday. Have not seen them since just after my last surgery. I miss them so much. This is life. X-ray showed bone graft healing. "Right leg is about half inch longer than the left." Neither doctor will address why legs are not the same length. Big milestone today. Drove to Tracy's. Got hair colored and cut. First trip driving alone and walking since last year. Mothers who love their grown children enough to spend hours and hours in doctors' offices. Saw family doctor; wrote an RX for Permanent Disabled Tags due to hip fractures and Medical Toxicity. This week should be my last until maybe next year. Cassie is enjoying being outside. Watching the Squirrels putting away for Winter. The Rabbits enjoying the new grass and clover. I am working on YMCA "Bucket Pole" for Warsaw Fest fundraiser.

I saw doctor on Thursday in pain. Bowel habits changed. Bulge in groin. Hot. Urinating constantly. A KUB on kidneys. Ultrasound on Monday to rule out a mass in left Kidney. PSA had gone from 0.5 to 1.7 in a year. Doctor is doing a biopsy on my Prostate next week. Bulge in groin is Diverticulitis. Doctors have scheduled more test on my Liver and Bladder. Cysts in the Kidneys. No cause for alarm. Need the Biopsy on Prostate. I was rushed to Emergency Room at St. Mary's Hospital. Have 'C Diff' bacterial infection in Colon. Hospitalized for five days. We stayed in Midlothian until after Thanksgiving. This year we have a lot to be thankful for. The Annual Shannon Hinson YMCA Auction Brunch for twelve. Started at 11 a.m. The last guest left at 8 p.m. Took me all next day to clean up the dishes. I have been off work since New Year's Eve. Plans to take more time off. The Biopsy is scheduled for January. Harvey Lee had Prostate Cancer late last year. Operated on. Made a full recovery. I am negative. Simonson is having a blizzard. I went to Albuquerque, New Mexico, for son Tom's discharge from the Air Force after serving twenty-two years. Is a proud day for all the family.

**TSGT Harold Thomas Hinson, Jr.
USAF 2003**

Hurricane Isabel

October 2003. Northern Neck is in the bull's eye of the first hurricane to hit the area since Hurricane Hazel in October 1954. We begin preparing for the storm. Shannon called Connie and Jim D. to see if we can move the boats and vehicles to their Circle Driveway. Two clean 40-gallon trash cans under the roof edge set up for toilet-flushing water. Northern Neck Electric will cut the power off soon. If there is an emergency no one will come. Rescue and Fire Departments will not even try. Understood. The decision must be made whether to ride out the storm or leave? Once the wind reaches fifty miles per hour the two bridges crossing the Rappahannock River will be closed. "I must stay. No way to know when anyone can get down Simonson Road. We are four miles from Rt 3."

Shannon filled plastic jugs with drinking water. Propane lanterns prepared. The gas grill moved to screen porch. Will be our stove. Everything that can become a hazard is tied down. We have plenty canned and dry goods. The power is cut off early that afternoon. "Now we are in the *shit*." Shannon has all our favorite games on the dining room table. Sun goes down. It gets dark quick. Reality. Winds of fifty mph gust are here. I see the look on Shannon's face. Maybe I should have packed her up. Sent her to Midlothian? This is going to be bad. Big unknowns. How high will the creek water come to the house. The patio doors will not slide open. Wind pressure.

We were still awake when the Hurricane hit. Midnight. Sounds unreal. Noises. Could not imagine what they were. It is pitch black except when lightning bolts strike. Objects hitting the house. We got very little sleep. Were up early the next morning. Cassie pacing to go out. There are dock decking boards and poles just four feet from the screen porch steps. All the screens blown out. Our dock is intact with a raised portion near the shoreline. Trees are down across the shore as far as seen. "Will never stay here again when a hurricane is coming."

"I won't let you stay Shannon." Weather is tropical. Hot and sticky. The electricity off. The fridge and freezer food will be good for three days. Checked on Rosie. "I never lost power here in Midlothian." Shannon put a pot of water on the gas grill for French Press Coffee. The roof shingles are damaged. Promised Shannon that when we replaced the shingles, would make some other house changes. There is a report on the local radio about the area damage. Road closures. Power outages. There was even a whole house floating down the Rappahannock River towards the Bay. Lancaster Creek has a lot of floating trees and debris. Simonson road is blocked, going to be days before anyone living on the secondary roads can get to the main highway. Power is out in town of Warsaw. Shannon will not be able to leave for three days. After trashing food that would spoil, I went to Midlothian on fourth day.

Things settled down. Contacted our friend Garland M. about the new construction plan for this Fall/Winter. Shannon approved the plans that I drew up. We met with Garland to go over the plan. Rebuild the Craft Room, Shannon's new Office, add a full Bathroom off the Master Bedroom, covered Porch at front door. "Work up the cost to construct a 24 ft x 24 ft room above the Garage, open room space, storage closet, windows all around."

"That is a lot more work, Harold."

"I want it for Shannon."

"Done, Harold."

November 15, 2003. The Richmond County YMCA Annual Auction Dinner is a great success. Exhausted. Did not matter how sick Shannon was, she was going to get it done. She would not let anyone know what she was going through every day of her life.

We were in the hospital all day with Ricky and Elsie, the last day of September 2005. Our next grandchild was due. At 8 p.m., baby not born. We decided to go back to Simonson. At 10 p.m. Shannon was stepping on the wood stool to get into the "granny" bed. The stool flipped and ripped her calf open. Severed an artery. Blood spraying with each heartbeat. I wrapped towels around her leg. "Hold pressure on here, Honey." 911 answered - "Middlesex County."

"My wife has severed her leg and is bleeding in spurts."

"Stay on the phone – going to transfer the call to Richmond County." Rescue came and took Shannon to Rappahannock General. When I arrived, they would not let me see her. "Please tell the Doctor if he is afraid of me seeing the wound, I already have. I am coming back there." The doctor used a Mattress Stich to close the wound. It took two hours. "Have not used that stitch in years." We left the hospital at 4:00 a.m. next morning. Both exhausted. Ricky left message on the home answering machine. "You have a Granddaughter. We named her Irina Kaye."

Shannon has a connecting tissue disease, Ehlers Danlos Syndrome. Wound is not healing properly. Doctors send her to the MCV Burn Unit. Takes a lot longer for her to heal after months of treatment. She is left with a terrible scar.

Shannon is feeling better. Decides to work from home. No more working for someone else. She has the office space to start a new venture. One smart lady, opens a store on eBay. HILANDLASS. Specializing in Vintage Mexican & Taxco Silver Jewelry. She is fascinated when researching this art in the known publications. In just a few years is Awarded eBay Top-Rated Seller Plus status. Becomes well known as the person to go to. "Who is this artist, Harold?" A piece has just been delivered by UPS. I began to see the difference between the artist styles. Never as good as Shannon. She spent hours looking at pieces on Websites. Can hear her now. "I think I have found something." Looking in the Book Silver Masters of Mexico. "There it is. A Book Piece." She has customers from all over the World. Known for her honesty and research on artist history. Recognized in the publication Mexican Silver Trade and Hallmarks, Billie H. Little Book. Shannon found Artist Hallmarks not previously known. Her listing on eBay includes a full writeup about the artist, pictures, description. She is a marketing genius. Other sellers attempt to do her way. Some try to copy. None have her style and flair. Talent.

May 2008. I have been diagnosed with Prostate Cancer, in the right lobe. Harvey Lee was diagnosed two years prior. Twins being seen at the same Urology Center is rare. Discovered early because of Harvey Lee. Things have convinced me to retire for good. Shannon beginning to have pain in the left hip. Doctors Ortho Virginia. "A pin has migrated out of the bone graft. Never seen that before." Shannon keeps smiling. Left hip again. Having trouble walking. "You have loss the cartilage in the hip. At least you had your own body parts for seven years." Shannon keeps smiling.

**Hinson Family, Five Generations
July 4, 2006**

Richard Dwayne Hinson, Sr.
Quest for Answers

Easter Week 2012. Our son, Richard, and his wife Elsie have been married for nine years. Have three children. Irina seven, Rachael five, Richard, Jr. fourteen months. Rosalie H. [Rosie], Shannon's mother was a big part in his life. He confided in her often for advice.

I had just left the Tractor Supply. Went there after the Wednesday Warsaw Rotary Club Breakfast Meeting. Started my truck when I looked at my cell phone. A missed call and voicemail from Shannon. "Go to your mother's. Call me." Mama lives on Islington Road just off East Rt. 3 outside of Warsaw. I often stop to check on her on the way home. There was no apprehension about the message to stop, or to call home. Arrived at Mama's. She was crying. "Please call Shannon. I am so sorry. You will never get over this." I have a sick feeling in the pit of my stomach.

Shannon answered. She is crying. Distraught. Her faint voice. "Ricky is missing. He did not come home from work." *What?* "Mama got a call from Elsie this morning. She told Mama that he was missing."

"This makes no sense. Is that all that Elsie said?"

"Yes!" "Are you okay?" I did not give her time to answer. "I am on the way home." Our first cousin Becky was looking after our mother. Mama was in good care. I left for Simonson. "Need to check on Shannon."

"Call us Harold."

On the twelve-mile drive home. I started processing the events. Ricky called me on Monday afternoon around 3:30. What date was that? April 2nd. Ricky sounded great. He had just started work on A Shift 7:00 a.m. to 3:00 p.m. after several years on C Shift 11:00 p.m. to 7:00

a.m. "How are you liking the day shift, Son? Are you bringing the family for Easter?"

"Why don't you call Elsie and ask her, Dad?"

"Okay, if you want me too."

"No. I will call her." That was my last conversation with him.

What does this mean? How could this happen? Was he in an accident on the way to work? He just started working A Shift a week ago. More time to spend with the kids. This is a short week. Easter. Four-day weekend. The family always came to Simonson. Ricky has his acre on Lanear Road. Cleared the lot for their home. Just had the septic installed by Tommy B. He was getting quotes on the well and electrical power. I helped him with the local Richmond County Zoning requirements. Made calls for him. We looked for house plans together. It is going to be wonderful having the family live just a 1/8 mile away. Ricky was supposed to ask Elsie about Easter. Wonder if he did? Elsie has a history of not making up her mind very fast. Annual Easter Egg Hunt. Shannon always made it a fun day for the kids. Her special meal for Easter. Plenty of Fresh Strawberries that the grand kids loved. First spring fishing trip with him. Dogwoods are blooming. Croaker will be biting. Night crawlers work best this time of the year. Need to get some. Stop at Thomas Store. Must talk to Elsie. Why did she not call me? Did Rosie hear Elsie correctly? She has a hearing problem, even with hearing aids. Need to talk to Rosie. Lot of questions. Do not like this feeling. Need to start taking notes. Hope I remember all that is going through my brain. Elsie has got to have more information. Okay. Simmer down and think. Home. Try to console Shannon. "We do not know enough about this yet."

We placed the call to Elsie. "Hello. Oh, Hi Harold." That was strange. Where is the emotion?

I called Philip Morris. Had to go through Security to make any Employee contacts. Contacted Ricky's Group Leader. I had worked with him in Engineering. Rickie C., one of the young Engineers I trained back in the day. He did not understand where Ricky could be. Why did he not call in on Tuesday? We were having a meeting that morning. "Can you go in the Philip Morris Parking Lot? Inform Security to also look. Tell Security about the situation as we know it. Security would have a record of Ricky's coming and leaving."

I called and talked with Ricky's Manager Jim Z. "Ricky was here Monday. He had a doctor's appointment on Thursday last week. The doctor gave him a note to stay out of work on Friday. Ricky seemed to be okay when I talked with him Monday afternoon. He badged out at 5:30. He did not come to work on Tuesday. It is not like him not to call in. I left a voicemail on Ricky's phone. 'Are you okay?' Did not hear back from him, Harold."

"This makes no sense, Jim."

My next call was to my former Group Leader Gary A. He is retired now. His wife answered the home phone. I told Mary what was going on. "Gary is on a fishing trip. I will get our son Chris to call you."

"Ask him how I can contact the Hunt Club. Maybe Ricky is there in his trailer." We have known for some time Ricky is not happy with Elsie and her lack of doing things at home. Who knows it all. He never confided with his father like he did with Rosie. Just what we are being told by Rosie.

I asked Elsie to take the kids, go to Rosie's. "We do not know what this is all about, but it may be safer for you to be with Rosie."

Next call to the Powhatan County Police. Asked to speak to the officer that went to Ricky and Elsie's home after receiving the Missing Person call. The officer called back. "Mr. Hinson, this is Sgt. Sullivan. We received the call at 5:30 Wednesday morning. I took the call, having just coming on duty."

"Thank you for calling me back, Sgt. None of this makes any sense to me."

"Mr. Hinson, I went to the home and met with Mrs. Elsie Hinson. She said that her husband did not come home on Tuesday after work. She fell asleep in the Lazy Boy. When she woke up Wednesday morning, he was not home. Mr. Hinson, you keep asking questions. I do not like what I see."

Gary's son called back. "How can I help?"

"Can you give me the phone number to contact the Hunt Club?"

"Will call Mr. Jones, President of the Club? The Clubhouse is on his property and give him your Phone Number. Sorry about this with Ricky. He is okay, I am sure."

"I am Mr. Jones from the hunt club. We had guys at the Club this morning feeding the dogs. They told me that they have not seen Ricky. My son and I are going out to the property to look around. Our hunting property is in Columbia County."

At 5:30 we received a call from the Buckingham County Sheriff Department. "Calling you, Mr. Hinson, to report that your son was found. Buckingham County had received a call from the President of the Hunt Club. He and his son found Ricky on land in the adjoining county with the Hunt Club. They were going to quit looking on the Hunt Club Property when a white pickup truck was seen on adjoining cut-over property. Recognized the truck to be his. His son found Ricky. This office has contacted Powhatan County to contact Mrs. Elsie Hinson. They have not been able to do that."

"Officer, I told Elsie to take the kids to my mother-in-law's. She lives at 12001 Bromwich Drive, Midlothian."

"We will call Chesterfield County to go to the house. We have called for the Medical Director."

It has not sunk in yet!

"Officer, is Ricky, okay?"

"You son is deceased."

"No!"

There are not words to describe this moment. "What can you tell me Lt. U?"

"Your son was found with a shotgun across his lap. He was leaning against a small tree."

"No way Lt. that my son would do this."

"Mr. Hinson, we assure you that we are continuing to investigate. Would you like us to contact Richmond County to send an officer to your home?"

"Yes." I called Rosie and Elsie. Chesterfield County had already been there. Rosie went to her bedroom when the police came to give Elsie privacy. She did not hear what they said or Elsie's reaction. "Have Elsie call me tomorrow."

Our Mother was correct. She had never gotten over losing a son. Shannon is screaming. Uncontrollably. Very worried about her. Helpless to do anything. Just hug. Midnight the Richmond County Officer, Bull, came to the house. No one slept this night.

"Elsie, would you like me to take care of the arrangements?"

"Yes." I called Welch Funeral Home.

"This is John, we have just been notified. So sorry for your loss. We have not received Ricky yet. Should be here by late afternoon." Next call is to Cobham Park Baptist Church to talk with Pastor D. Bowen. He agreed to meet at Welch's to go over the service. "Will give me the opportunity to know more about your son." That afternoon at Welch Funeral Home with P. Welch and Pastor Bowen.

"Paul, Elsie has asked if she can see hold Ricky's hand one more time."

"Harold, we do not recommend that the casket be opened. Trust me on this. No one should see Ricky."

This Sunday is Easter. Pastor Bowen said that we could have the church after the Easter service. Late in the afternoon. I declined. "Will have family and friends, co-workers coming from out of town. Need to give them time to get here. Would like to have the service on Monday morning. Have talked to my cousin Pastor B. Hinson to do the graveside service. We would like to use the Church Gathering Hall to meet after the service." Completed all the Funeral Arrangements for Elsie. Instead of Flowers, donate to the Richmond County Little League. Service at Welch Chapel beginning at 11:00, our Pastor W. Winegar. Harvey Lee has requested to speak for me, niece L. Orlosky will sing, B. Omohundra will play the piano. A Graveside Service will follow. Ricky is to be buried in the Hinson Family Plot. His grave site will be above Brother Sammy's. Up on the Hill. Elsie asked to visit with Ricky. Tom and Chris flew in from Florida on Friday afternoon. This is going to take a toll on Shannon's health. Life will not ever be the same. Why did you not call me? Who did this? I have many questions. Not getting answers.

At Cobham Park Cemetery. The Gravestone is in line with the Veterans Memorial, our mothers name is on it with Warfield. Her final date not known. Pastor Bobby was giving a prayer. "We are here on this hill where many of our Hinson family are at rest." At that moment a breeze blew up as if on cue. Deed it is![10] Harvey Lee and I will be there one day. I took Rick, Jr. from Elsie. He clung to his grandfather's neck. Does he realize what is going on? Only fourteen months old. We gather in the Fellowship Hall. Rick Jr. still clinging to my neck. Do Irina and Rachael know what is happening? Do they know anything? Cannot tell. Where is the emotion from Elsie? Will we ever know what happened? No one believes. Cannot believe what we are being told. I have the feeling that something is not right.

The following week I contacted the Buckingham County Sheriff's Department. Set up a date to meet with them. Discuss events. Contacted Elsie. "Want to let you know I am going to meet with the Buckingham Detective handling Ricky's case, Lt. Brent U. Will you give me the keys to Ricky's trailer? The Detective wants to go look at it." I arrived at their home in Powhatan. Elsie and the three kids are sitting in the family pickup truck parked in the driveway. Man, that is strange. How long have they been out here? Elsie - not wanting me to go into the house? Why? Is she hiding something? She will not talk to me. Few words are exchanged. I continue to Buckingham, realizing Ricky traveled this same highway on his last day. That memory keeps going through my

---

[10] Richmond County Virginia, Page 368, Can be found only in the Northern Neck – the true Home Spun Expression.

brain. The trip is over an hour and a half from his home. Two counties away. What was Ricky thinking? Did he have a plan? Was he alone on his last day? Some good memories came to me at Spruces Corner. The times our mother took Route 60 West to Marion, Virginia. Us going to spend the rest of the Summer with mountain family. Looks a lot different than those days in early 1950s. That long stretch of highway. Nothing but road and trees in the distance as far as you can see. A straight line to the mountains. Seemed to roll on forever. Rise and fall. A very boring ride. Not much of a view from the back seat of that Plymouth sedan. Left or right. Mama with the cigarette hanging from her lips. Ash forming on the end. How did it do that?

"Roll that window up." No escape for us from the smoke. "I told you to roll the window up. I can feel the draft on my neck." Not even a small crack would get pass her.

At the Buckingham Sheriff's building. I am escorted to a room. Probably the Interrogation Room? Detective Lt. Brent U. is waiting. "Sheriff B. Kidde is going to join us. We call him Billy the Kid. [Little Man in Head: *"Are you kidding me?"*] The three of us talk in detail about Ricky. "We can show you some things. Tell you some things. We will not show you any pictures. The white pickup truck was parked on the side of an access road. Locked with the truck keys on the open glovebox door."

I had asked Elsie what vehicle Ricky was driving. She did not know. "He would drive a different one each day." Does not make logic. Look in the yard. What is missing? Ricky had moved the Datsun 260Z to Rosie's garage months ago.

"Did your son smoke? There were many cigarette butts on the ground."

"Ricky did not have a habit of smoking."

"In the truck driver door pocket was a box of Buckshot Shells. On the truck seat was a Finance Statement for removing funds from his 401K. We found his wallet in his right back pocket." [Little man in Head: *"Strange, carried wallet in left rear pocket like you, Harold."*]

"A beeper on his belt. There was a doctor's note in his wallet to excuse your son from work. There was $150.00 in the wallet. We did not find his cell phone." [Little Man in Head: *"No Cell Phone makes no sense."*] "Your son was found against a tree. There was a Remington Model 870 Pump Shotgun laying across his lap. The Shotgun had one spent shell" The shotgun was loaded with five shells. His arms were folded loosely around a shotgun. The shotgun safety was off, and a barrell was pointed toward his head, tucked into the chest with his right arm lying across his chest and his forehand resting against it. Your son was dressed with his safety toe shoes. Like he was going to work." [Little Man in Head: *"Or dressed when he came home after work."*]

"Lt. Brent U, my son was an expert marksman. He knew how to handle weapons. He would not have loaded a pump shotgun with more than one shell. Ricky would know there would not be a second shot. He would not have committed suicide. No way he would have done that. He would have called his dad for help. Why was the doctor note in Ricky's wallet? He went to work on Monday. Would he not have given that note to the Nurse? The E. Beam family and his mother B. Bailey were always asking him for money and recently asked Ricky to send money. Ricky's half-brother Roger was in trouble with the Law. Drugs. I was told by Elsie that Ricky was tired of sending money. Told Beulah, his mother. Roger is a big boy. Not sending any more money. Elsie told me that Ricky woke up dizzy on Thursday morning. She carried him to the doctor. Also told me that everything was okay on the weekend. The family watched a movie Saturday night—Ironman. Sunday, they were cleaning up, he got upset when Irina broke a glass. He got a haircut on Sunday afternoon. Elsie said there was a call on his cell phone Monday Night at 10:35 p.m. She said it was from a land line. [Little Man in Head: "H*ow did Elsie know call from Land Line?"*] I have talked with the Powhatan County Officer that went to the home on Wednesday morning. Asked him about getting Ricky's cell phone records."

"What do you want to know, Mr. Hinson?" The officer read me the phone call record by phone numbers. I told him what each number was and who's phone it was.

"Is that all, Mr. Hinson?"

"Officer, you did not mention the Monday night 10:35 p.m. call."
"There was no call, Mr. Hinson." That really bothered me. [Little Man in Head: *"Elsie trying to establish Ricky was home in bed Monday."*] Was he? She told me that the last time she talked to him was during the day on Monday. She did not call him at all on Tuesday. Elsie called in a "Missing Person" at 5:30 a.m. Wednesday to the Powhatan Police Department. She will not talk to me any longer. Says she does not like confrontation. Just asking simple questions that should not be hard to answer." [Little Man in Head: *"Unless you forgot what you have already said."*]

"Mr. Hinson. Do you think Elsie had anything to do with this?" [Little Man in Head: "H*ow the hell do you answer that?"*]

"Have no idea. Hope not."

"Do you have the keys to the trailer at the Hunt Club?"

"Yes, I do."

"Then follow me over there into Cumberland County. I have permission from the Cumberland County Sheriff to go and look." At the Hunt Club. "Let me go in first, Mr. Hinson." The Lt. hands me a pair of blue gloves and socks for my shoes. Unlocks trailer door and goes in. Calls me. "Nothing wrong here." We part after he drew map directions on an empty cigarette carton. Not a Philip Morris brand. "Call me if you come up with anything that you think we should know. Number is on this Card."

Ricky was right-hand dominate. The autopsy noted that his right arm is an inch longer than his left arm. [Little Man in Head: "W*ouldn't head shot cause arms to fling away from body?"*] Buckingham County requested Elsie come and talk with them. She did not as far as I know. Elsie told me that Beulah had stopped at Buckingham County on her way back to Georgia. Buckingham County had the white pickup hauled to the home in Powhatan County. I do not know where Ricky's clothes, things found on his body are. Buckingham County told me that they have not been able to track through ATF where the Remington Model 870 came from. [Little Man in Head: *"How can that be possible?"*]

Before Elsie quit talking to me about Ricky days after he was found, "What if someone hit him in the face with a cast iron frying pan and then shot him. Would they be able to tell?" Harvey Lee phoned Elsie and asked the same questions I had. Elsie gave him the same answers and repeated the "What if" question. Should I have called Buckingham? I did not. There are two other Datsun Z cars at the home in Powhattan. Ricky had both Z Cars on the road. The Datsun 280Z is parked in the carport. Per Elsie.

"The owner of that Z had a disagreement with Ricky."

"Over what?" Did this have anything to do with Ricky's death? At the Warsaw Rotary Meeting K.K. asked if I would like him to take the binder with records on Ricky to the Commonwealth Attorney Wayne E. of Richmond County. The CA and his Lead Investigator John H. reviewed the records. Kerwin called me to meet him at the Daily.

Did not think I would get any response. This is what they reported! *"Do not know what this is, but it is not a Suicide."*

I received the Powhatan Sheriff, Buckingham County Sheriff, and Department of Health autopsy reports by June 11, 2012. Specifically noted in the final autopsy report are comminuted skull fractures and facial fractures without

Ricky with Kids at SC Beach On Vacation, March 2012

evidence of shotgun pellets, but the oral cavity is remarkable for an intraoral shotgun wound of the hard palate (Lt. Brent U.).

Ricky and Irina

Ricky's Kids with Pop Pop

Ricky and Dad Fishing Trip
July 2004

YCUP RCYMCA

Breakfast at Henry's, Nags Head

Datsun 260z Title

October 2012. Friday. "I have decided to give the Datsun 260Z to you." This was what I had been hoping for six months. Had no idea what Elsie was planning with the Datsun. She met me at the DMV Building in Midlothian. Title is changed to me. The clerk came back to the counter with the antique tags. "This was meant to be." I looked at the plate. "AT 1942." What were the odds of that happening?

    I contacted the ZCAR Association of Richmond. Their Annual ZTOBERFEST is scheduled this Saturday at Pence Nissan in Mechanicsville, Virginia. Entered Ricky's 260Z for him. I returned to Rosie's. "Need to get the Z ready for the car show tomorrow." I have never been in a car show before. The 260Z had been sitting for almost a year. There is a lot to be done. By Friday night I was exhausted. Started thinking of the best route to Mechanicsville. Stay off the interstate. "Going to take a route where the Z can be pulled off the road into a parking lot if needed. Not sure how sound the Z is for a forty-mile-each-way trip." That ride I will never forget with the feeling that Ricky was with me. All the people trying to get a view of the Gold 260Z. They know what it is. "I have not seen one of these in years." Indeed. This Datsun 260Z is rare, only imported to the United States market for three months. September, October, November 1974. Shannon will drive over to the show later. There were forty Model S30 Datsuns in the show. Ricky's 260Z won! I cried. He had a love for sports cars, same as I. Keep Ricky's memory. "Wolf Z." Name that his kids gave the car. Shannon's stuffed Wolf in a Sheep's Cape became the mascot. I had a Show Board made detailing the history. The full documentation from Dream Car Restorations details how the Z was brought back to life. I wish we could be together.

P. Ray created a Facebook site to have known Datsun Z cars registered. "I am ready to start the Datsun 260Z Registry of America. Your 260Z will be Number 000001." For Ricky. The day he called and asked me to be out in the driveway at Rosie's. Heard it coming. He came in sight driving it. Gold. Smiling ear to ear. "It belonged to M. Sterchele. Loren had it stored in his barn. Mike moved to Florida years ago. Loren called him because he needed the space. "Get it running. Sell it."

"Dad, you drive. Let us go to Uncle Harvey's."

Ricky did not have the time or funds to restore my first Early Model Datsun 260Z. "Do what you think is best, Dad, with the Z." We donated it to Northern Neck Tech Center.

First Place, 2012 Ztoberfest

Last Gratitude Journal Entry
Medical Problems

October 2016. It has been years since Shannon had written in her Journal. So, much has transpired during that time. She had several more surgeries. Three beautiful grandchildren. Three great-grandchildren. The loss of our son, Ricky. I am fully retired. Shannon has a few "buy-it-now" auctions on eBay. Really have slowed down. It has been five years since the death of her best friend, Linda Dotson. Linda was a 'gatherer.' She brought folks together, no matter their differences. She loved to cook and entertain. So did Shannon. They hosted many memorable parties together. Including the Buffet at Indian Banks[11] for Connie. Jim Durham's Memorial Service. We all miss Linda. After Harvey was diagnosed with Prostate Cancer, I was tested again. Cancer. Had my Prostate removed.

    2017. One morning I was up in my office when I overheard Shannon talking to her mom. "I had this strange feeling last night in my chest."

    When Shannon got off the phone, I was standing next to her. "Why did you not tell me. We are going to call the doctor."

    At doctor's office Shannon come back holding a bottle of Aspirin. "Doctor wants me to go directly to the hospital, chew some Aspirin on the way." Rappahannock General Hospital is just up the street. Overnight Shannon is transferred to Henrico Doctor's Hospital in Richmond. Unstable Angina. She has a 98% blockage in the "Widow Maker." Operation scheduled the next morning. Two stents. Shannon never quite smiling. "I will be okay, Honey." Okay did not last long.

---

[11] Indian Banks, Richmond County, Page 46

Shannon's medical problems start building on each other. Kidney function numbers are not good Not improving with meds. Our days are spent going from one doctor to the other. There are many tests… blood and urine. Shannon is referred to Nephrology Specialist and Virginia Cancer Institute. After months of more tests, doctor believes that he has pinpointed Shannon's kidney problems. "It will require a Biopsy on your kidneys to determine what I suspect."

We meet with the Biopsy Doctor. "I will not know which Kidney will be performed on until I do the Biopsy using a Cat Scan guiding us. The Biopsy will be sent to a Lab in Louisiana. They are experts in this field. Should have results in two weeks. Be at the hospital by 6:30 a.m. There is a 'window' of four hours to do all Biopsies. You will be the first of four patients." Shannon has a history of High Blood Pressure. White coats do not help. Left our home in Simonson at 5:15 a.m., one hour to Mechanicsville. Shannon in the staging area of the operating room when they call me to sit with her. All prepped. "Will need a blood pressure of below 140/90, or Doctor will not perform the procedure. Risk of bleeding." Blood Pressure 190. Shannon gets bypassed from her number one position. Two hours later, no change in blood pressure. "You have missed the window for today, Mrs. Hinson. We are going to send you back home today. Come back tomorrow morning. We will try again." Next morning, we do the same thing. Blood Pressure again. "You have missed the window for today. Doctor cannot give you meds for High Blood Pressure because you are under the care of a heart doctor. Come back tomorrow morning." Day three, blood pressure. "Doctor wants you moved to the Short Stay Room. We will continue to monitor your Blood Pressure." One and a half hours later. "I am going to remove the IV. Get dressed. You have missed the window for a Biopsy today."

I have had enough. "Nurse. Please wait a minute. This is crazy. It is the third day that Shannon has left home to get here, only to be sent back home. Why can she not stay here over night. Maybe her blood pressure will be better in the morning without all this stress. Why not have Dr.

A. call Dr. B., maybe Dr. B. will give him some instructions on meds. What we have here, Nurse Nancy, is a 'Catch 22'."

The Nurse looks at me. Thinking. Shannon has done as instructed ... put her clothes on. "Mrs. Hinson, sit on the bed. I will be back in a minute." Twenty minutes later Nurse Nancy returns. "Dr. B. has prescribed meds. Sorry, Mrs. Hinson, going to have to put the IV back in. We are going to keep you overnight here in this Short Stay Room. You will be number one in the morning." Shannon gives me that smile. Next morning Blood Pressure 135. Biopsy performed. Go back to Simonson and wait for the results.

We are waiting in Nephropathy Specialist doctor's office. Today we are going to hear the report from Louisiana State University Health Sciences Center Department of Pathology. Dr. A. A. is looking Shannon in her eyes and speaks directly to her. "What your Kidneys have is called Focal Segmental Glomerulosclerosis C1q. Some sections of your Kidney Filters are scarred. There are no known FDA-approved drugs. There is no cure. Because of your advanced Kidney condition there is only one drug that can be prescribed. If you have any infections, it will kill you."

Shannon has that smile. "I want to try it." Doctor hands the report to her.

Interpretation Renal Biopsy: C1q nephropathy (focal, segmental sclerosis mesangiopathic pattern) associated with focal mild-to-moderate interstitial fibrosis and mild vascular sclerosis. Acute tubular injury.

Shannon continues to get weaker. She must use the wheelchair whenever she leaves her Lazy Boy recliner. Her blood count is down to 7. Should be 16. Now seeing doctors at the Virginia Cancer Institute. The next month three Mondays for Iron Infusions. Takes two hours for each.

March 17. York High School Annual Car Show. "You must go, Harold. You must do something for yourself. Fix me some food and something to drink. I will be okay." The Wolf Z placed with a Top 75 Award out of 300 plus entries.

After infusions, we go to Nephropathy Specialist for more blood tests. Does not show the change that the doctors expected. Shannon is exhausted. Weak. It is all in the effort. Shannon's body has gained so many fluids. She wants to be in her home. "Do not call Hospice."

March 27. Shannon's Birthday. I fixed a special dinner. Gus at Bluewater Seafood had some nice Alaska Salmon. "Cut me a pound off of the thick end, Gus." I pan-sautéed it. Made a Butter Caper Sauce. Fresh Asparagus Spears.

Shannon takes a few bites. "I cannot eat." Starts crying. "Have no taste for anything."

"It is okay, Honey. Can I fix you something else?"

"No need." Canceled out of two car shows for the month of April. No time for that now.

Shannon's Birthday Lunch with Melinda, Rosie. She wants to go to Denson's in Colonial Beach. Her favorite place. Blair set up a table for wheelchair access. Lunch was special. Not the same fun time we normally have. We are feeling this may be our last time together at Denson's.

May 2. 2 a.m. in the morning. My wake-up call. Kidney Stone Attack. I know the routine. Start taking Flowmax. Virginia Urology. Get a KUB. Riverside Hospital Tappahannock. Kidney Stone is 3MM. "You should be able to pass that without blasting." That is good. We do not have time for me not being involved. The most important thing in my life. Shannon. Two days later the "stone" is sitting in the "urine strainer." Carry on.

Shannon thinks she has developed a Fistula. "When I Pee, can hear it."

Renal Failure

Colon & Rectal Specialists put Shannon on a routine of Steroids for six weeks. She is not getting any better. Next appointment for Shannon is at the Virginia Urology Tappahannock Office. A Cystoscopy exam to see where the fissure is. Found between her Bladder and the Colon. "We have to operate." Regional Memorial Medical Center for pre-op testing. Operation scheduled in two days. On the way back home, I stop at Food Lion in Tappahannock. "Pick up a Roasted Chicken for dinner." Shannon waits in the Buick.

When I return. "Nurse Jill just called. All my Kidney Numbers are off the chart, bad. She wants us to wait here; trying to get in touch with doctor. May need to go back to the Hospital."

We wait ten minutes for the call. "We are twenty-five minutes from home. I think we should go home and get a bag packed in case you do need to be admitted today."

At home I have just gotten Shannon to her Lazy Boy when the phone rings. "Come back to the Hospital through the Emergency Room." I follow instructions, pack her bag. The Roasted Chicken goes in the frig. The hour drive back to Mechanicsville. Thirty-minute wait, a space comes available for her. It is 9:45 p.m. Our day started at 6:30 a.m. Shannon is smiling. Amazes me. "We are going to admit you, Mrs. Hinson."

"You might as well go home, Harold. I will be okay. See you first thing in the morning." She gets her room at midnight. My leaving Shannon's bedside every day has only begun.

On the drive home my mind wonders. Our Wedding Party with many friends and family. The look of joy on Shannon's face. The Honeymoon in Nags Head. Two people meant to be together. Love at first sight. For all time. Shannon has been through so much. Why does this happen to such a giving – sweet – caring soul? Lived a whole lot of life. Travels to Ireland, Scotland, Italy, Canada, Nova Scotia. There is more life to live. "God please. Grant Shannon more life."

The next morning up at 5:30 a.m. Nothing new. All those years commuting to Richmond. Body has an alarm clock. No need to set one. "Can you tell me which room Shannon Hinson is in?"

"We do not have a Shannon Hinson."

"Try Mary Hinson."

"Mary Hinson is in Room 2156, General Surgery Floor."

Surgeon on his morning rounds explains the upcoming operation. "Must get her Kidneys in better shape." Nephropathy specialist doctors are providing care. Doctor that was most involved with Shannon does not practice at this hospital.

I leave Simonson not later than 5:45 a.m. every morning to be in Shannon's room when the doctors make the rounds. "Where have you been?"

"I forgot my wallet and had to go back home."

"Got you a Hard-Boiled egg on my Breakfast tray." Most mornings in the Hospital Café all Hard-boiled Eggs gone by 8:00. She looks forward to seeing me first thing in the morning. Wants me to be there every day. I am. Looking after her wellbeing, asking questions of the doctors and nurses. Writing down their names. A Single Subject Notebook keeps the record. "Have you a business card?" Make sure that they know who to contact. Write my name and cell number on the White Board. They tell me it is good to ask questions. I believe they mean it.

Shannon was in the hospital for a week. We are back home in Simonson. Sue Hinson called to welcome us back home. "We are getting some of the best-looking Soft-Shell Crabs seen in years. Come and get you and Shannon some." Sue picked out six of the best I have seen in years. "Shannon is going to love these."

"They will be an early evening dinner treat. Thanks, Sue." After cleaning the Crabs, cut off mouth, remove lungs, wash. Dry the Crabs on paper towels. Transfer to a plate containing a combination of White

Corn Meal, Flour for a light dusting. Do not want a heavy coat. Heat up a cast iron pan with Peanut Oil and Butter. Carefully keeping the claws folded at the body. Lay two Crabs at a time, bottom side first in the pan. Three minutes. Carefully turn over. Three more minutes until brown and crisp finger legs. Remove to a sheet pan lined with paper towels. Pan in a warm oven. Continue with the next two. Have some String French Fries cooking in the oven. It was a 'special' dish that I know will please her. Shannon took two bites. "I cannot eat this, Honey. Cannot taste anything. Just bring me some hot tea with honey and lemon."

Italy Trip – Amalfi Coast

The wear on us not describable. She does not want me to call for anyone to help. Sometimes Shannon is too weak, cannot handle her alone. I must get someone to help. Thankful for cousin Martin Hinson, comes when I call. Days are consumed going to the doctors. Walgreen Drug Store. Walmart. Food Lion. The things that we use to love to do together. All gone. Shannon does not even want to stop on the way home to get something to eat. "Cannot go inside, Harold." Drive through Burger Joint – okay. The Triumph boat is on the lift. We purchased this boat so that Shannon can stretch out in the bow. We will not be in the boat this year. No way that I will go fishing and leave Shannon at home. Jim and Mary Kay came one day before Shannon got so ill. Shannon drove the repurposed lawn mower to the dock. Jimmy and I helped get her on their party boat. The TCYC gang and friends from our trip to the Amalfi Coast are meeting for lunch at Merrior. Our only trip together overseas was Italy. We were looking forward to going again. Positano. Stay in town and travel on the bus system to other sites. The memory not known.

She is too weak to walk to the bathroom. I roll her in the Wheelchair. Everything an effort. We made the right decision putting the Master Bathroom near the front Family Room. I sleep on the couch to be near her. She can see Lancaster Creek, Porch, Yard from her Lazy Boy.

Professor and Raven come to the door and look from the porch. Zorro spends most of his day sleeping in Shannon's lap. They love it. Someone dropped a Tuxedo Male Kitten around Christmas years ago. The Richmond Grandkids had several names Oreo, Zor-oreo. The kitten was malnurished and wanted all the food. Not mean. Just hungry. I started feeding him on the side deck away from Professor. He was very protective of 'his' yard. Getting into fights with any stray that came. Professor would just sit and watch. After the last Vet bill and scare from infection, we decided to bring Zorro indoors.

June 21, 2018. Traffic Court in Essex County. Road trailer lights not working. Dismissed. June 23, 2018. Classics on Main. "You have to go, Harold." The Foxy 5.0 was judged to be Third Best Ford in the Show. When leaving Gloucester, ran into a very bad thunderstorm on the backroads home. Checked my phone. Shannon had left a voice mail. "I do not know where you are. There is a severe Thunderstorm Warning. Be careful. I am okay, Honey. Can you go to Tappahannock and get me a Gero?" Continue to Route 17 and Bella Pizza.

She was not able to eat. "I can't taste anything."

"We are going to operate, cannot wait any longer."

I do not remember my birthday on the 4th. Shannon asked Elsie to bring her mom Rosie and the kids for the day at Simonson. The things she would do. "Take this grocery list and get me everything on it." She has planned to have each of the kids make their own Pizza's. "Pop Pop will cook them for you. Make one for us adults." Always thinking how to make each visit at the river special.

"Honey, will you shave my legs and polish my toenails? I would but cannot reach them." She did not tell me what the future was going to be.

Regional Memorial Medical Center

"Call from Shannon Hinson." I was stopped at the traffic light on Rt. 360 at West Store.

"Honey, they are here taking me down now." Shannon was scheduled at 7:30 a.m.

"Going to try to make it." At 6:05 a.m. I walked in Shannon's Room. The two nurses were helping her get on the scale to weigh.

"You made it."

"Glad there were no police on the road this morning." I walked with her to surgery floor.

Shannon was in surgery for three hours. Melinda and Rosie came to the hospital. We met with the surgeon. "The surgery is a complete success. We will have to wait to see how Shannon heals. She has a bag on her right side. Can be removed in eight weeks." Physical therapy works with Shannon every day to get her strong enough to come home. They wish that Shannon would go to Sheltering Arms. Shannon convinces them otherwise.

"Harold can handle it when we get home. He made me a step to get in the Utility Room that I have practiced on. Show Nurse Joyce the video, Honey."

"That looks like it should work, Mr. Hinson."

The nurses send us home with supplies and instructions for the care of her bag. Give Shannon a hug. Lots of smiles. A happy day. Did not last. We arrived at our home. She goes up one step. "I need to sit back down. You need to get some help." This was the moment that I should have done another method we had done before when Shannon could not go up the steps. Lift the wheelchair with Shannon in it into the Utility Room. I did not think of it. Do not know why.

I called Cousin Diane. "I am in Richmond. I will call Don. He can help you." Don and I get Shannon out of the chair. She walks all the way up the steps and has her right foot into the Utility Room.

"I cannot pick up my Left Leg." I am in the Utility Room behind the second wheelchair.

"Don, just pick up her foot enough to get it over the threshold."

Shannon loses her balance. Falls to her knees. I moved the wheelchair out of the way and grab Shannon to kept her from falling on her face. "You have to let me go down, Harold." She comes down and screams. Lying face down with both legs out of the door.

"Help me roll Shannon over." That is when we see Shannon's legs. She scraped both legs on the threshold, ripping skin and flesh. I called 911. Got a pillow and blanket to cover her.

Rescue Squad arrives. They are working through the standard questions. Cousin R. Hinson is one of the members. "This man is trying to take care of his wife by himself. He is 76 years old. Where do you want us to take your wife?"

"Rappahannock General in Kilmarnock." I arrive to check Shannon in with the hospital staff. The hospital waiting room is a mess. Construction going on around the Emergency Room? There was a person at the check-in desk I was talking to. Where the *hell* did, she go? A different person comes after about fifteen minutes. Started going over the same questions as the last person. "What happened to the lady I was talking to?" "Oh, she went to dinner." [Little Man in Head: "*WTF.*"]

Allowed into the Emergency Ward and directed back to Shannon. Lying there. "Has anyone seen you yet?"

"A Nurse took my vitals." Blood all over the sheet covering. A doctor comes, begins looking at Shannon's legs.

"We do not have any way to treat these wounds." Told the nurse to wrap them up.

Discharged. I was handed an Instruction Sheet: "Find a facility that does Wound Care." [Little Man in Head: "*You got to be kidding me.*"] Two nurses help me get Shannon into her Buick. On our way back to

Simonson: "Shannon, call Martin. We need him to help get you in the House." Martin is waiting when we arrive. We keep Shannon in the wheelchair and roll her to Lazy Boy.

"I cannot stand."

"Wrap your arms around my neck." Martin picks Shannon up out of the Wheelchair. Lowers her down into the Lazy Boy. It is now 11:30 p.m. Thank God for Cousin Martin. I make Shannon comfortable for the night.

Home Care

Nurse calls at 11:00 a.m. "Running a little late. I am on the way. Should be at your house by 11:30." When the nurse sees Shannon's legs, does not even take Shannon's vitals. "I am not authorized to deal with this. I will have to call the Home Office."

"Can't you at least change the 'blood-soaked bandages?"

"I will look and see what I have in my car." Changes the dressings. "Someone will call you. Got to go. I am going to be late to my son's graduation." [Little Man in Head: *"What?"*]

During the day Shannon continues to say she is fine. A light breakfast of Coffee, Yogurt with Fruit. I fixed some soup for lunch. No one has called. It is now 3:30 p.m. "Harold. I am having trouble breathing. Bring me a bag to breathe in."

I call 911. "My wife Shannon is having trouble breathing."

"We are on the way, Mr. Hinson." Two Rescue Squad Units arrive with seven members. They try to take Shannon's vitals. It is not good. Two members get Shannon to her feet.

"I am going to faint."

"Take the quilt with Mrs. Hinson in it." They lay Shannon on the gurney and carry her to the ambulance.

"Where do you want us to take Mrs. Hinson?"

"Riverside Hospital, Tappahannock. That is closest to Mechanicsville."

Squad lets me in the ambulance with Shannon. "Cannot get a blood pressure. Want you to leave now, Harold. Do not follow us too close on the way to Tappahannock." Minutes have passed. The ambulance does not leave the driveway. [Little Man in Head: *"What is going on?"*] All

I can do is watch through the Kitchen window. Fifteen minutes pass before the ambulance backs out of the driveway and leaves with Siren and Lights. Tappahannock, thirty-five minutes from Simonson.

Riverside Hospital Emergency Room

"Richmond County just brought my wife Shannon Hayes Hinson here. I am her husband, Harold."

"Take a seat while I got her information." A nurse takes me to the Emergency Room wards. Shannon is hooked up to lots of equipment. Something coming out of her left shoulder. She gave me that smile.

"What is that, Honey?"

"When they could not get a blood pressure, had to drill into my Collar Bone marrow to get one. Could not deaden it before they did."

"Mr. Hinson, I am Doctor Atkins. We have started a Blood Transfusion." I brought the doctor up to date, just leaving Memorial Regional the day before. Falling. Discharge from Rappahannock.

"They do not have an ICU, Mr. Hinson. We are having trouble finding a place to put in the IV." I watched as a nurse used an instrument with screen. "Found one." He guides the IV in. "Your wife needs to be admitted. We can do it here or would you rather somewhere else?"

"Doctor, I want her to go back to Regional Memorial, where she was just discharged."

"We will arrange for that." The Ambulance Service arrives and agrees to give Shannon the second Blood Transfusion on the way to Mechanicsville.

"We cannot let you ride with us. Are you going to follow?"

"Afraid that I will not be able to drive tonight. Exhausted. Will go home and pack a bag. Come first thing in the morning." Kissed Shannon.

"Drive careful, Honey." At the light to turn right and cross the Rappahannock River. [Little Man in Head: *"Go back to the hospital, Harold."*]

"I thought you were going home?"

"Wanted to make sure you are okay." Shannon smiles.

"I am. Please, go home and get some rest." It is now 10:45 p.m.

Back To Medical Center

5:30 a.m. on the road from Simonson to Mechanicsville. Getting to know this road well. Will be getting to know it even better. At the front desk. "Can you tell me which room Shannon Hinson is in? They may have her in the system as Mary Hinson."

"Let me check. There is a Mary Hinson in the Emergency Room." [Little Man in Head: "W*hat?*"] My heart skipped a beat. Shannon is getting another Blood Transfusion.

"They got her there around midnight."

"Mr. Hinson, my name is Doctor Davies. Mrs. Hinson is still here because there was not a room available on the second floor. There is one now. We are going to take her for an ordered Cat Scan and then transfer to Room 2256. You can walk with us if you like. They are also putting three lines directly into her neck artery." I stayed with Shannon until the Cat Scan was complete. Followed her to the Critical Care Unit, Second Floor. Her Day Nurse, Robin is aware that Shannon is coming back. Maria is Shannon's Bag and Wound Care Nurse.

Case Manager Amanda brings me a list of health and rehab facilities. "Pick the one that you want Shannon moved to. Will need to know later today." Three Doctors are in and out of the room. Shannon's blood count continues to be low. Pain meds have been ordered. Nephropathy Specialist reports that Shannon's kidney numbers are improving. Her blood pressure is 125/72.

"Amanda, I picked Lee Davis for health and rehab. How will Shannon be moved to the facility?"

"We will do that by ambulance, Mr. Hinson. Not to worry. Lee Davis is a great location."

Melinda and Rosie are at the hospital. I washed the Lazy Boy quilt, pillowcases, and sheet. Ready for when Shannon returns home. Took Buick to Standard Garage. Wayne followed me and brought me home. State Inspection is due in September. Told W. Angolia to inspect the Buick. Fix anything that is close to wear limits. This SUV is for transporting Shannon. I measured the car port to see if the Mustang LX would fit. Winter is coming. Wet, snow and ice. Cut the grass front and backyard. Lowes Store Manager helped to special order an Aluminum Handicap Ramp. Two-week delivery. Wayne A. called. "Buick is ready to go."

"I called Mahan. He is coming for the Buick and take home for me. Thanks again." Good to have these two in my life. Cleaned the car port. Exhausted mentally and physically.

Personnel came to transport Shannon for the Cat Scan and brought a special bed. "Why can you not keep Shannon on the bed she is in? It is going to be hard on her to be transferred."

"Because that is how we do it." I called Nurse Robin and she intervenes. Shannon was taken down in her bed, I walked with her. The Cat Scan shows something. Cat Scan used to put in a Drain Line shows a small leak.

I walked down to surgery with Shannon. On the way to the elevator, "There is Mary Kay."

"Shannon, that is not Mary Kay."

"You would tell me if it was, Harold?"

"Do you want to see Mary Kay, Shannon?"

"Yes." I called Mary Kay. Told her what Shannon said. They have been close friends since working at Foley in the 1970s.

They had a good time. Lots of laughs. It cheered Shannon up. She was in good spirits when Mary Kay left. I did not go to the hospital this day. Spent Friday afternoon getting the garage ready for the ramp. Moved the Mustang into the car port. Put the cover on the 260Z and called nephew Jason. "Lowes has called, the ramp is in the store. Should I go and get it?"

"I need to stop for supplies in the morning. Do not go. I will pick ramp up in the morning." I fell asleep on couch with Zorro on my legs.

Jason, Ben, Taylor arrived with the supplies. This is the second day that I am not at the hospital. When I called, Shannon did not answer the phone. Rosie was supposed to be there. I called back again. No answer. I called the Nurse Station. "Your wife is sleeping most of the time. She is doing well."

The ramp construction takes all day, into the late afternoon. We tried the ramp with Ben in a wheelchair. "This will not work. Need more room to turn the wheelchair." Tore down the railing and added more decking. Redid the railing. Finished. Jason and the boys packed up and headed back to Henrico County. Sun is going down. I want to go see Shannon. Make it to the couch. Collapsed.

I woke up exhausted. Called Shannon's room. Did not get an answer. Called the Nurses Station. "Mr. Hinson I am first time new to your wife's care."

"Nurse, I want to talk to my wife. She is not answering the phone. Will you go in her room and see if she can reach the phone?"

"Mr. Hinson, she is on pain meds and sleeping. Pain level 9-10." Soon, Shannon called me on her cell. She was upset about a call that keeps coming from Ohio. Did not tell me if anything was wrong. The Nurse reported that hospital doctor ordered a unit of blood. More pain meds. Ordered a PCA Pump. Right then a "red flag" should have gone up for me. It did not. I was so exhausted that I was not sure driving to the hospital was possible. Thinking that Rosie was with her. Did not know Rosie was not there. She had gone on Saturday. "Could not find a wheelchair as promised." Did not go see Shannon. Went home, did not call me.

7 a.m. I enter Shannon's Room. The Night Nurse Shelly is debriefing the Day Nurse Beth. I went to Shannon's bedside. Call her name. Shannon jerked her head to face me. Stares through me. Does Shannon know who I am? I crossed the room to the nurses standing by the window. "What has happened?"

"Shannon became non-verbal last night."

Hospital and Colon & Rectal doctors are now standing by her bed.

I overhear the doctors talking. "This is worse than last night. She may have had a stroke. Nephropathy Specialist ordered Ultra Filtration. Was started at 5:30 p.m. Shannon's blood pressure dropped. She became unresponsive! I called a Code S! We did a full work-up. Ordered an MRI Brain w/o Contrast. May have been the pain, meds. Shannon cannot, swallow. Shannon was alert and talking before the Ultra Filtration."

Dr. C. shouted, "YOU DID NOT CALL ME."

"I have ordered a Cat Scan Stat. Pain Meds have built up in her kidneys. Shannon's belly pain may be infection. Abdomen a concern. May have gone Septic. The White Count is up. Will do surgery this afternoon."

I called Melinda. Shannon is back in her room from Cat Scan. Nurses from Wound Care begin to work. Maria asked Shannon if she recognized this guy?

She looked at me. "Yes, he is my husband." I cried.

2:35 p.m. Doctor from Nephropathy. "No Stroke." Infectious Disease takes culture for lab. 4:20 p.m. Shannon taken down to the Operating Room. I walk with her.

Talk with the doctor. "Mrs. Hinson will be kept asleep for one-to-two days with a breathing tube in. She will be taken directly to the ICU. Give your wife a kiss." Shannon said she loved me. Nurse gave me a phone number. "We leave at 6:30 p.m. Gather her belongings. Shannon will go directly to ICU Room 2516." I walked back to Room 2266. A nurse came in. "There is no need to rush. Colon & Rectal Doctor C. will come to this room after the surgery is completed. I packed Shannon's belongings. Have had nothing to eat all day. Cut the lights off. Rolled up my coat for a pillow. Was asleep in minutes on the seating area under the window when my cell wakes me.

"I am on my way from Maryland coming directly to the hospital. Can I bring you anything?" "Just bring me some of whatever you are having."

7:00 p.m. We are waiting in Room 2266 when surgeon Dr. C. comes, still in his surgical clothes. "Found a leak and was able to re-stitch. Used glue. Never had to do that before. Elois Danlos, we have found also affects the healing of internal organs. When Shannon came to the ER on August 1, her Cat Scan showed that the Colon and Rectum were connected. The fall did not cause this. Breathing tube overnight. Shannon will be in ICU for weeks." He made a drawing in my Notebook showing the surgery location. "More Optimistic." I am too exhausted for this moment to sink in. We go to the ICU Room 2516. Set up Shannon's things. Wait for her. Helpless.

Intensive Care Unit

August 14, 2018. ICU Room 2516. "Numbers are good. Cancelled Dialysis. May try to wake Shannon today. No Meds needed." On my walk down the hallways to the ICU each morning, there is a doctor sitting at a Nurse Station on the Critical Care Floor. He always nods like he knows who I am. Never stops me. I wonder who this doctor is. Have not seen him caring for Shannon. Will know August 22nd.

August 15, 2018. Since 6:30 p.m. yesterday Shannon is breathing on her own and awake. "I will keep you updated, Harold. No need for you to come every day." Another doctor enters through the glass doors.

"I am Shannon's husband." The doctor observes me writing in the Notebook as he talks.

"I guess that I am in trouble?"

"No sir. Just want to know who is taking care of my wife and what you are doing for her. Do you have a business card?" The doctor hands his card, MD Pulmonary Associates of Richmond, Inc.

"Mrs. Hinson is not following commands. Will not remove the tube until she is more alert to commands. Your wife is better than yesterday." Another doctor enters. Introduces herself as she hands her business card. [Little Man in Head: *"Word has gotten around."*] MD, Nephropathy Specialist. "Mrs. Hinson's lung fluids dry. No Ultrafiltration today." Every morning the ICU Staff have a meeting in the Command Desk area. I can see this area through the glass doors, just across ten steps. Looks as if they are discussing each of the patients. Doctor and nurse speak in turn as they look at their laptops.

2:30 p.m. Another Doctor, seen her before. Business Card. MD, FACP Infectious Disease, Bon Secours. 5:20 p.m. I have arrived home when Nurse Virginia called as she promised. "Shannon is more awake.

Doctor gave me instructions on changing her dressing. She is going to be okay, Mr. Hinson."

August 16, 2018. 7:00 a.m. Shannon squeezed my hand. First time she has done that in many days. Her hands are not puffy with fluid this morning, look like the ones I have held for years. She is breathing on her own. "We are taking the breathing tube out soon."

7:15 a.m. Code Blue Alarm. The Response Team enters room next door. Doctors and nurses are coming from everywhere. A woman well-dressed in a suit carrying a clipboard enters Shannon's Room. Does not provide a business card. "Are you okay, Mr. Hinson?"

"Yes, I am fine." She closes the drapes. [Little Man in Head: *"Who was that person?"*]

I will know August 22nd. 8:40 a.m. Second Code Blue, Room 2514. The lady in the suit is joined with others. I think they are family members. She closes the glass door this time. Does not speak to me. If Shannon knew what was going on, did not indicate it. They leave the ICU Ward and enter a room just off to the right. On the way to the bathroom, "Family Conference" name plate on door. I noticed that my name and phone number had been erased from the white board. M.D. Nephropathy came. I asked doctor to step outside Shannon's Room. "Doctor, am I observing this correctly? Appears to me that doctors are not agreeing with each other?" I know that look. Seen it before. 10:35 a.m.

The lead nurse came to check on Shannon. "What are your concerns, Mr. Hinson?"

"I know that the Code Blue was the most important event this morning. *But*. There has not been a nurse checking on my wife in quite a long time." [Little Man in Head: *"Think M.D. had a word."*] The lead nurse begins to work on Shannon. Cleaned her breathing tube. Swabbed her mouth. Reposition her in the bed so her neck was not in a bind. Loosened the blood pressure cuff. Took care to remove bandage on her nose. No other nurse has come. 4:00 p.m. Surgeon called me. "Shannon's numbers are good. Will increase the pain meds."

Intensive Care Unit

"Doctor C., we need to discuss what happened on Sunday. No doctor call from hospital to you or me."

"Harold, I will talk to the Staff." [Little Man in Head: *"Knows it was not right."*]

August 17, 2012. 7:00 a.m. "Will try to remove breathing tube today." Doctor leaves. Shannon is looking at me, chewing on the tube. I have seen that look for many years.

"Honey, I cannot do any more." She knows me. 8:20 a.m.

"We are taking out the breathing tube." 1:35 p.m. "Surgeon has given instructions. If during Ultra Filtration Shannon's blood pressure drops, we are to stop the procedure."

Nurse Virginia confirmed. "Dr. C. comes twice a day. Blood pressure is better. Dr. C. did order to stop Filtration." [Little Man in Head: *"Appears Doctor had talk with Staff."*]

August 18, 2018. Saturday. Melinda and Rosie are at the hospital as promised. I am home cleaning the house and washing clothes. Melinda called. "We have not seen Nurse Virginia. Physical and Occupational Therapy working with Shannon moving in bed. She was able to lift legs on her own."

11:55 p.m. Nurse Virginia called me. "They were doing a Short Run Ultra Filtration. Shannon did not tolerate. Blood Pressure dropped. Doctor will try again today. She is sleeping now." 3:25 p.m. I called Nurse Virginia. "Shannon is sleeping a lot. She did not sleep well last night." 5:20 p.m. Nurse Virginia. "Davita Filtration is here, starting Continuous Ventral Veno Hemodialysis CVVH. Finished Filtration without any issues. Shannon is sleeping now. Melinda and Rosie are here. They brought framed pictures of the family for Shannon's Room. Put them on the windowsill so she can see them.

Melinda talked to me. "Going to leave for home tomorrow. Shannon has Delirium. She is stronger today and sat on the side of the bed. Said to tell Harold that I miss him."

August 19, 2018. Sunday. 10:30 a.m. Called Nurse Owens. "Shannon is doing well. Changed her mind about not wanting pain meds for the stomach. I will tell her you called. Doctors doing Ultra Filtration, continuous Dialysis 24 hours for several days. Must get fluids out of her body." 12:30 p.m. "Dr. V. is here, and he concurs with Dr. Patel. Special procedure with CRRT Machine in room. Runs at a slower rate. Removes toxins and waste fluids. Nurse Leeann: "The Nurse Station phone number 764-7803. Ask for Shannon's Room 2516. I started today at 2:30–3:00 p.m. Night Nurse Rob."

August 20, 2018. Monday. 7:00 a.m. When I got to Shannon's room, she is wrapped in a "Bear Hugger" warm cover. "Shannon was cold and we use this to warm her body."

Doctor C: "Shannon has less belly pain. Will do a CT Scan this week. There is a high risk for an Abscess. We may remove the nose tube tomorrow. Shannon will get stronger each day. At least another week."

Care Manager Bon Secours; Guest House, 1100 Libbie Ave. Call 764-6702. "The house is available for you to stay."

"Thank you very much, but I can drive home from here in the time it would take me to get to Libbie Ave. We have an indoor cat, Zorro. He has not been doing well since Shannon has been here."

Shannon motioned me to lean over her. She can only speak in a whisper. "Rob's family are giving him a birthday party on Saturday. Steam Crabs. Write this down and go get it. Twenty-four Wooden Crab Knockers; French Bread; Old Bay; Bibs; Birthday Balloon. I want to do something special for Rob; because he sings to me." One hour later. No luck. Wooden Knockers not found in any store. I called Harvey Lee. He sent me on a wild goose chase far out in the West End. Look for Harvey's store.

"I am not coming to help you look." [Little Man in Head: *"Nothing new."*] Harvey Lee does not realize how much I need some help. I gave up and started back towards the Hospital. [Little man in Head: *"Go to Sam's Club."*] Box of 36 Butter Knives. Large container of Old Bay. 52-oz container of Extra-large Virginia Peanuts. Package with two French Breads. A Sam's Club insulated bag to put the supplies in. It has been over two hours when I return to the Hospital to show what I got.

Shannon was pleased. Gave me that smile. Then motioned for me to lean over her. Softy. "You forgot the Balloon."

"Okay, Honey, going to the Hospital Gift Shop, see if they have one. I find the clerk. "Do you have a Balloon that can be inflated?"

"Which one would you like?" The lady pointing to the display case?

"Any adult one that has Happy Birthday on it."

While the lady was blowing up the Balloon, I looked around. Stirring right at me, was a Cast Silver Elephant. *OMG!* Shannon has loved Elephants since she was two years old when Mother Rosie carried her to Train Yard in Richmond to watch the Ringling Brothers unload the Elephants.

"Is this Elephant for sale?" I am holding it for the lady to see.

"Yes, it is your lucky day. That is the last one we have."

"Please, wrap it for me? My wife is in the ICU. Loves Elephants."

I am holding the Balloon string with the other arm behind my back.

Softy. "What is this?" I had laid the box near Shannon's hand. She opens the box. Starts crying.

"How did you know this is what I wanted. Tie the Balloon String onto the Sam's Bag Handle. Sit the bag in the chair before you leave. Rob will see it when he comes on duty this evening. Thank you, Honey."

August 21, 2018, Tuesday. The doctor that nods to me is in Shannon's room when I arrive. Hands his business card. A. Gilrod., MD, Hospitalist Regional Memorial Medical Center, Sound Physicians. "We are preparing to move Mrs. Hinson to the General Surgery Floor. She will be in Room 2176." Her belongings are packed on a cart. As we pass the Nurses' Critical Care Floor, they are clapping and wishing her well.

General Surgery Floor Room 2176

The Elephant was placed where Shannon asked. "So, I can see it!"

"The tube was in for four days. Causing the muscles to get weak. Yes, she can have Ice Chips, but only with the nurse present."

G.E. K. III, M.D. Nephropathy Specialist: "We will do Dialysis today, tomorrow, access for next." [Little Man in Head: "*Arrogant.*"] Wish that Shannon's care was by Trudy R., MD.

11:45 p.m. I went to Café to get a quick lunch. Patient Advocate saw me, came over. "How is your wife, Harold."

"They just moved her this morning to General Surgery Floor."

"Harold, now it is even more important to be the Advocate. Nurses one to four Patients now."

4:50 p.m. I left the hospital for Simonson. Should have spent that night in Shannon's Room. Beyond exhausted. Mental state not any better. What happened!

August 22, 2018. 7:00 a.m. Wednesday. General Surgery Floor, Room 2176. Surgeon Dr. C. is walking towards me from the other end of the long hallway. I stopped at Shannon's door and waited. "Good to see you this morning, Harold." I follow Dr. C. into her room. We see Shannon at the same time sitting up in her bed. Bent over at her neck.

Doctor C. pulls the Rapid Response Team Alert, as he 'YELLS OUT'. "What happened here?" A nurse appears. I left the room as the Rapid Response Team came pushing in. Only able to get one glance at Shannon. Surgeon joins me in hallway. "I pulled the Rapid Response out of caution." I do not remember anything else if he said it. Hospitalist and Nephropathist are in hallway. We stand in stillness for minutes when the hospitalist breaks the silence. "We are taking Mrs. Hinson back to the ICU. Getting that room ready." [Little Man in Head: *"Why did you move her out of the ICU?"*]

Doctors begin talking. "If your wife had Cancer; Diabetes; a Broken Leg we could fix her. We cannot fix this." That dagger came from the Doctor K III. I was not prepared to hear this.

"Hospital does not have a Medical Directive." That came from Hospitalist Dr. A. G.

"What do you mean? We provided a directive with registration desk when Shannon came here." A Response Team nurse was sitting at the computer desk banging away on the keys as we were talking.

"Here it is." As she turns the screen towards the hospitalist. He reads the screen.

"We have already done more than we should have." My heart sank again.

I called Melinda. "They are moving Shannon back to the ICU. Not good this morning."

"I am leaving Maryland now and will get Mom. Bring her when I come. I will call Mom."

I have no memory of how Shannon looked when I next saw her. A nurse starts to pile Shannon's belonging on her bed.

"Wait a minute. Why don't you get a cart for those things? Do not put things on her bed." An attendant with cart helped me move belongings back to the ICU. Same room moved out of fifteen hours ago. As we follow Shannon's bed passing the Nurses' Station.

"We are so sorry."

Losing Shannon

9:00 a.m. Intensive Care Unit, Room 2516. The nurse is talking to me as she gets Shannon comfortable in bed. "When they were giving Shannon Dialysis last evening, her Blood Pressure dropped to 80/40. Her lungs are filling with fluid. Per the Medical Directive, we will not be putting in a breathing tube. Nurse Tim Ford will be taking over for me, Mr. Hinson."

I had not grasped the total situation until this point. My brain is overloaded. Everything moving too fast. Shannon holds my hand. Having trouble talking. Whispers; murmurs. I constantly follow the changing numbers on monitors. Never been more helpless in his life! [Little Man in Head: *"Broken."*] Nephropathist enters. "Ordered Slow Dialysis. Mrs. Hinson's condition is a lot of things. Cannot fix this." [Little Man in Head: *"Heard you the first time."*] "Ordered Blood Pressure to be taken every fifteen minutes."

Dressed in all white, Nurse Tim enters. Introduces himself. Talks with Shannon, calling her "Honey." This man is very compassionate. The only one looking after Shannon. I looked at her blood pressure reading. 10:03 a.m.-142/51. 10:30 a.m. A dialysis machine was brought. Alice introduced herself. Ran a short test with Tim. Alice was preparing to leave. "Aren't you going to stay?"

"No, Tim knows everything that needs to be done."

12:30 p.m. Dialysis machine goes into "Alarm." "Extremely Negative" flashing in red. Shuts down. Tim starts checking the hoses. "There are two people trying to get into the ICU, Mr. Hinson."

"That would be Shannon's Sister Melinda and Mother Rosie. Please let them in."

Melinda appears at the opening doors pushing Rosie in a Wheelchair. "Have you had anything to eat?"

"Nothing today."

"Go down to the Café. Brian is down there. Get something to eat."

"Brian, do not have an appetite. Going to just have a quick bowl of Soup with some Crackers. Need to get back to Shannon."

"I am going to stay down here, Harold."

1:40 p.m. I return to the Nurse Station area outside Shannon's room. The lady in the suit is leaning over her bed. Talking with Shannon. Melinda was standing near her. As the lady is leaving the ICU Room. "Do you have a business card?" Nurse Practitioner, Palliative Medcine, Bon Secours Medical Group. [Little Man in Head: "*Now you know.*"]

I returned to the ICU Room. Rosie is very upset. "Harold, she kept asking Shannon what she wanted the hospital to do? Shannon told her. '*I may be nearing the end!*'"

"What, Melinda? She had no right to ask that question. The Medical Directive was found on the hospital computer this morning. They have had it this whole time." I looked around. Ms. H. was not in sight. "Also, Tim started running the Dialysis Machine. He shut it down when it went in "Alarm, Extremely Negative."

2:00 p.m. Ms. H. comes back to the Ward. "Ms. H.!" She stopped and turned to me. "Why were you asking Shannon what she wants this hospital to do? Her Medical Directive is on this hospital's computer."

"I have not seen it, Mr. Hinson."

"*You have got to be kidding me.* Have you talked to Doctors G. or K.?" No answer from Ms. H. as she goes into the Nurse Station area. Signs on a computer, starts banging on keys. I stand waiting outside the computer area, leaning on the counter. Watching her.

"There it is." Prints the document. [Little Man in Head: "*Do not say it, Harold.*"] Leaves the ICU Ward. I return beside Shannon's bed. Start talking and kissing her. Melinda joins me. She is looking at us with that smile.

2:30 p.m. Ms. H. comes into Shannon's room again. Starts talking. I hold up my hand to stop her from talking. [Little Man in Head: *"Do not upset Shannon."*] Ms. H. motioned me to come out of the room. Starts talking again.

"Don't you have somewhere more private that we can talk?"

"Yes, we do." By this time Melinda is standing by my side. Ms. H. directs us out of the ICU Ward and unlocks that door. Family Room. She is holding Shannon's Medical Directive. "This was written in 1986. Things have changed a lot since then. *'This document is missing a key statement'.*" "What do you mean?" "Needs to say the words, *'Do Not Resuscitate.'*"

My emotions begin flowing. "When I met Shannon, it was love at first site. I was smitten. Before turning thirty years old: two failed marriages and two sons. My life became going to college and work. Find a better job. Get my life in order. Make enough money to take care of the obligations. Purchase my first home. An Engineering Job. I did that. Then I met the one that made my life complete. All the fun things we did together. We would finish each other's sentences. Drafted our forever home plans. *Shannon is the love of my life!*"

"Mr. Hinson, Mr. Hinson, Mr. Hinson! You need to say the words." I lost it. Melinda grabbed me. We held each other and cried together. "Mr. Hinson, we know Shannon wants to go home, and we do not think she will make it. You would not want Shannon to die on the highway. We have a Hospice Unit in the lower level of this facility. A room for you to stay with Shannon. We will make Shannon comfortable. Mr. Hinson, Mr. Hinson: you need to say the words."

I uttered those words. *"Do not resuscitate."*

"I am proud of you, Harold. Shannon knows that you have done everything that can be done for her. You have done more than most men would have. Most men would have not even tried." We walked back to Shannon's room, Tim waiting there with Rosie. Do not know where the lady in the suit went.

"She is having trouble breathing." Laboring. Tim gave her a shot. "Will help her to relax." Then a second shot. Disconnects most of the equipment. One monitor seen working. Blood pressure. 4:00 p.m.– 40/14. Nurse Tim leaves us and returns to the Nurse Station. Her surgeon is there. Looks upset as he gestures to the nurses. Me on one side of the bed, Melinda the other, talking to Shannon. Rosie is weeping, sitting in the wheelchair. A mother losing her beloved daughter too soon. I wipe the bubbles from Shannon's lips.

5:45 p.m. Nurse Tim returns. Walks over to me.

"Is she gone?"

"Yes, Mr. Hinson. Is there anything you wish me to do?"

"Will you call the Lead Chaplain?"

A doctor enters and listens to Shannon's heart.

The Chaplain comes. "Mr. Hinson, Shannon, and I spoke a few days ago. Shannon was ready to let go." We gathered beside her bed as Jennifer gave a prayer. Rosie kissed Shannon on the forehead. We packed up Shannon's belongings.

Tim stopped me when we passed the Nurse Station. "Have paperwork for you to check/correct/sign. You did everything the way it should have been done, Mr. Hinson. Not many people do. God Bless you."

Nurse Robin is waiting in the hallway outside the ICU. Comes to me. Takes an arm and wraps it around her waist. We walk to the elevator. "This is as far as I can go." Kissed me on the cheek.

Voice in My Head: *"I am your brother Sammy"*

The End

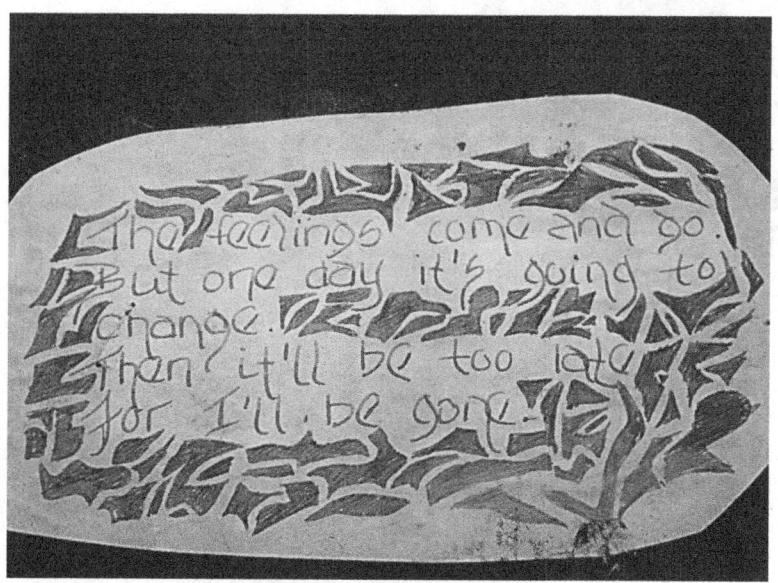

Shannon's Art and Words

Harvey Lee and Harold Hinson
Provided by Olin Mills

Harvey Alexander, H.A. Hinson, Jr.

1991 Mustang LX 5.0, "Foxy 5.0"

1994 Datsun 260Z, "Wolf Z"

Appendices

A. Obituary of Mrs. M.C. Hinson
B. Lucy Hall and Lewis Alexander Washington Hinson
C. Recipes
D. Hinson Genealogy
E. Letter from Warfield
F. Collage of Family Pictures

Appendix A
OBITUARY OF MRS. M.C. HINSON

Mrs. M. C. Hinson.

Mrs. Ada B. Hinson, aged 43, passed away Dec. 4 at her home.

Mrs. Hinson had been confined to her home for eight weeks. She was a great sufferer, but bore her suffering with patience and was willing and ready to go when the Master called her. All that was possible was done for her comfort, but God, who doeth all things well, knew best to take her from this suffering world to a home not made with hands, eternally in the heaven.

Mrs. Hinson was a devoted and loyal member of Cobham Park Church She was a good neighbor and friend and a devoted wife and loving mother.

Her remains were laid to rest on Saturday, Dec. 6, in Cobham Park cemetery, her pastor, Rev. R. O. Reamy, conducting the services.

Active pallbearers were Walter, Virgil, Joseph and Lyell Scates, Harvey Hinson and Russell Morris.

She is survived by her husband, M. C. Hinson, and daughter, Mrs. Lawrence Rock, and two sons, M. C., Jr., and Lewis; her mother, Mrs. Eva D. Scates; four brothers, Walter, Virgil Joseph and Lyell Scates, and two sisters, Mrs. Russell Morris and Virginia Dot Scates.

Much sympathy is felt for the bereaved.

Appendix B

LUCY HALL AND
LEWIS ALEXANDER WASHINGTON HINSON

**Lewis Alexander Washington Hinson (Law),
Our Great Grandfather with Wife Lucy Hall**

Private Lewis A.W. Hinson talked about his experiences especially at the Battle of Cedar Creek when his horse was killed under him. Hinson grabbed the tail of another horse and was dragged out of danger. Until his death at the age of 80, he would tell his children and then his grandchildren that if it hadn't been for that horse's tail, none of them would have been born (Gettysburg Book, Page 107).

Great Grandfather Lewis Alexander Washington Hinson in His Civil War Uniform

"If it hadn't been for that horse's tail, None of you would have been born."

Appendix C
RECIPES
Steamed Crabs
(H.A. Hinson Style)

You will need:
ONE DOZ HARD SHELL BLUE CRABS
CRAB COOKING POT WITH LID / HOLD DOWN
GAS BURNER
PROPANE GAS [Outdoor Cooking Recommended]
OLD BAY SEASONING
MONTREAL STEAK SEASONING
HOT SAUCE
APPLE CIDER VINEGAR
COOKING:
Add 2 INCHES of WATER to the POT with the COLANDER

Add ONE CRAB at a TIME to the POT. [KEEP THE LID HANDY]

SPRINKLE EACH LAYER OF CRABS WITH OLD BAY SEASONING [Usually Three to Four]
SEASONING IN THE EYES SETTLES DOWN FEISTY ONES] -

LIGHT THE GAS BURNER – SIT THE LOADED POT ON THE BURNER. CHECK THE TIME.

While the CRABS are STEAMING, MAKE THE SLURRY MIXTURE:

IN A SMALL BOWL – ADD 2 Tbsp OLD BAY SEASONING – 2 Tbsp MONTREAL STEAK SEASONING – 6 OZ HOT SAUCE – 4 OZ APPLE CIDER VINEGAR – STIR WELL

POUR THE SLURRY MIX ON THE CRABS AT THIRTY FIVE MINUTES – STEAM FIVE MORE MINUTES. CUT OFF THE BURNER. LET THE CRABS SIT IN THE POT WITH THE LID OFF TO START THE COOLING. CRABS ARE DONE WHEN THE APRON IS LOOSE FROM THE BOTTOM OF THE CRAB. REMOVE CRABS FROM POT.
We Eat CRABS on Small Plastic Dinner Trays. EZ Clean Up!

Crabs H.A. Hinson Style

Microwave Party Mix

MICRO WAVE PARTY MIX [Shannon and mother Rosie]
You will need: Four-quart Mixing Bowl – Large Baking Sheets
[Cooling] – Parchment Paper
ONE BATCH Per Four Quart Bowl
The Dry Mixture:
Two Cups Each – CHEEZIT Wheat Chex, Rice Chex, Corn Chex
3 Cups CHEERIOS
1 Cup Cocktail Peanuts

Stir Mixture Up
The Seasoning Mixture:
2 Tbsp WORCESHIRE SAUCE
1 Tsp GARLIC POWDER
1 ¼ Tsp CURRY POWDER
½ Cup WESSON OIL

STIR into Dry Mixture

TO COOK:
MICROWAVE – HIGH – TWO MINUTES
REMOVE BOWL AND STIR
REPEAT FOUR TIMES

COOLING:
Pour Mixture on PARCHMENT PAPER-LINED BAKING SHEET
Sprinkle Mixture with MORTON SEASON ALL SEASONED SALT

Hins Bloody Mary Mix

You will need:
64 oz Clamato Juice
20 oz V8 Juice
1/3 Cup Lemon Juice
1/3 Cup Lime Juice
¼ Cup Hot Sauce [You Choose; I prefer Old Bay] If you want more Heat – 1/3 Cup
½ Cup Worcester Sauce
Lemon Pepper
VODKA

Garnish Suggestions:
Celery Stark; Green and Ripe Olives; Caper Berries; Slice Lemon; Slice Lime
To Make one Drink:
Fill a Tall Glass with Cracked Ice – Add 2 oz VODKA – Fill Glass with Bloody Mix – Stir with Celery Stick – Add the Garnish – Finish with a Dash of Lemon Pepper

See the story in the book how this came about.

Appendix C. Recipes

Simonson Oysters
(Shannon & Harold)

LARGE CAST IRON SKILLET - PREHEAT OVEN 375 DEGREES

INGREDIENTS: [Double the ingredients for a quart of OYSTERS]

1 PINT NORTHERN NECK OYSTERS
1 Fresh Garlic Clove [Minced]
1 Large Sweet Onion [Finely Chopped]
1/4 Cup Fresh Graded Parmesan Cheese
4 Strips Bacon [Cut into One Inch Long Pieces]
1/4 Cup White Wine
Kosher / Sea Salt– Fresh Ground Black Pepper to taste
1 Tbsp Fresh Lemon Juice
2 Tbsp Butter
2 Tbsp Olive Oil
1/4 Cup Fresh Parsley [Chopped]

COOKING:

Cook Bacon until Crisp [Remove and sit aside for latter]
In Bacon Dripping – Add Butter and Olive Oil – Lower Heat
Add the Onions – Sauté until Caramelized – Add Garlic
Add White Wine – Bring to a Boil – Turn down to Medium Heat
Continue to Cook Sauce until Light Brown – Salt and Pepper to Taste
With a Large Spoon – Add the Oysters [Use as much of the Liquid as desired] -   Cook the Oysters until they have Slightly Curled Edges [<u>DO NOT OVER DO IT</u>]

Layer the Bacon Pieces on Oysters – Sprinkle Parmesan Cheese on Top

Put Skillet in Oven <u>ONLY LONG</u> enough to <u>MELT</u> the Cheese – Remove

Garnish with Parsley – Serve Oysters on Small Plates / Bowls / Cups or Cleaned Oyster Shells.

Simonson Crabcakes

Yield: Four/Six Cakes
You will need:
1 pound Fresh Lump Crabmeat
1 Egg [beaten]
1 tbsp Baking Power
1 tbsp Dukes Mayonnaise
1 tbsp Fresh Lemon Juice
1 tbsp Unsalted Butter [melted]
1/2 tsp Old Bay
1 tsp Prepared Mustard
1/4 Cup KIKKOMAN Panko Japanese Style Bread Crumbs [to bind mixture]
KIKKOMAN Panko Japanese Style Bread Crumbs [enough to coat cakes]

Mix all ingredients [except the Panko to be used to coat the finished cakes] in a large mixing bowl being careful not to break up the Lumps of Crab.
Scatter the Panko for coating the cakes on a Sheet Pan. Shape the Crab Meat Mixture into equal cakes and Roll/Coat with the Panko. Place the Cakes on a Parchment lined pan suitable to go in the Freezer or Refrigerator until ready to cook.

COOKING:
In a Cast Iron or Heavy Bottom Frying Pan suitable for how many cakes are to be cooked –   Heat 1/2 Butter and 1/2 Olive Oil to a temperature that will splatter with a drop of water.
  Use a large Spatula to put one cake at a time in the Hot Pan – I prefer to cook two at a time. Cook until Brown on one side and carefully turn the cake over and brown the other side – the crispier the better on the outside!

Shrimp & Grits

1 LB SHRIMP [24 MEDIUM]
4 STRIPS BACON   [CUT INTO SMALL PIECES]   ONE LOAF ITALIAN BREAD [SLICED]
1/2 CUP WHITE GRITS AND 1/2 CUP YELLOW GRITS
1 CUP SHREDDED SHARP CHEDDAR CHEESE
1/2 CUP SHREDDED PARMESAN
3 tbsp SALTED SWEET BUTTER; 3 tbsp OLIVE OIL
1 LG. SWEET ONION; 2 GARLIC CLOVES   [CHOPPED FINE]
1 CUP CHICKEN BROTH   [BETTER THAN BOUILLON ROASTED CHICKEN – FOLLOW INSTRUCTIONS]
1 tbsp LEMON JUICE;   1 tbsp WORCESTERSHIRE SAUCE
1 SCALLION [THIN SLICES ENTIRE – GREEN & BULB];   1/2 CUP FRESH ITALIAN PARSLEY   [CHOPPED]
SEA SALT & GROUND PEPPER [TO TASTE];   1 tbsp HOT SAUCE   [add more to taste]
CHOP 1/2 STARK OF CELERY AND 1/2 CARROT -   4 THIN SLICES LEMON [GARNISH]

1 CUP WATER IN SMALL SAUCE PAN – CLEAN SHRIMP KEEPING SHELLS AND OTHER 'BITS' IN THE PAN. – ADD CELERY AND CARROT TO PAN.
1 tbsp WORCESTERSHIRE SAUCE.   BRING TO A BOIL. REDUCE BROTH BY HALF.   STRAIN into CUP CHICKEN BROTH COVER & SET ASIDE.
COOK THE GRITS ACCORDING TO PACKAGE – ADD CHEDDAR; PARMESAN; 1 tbsp BUTTER   SEASON WITH SALT
COVER SET ASIDE   [ADD WATER TO THIN IF NEEDED]
HEAT OLIVE OIL AND 1 tbsp BUTTER IN TWELVE INCH SKILLET –
COOK BACON UNTIL CRISP   REMOVE – SET ASIDE
MED HIGH HEAT - SEASON SHRIMP WITH SALT & PEPPER — COOK SHRIMP UNTIL PINK   [ONE SIDE 2 MINUTES; TURN OVER 2 MINUTES]   REMOVE SHRIMP – SET ASIDE
MEDIUM HEAT – COOK ONIONS; SHALLOTS; GARLIC; UNTIL TENDER
RAISE HEAT TO HIGH - 1 tbsp BUTTER; 1 tbsp LEMON JUICE; 1 tbsp HOT SAUCE; SHELL SAUCE –   STIR UNTIL SAUCE THICKENS.
LOWER HEAT - RETURN SHRIMP TO PAN
   SERVE: DIVIDE GRITS IN FOUR BOWLS - TOP EACH BOWL OF GRITS
   WITH 6 SHRIMPS & SAUCE -   ITALIAN BREAD
SLICES   TOAST - WITH BUTTER or OLIVE OIL and GARLIC POWDER
        -                GARNISH BOWLS WITH LEMON SLICES

Appendix D

HINSON GENEALOGY

Samuel Allen Hinson   b. 1944 d. 1951

- Harvey Lee Hinson b. July 4, 1942 plus 15 hours; 5 minutes
- Harold Thomas Hinson Sr b. July 4,1942 plus 15 hours
- Harvey Alexander Hinson Jr.
  - b. February 22, 1921, d. November 18, 1996
- Harvey Alexander Hinson (b.1887, d. 1955)
- Lewis Alexander Washington Hinson (Mary Catherine Sofia "Willie" Fones Hinson)
  - 10th VA Calvary; Company D
- Daniel Hinson (b. 1817; d. 1848)
- Epaphroditus Jennings Hinson (1777 Richmond, Wise Virginia, United States; May 7 1848). First name also spelled Eppaphrodities.
- William Hinson (1778 Richmond, Madison, Virginia, United States; October 30, 1830 Richmond, Wise, Virginia, United States). Reported living in Richmond 1810 and 1820. Married Alice Carter (1779; 1822).

Jonas Hinson (1728? too late) of Lunenburg Parish, Richmond Co, Planter married 1785 to Henrietta Haney "Haney" (1729)

- https://www.familysearch.org/tree/person/details/LDS7-V54
  - Richmond Co, VA Deed; 11 Nov 1776: Griffin Murdock FAUNTLEROY of Northfarnham Par, Richmond Co, Gent. and Jonas HINSON of Lunenburg Par, Richmond Co, Planter; ... do demise grant and to farm let unto Jonas HINSON ... parces in Lunenburg Par ... 60 acres ... bounded by John EIDSON, Thomas BARTLETT, the Main Road and the Road leading to Naylors' Hole... said Johas HINSON and Henrietta his now Wife ...paying yearly

3 pounds; Sig: Griffin M FAUNTELROY, Jonas HINSON; Wit: John BELFIELD, Willifred BELFIELD, Joseph BELFIELD; rec: 2 Dec 1776
- George Alvin Alexander Hinson Jr? (1657 Richmond, Virginia, British Colonial America; 1727 Sittingbourne Parish, Old Rapphannock County, Virginia) https://www.colonial-settlers-md-va.us/getperson.php?personID=I28253&tree=Tree1
    - Married to Mary Jane Wood (b. 1658)
- Robert Tobias Hinson (Robert Hanson b. 1615 Charles, Stafford, Virginia, United States and lived in Charles County, Maryland, then Old Rappahannock County, Virginia, then Stafford, Virginia. He died in 1675 and he is listed in this "Descendants of Hanson" genealogy as being killed by Doeggs Indians, Stafford, Virginia.) https://www-personal.umich.edu/~bobwolfe/gen/pn/p17094.htm
    - Christening 11/2/1626 Norton le Moors, Staffordshire, England, United Kingdom
    - Thomas Hynson ? Brother. http://daysgoneby.me/hinchingham-maryland-surveyed-early-1659/
- James Tobias Hinson (1593 Suffolk, England, United Kingdom- 1650 Stafford, Virginia) Married 1612 to Nancy "Ann" Quisenberry (1595-1693). He's also found in Ireland, which could be before passage to the new world. They had 10 children by one source.
    - on the John Smith Manafest in 1609
    - https://encyclopediavirginia.org/entries/second-charter-of-virginia-1609/
    - https://www.wikitree.com/g2g/24935/was-tobias-hinson-on-the-virginia-colony-chart er-of-1607
    - There were 3 charters of Virginia, the 1st was April 10, 1606, The 2nd was May 23, 1609 and the 3rd was March 12, 1612. Tobias Hinson, grocer, appears on the 2nd Charter of Virginia of May 23, 1609. His name also appears in Smith, John, 1580-1631: The complete works of Captain John Smith

Appendix D. Hinson Genealogy

[vol. 2] & [vol.3], as well as in the minutes of The Virginia Company. The differences among the three charters lie primarily in the territorial jurisdiction of the company, not in the right to govern the colony. Many members of the Virginia Company, were merely 'investors' and never came to America, and you can check the names of early passengers to Jamestown via this link https://www.historicjamestowne.org/biographies/list.php?letter=H. The Virginia and Jamestown Settlements are often confused with the Mayflower Pilgrims, but they are two distinct settlements. The Mayflower ships did not arrive in New England until 1620--much later than the Virginia settlements. Hinson's name does not appear on the passenger manifests for Mayflower ships that arrived in New England or the Mayflower Compact of 1620.

- Early Origins of the Hinson family The surname Hinson was first found in Yorkshire, where we find Henry Hynson, Ellen Hyneson and Thomas Hynson, "ploghwryght," (plough wright) listed in the Yorkshire Poll Tax Rolls of 1379. Henry and Thomas were either brothers or father and son, and were the scions of their respective branches of the family name. [1]

Appendix E

LETTER FROM WARFIELD

21 March 61

Harold -

    I just wanted to write you a few lines to say Hello. Honest, we have been so busy trying to fix up the other house and work too that I hardly know which end is up. Believe you me you just don't know how much work there is to moving. We have painted the bedroom, kitchen, and bath. All we have to do now is some more wood work and then move. We expect to move Saturday. I have a sales meeting Friday, move Saturday, and we want to go down to Little Creek (Norfolk) to be in a First Aid contest Sunday. How does this sound for a full week end?

    I have been reading most of your letters to your Mother. Am real glad to hear that you are making out Ok. Of course I knew you would. You are the kind that will get along. Just take an old fools advise and don't try to fight them. If you go along with most of it you will find it so much easier. Son, you'll never know how your Mother misses you and how much your letters mean to her. Of course I miss you too, but you know its not like your mother does. You said in your letter tonight that you would like to call us soon, but had to make your money last. You can call us collect. Just don't make it a habit of calling too much, because it does cost right much.

    Every body I see asks about you. Every one of them say they know things are a little rough for you right now, but just wait until basic is over and it will seem like a different world. Just like I told you, this is the only hard part of it, and you'll never have to go thru basic again. I talked to some old air force men today, and they say if you get a choice to take Chenute (Spelling?) over Shepherd any time. Personally I think you will like electrical maintance. Wh not try to get into jet aircraft maintance rather than missels, and maybe you will get some flying to test your work. Its all up to you, you know. I'M not trying to tell you what to do.

    Harold you had better be glad you are in the Air Force. Boy, business really is rotten down here. They are cutting things back to the bone. It looks like we have one fair day and then two rainy ones. Its been hailing all night tonight, but the temperature is up around forty and the weather may says it will be seventy tomorriw with a thunder storm or so. Its too wet for the farmers and saw millers, and the fishermen could do all right if they could get anything for what they catch. Rock fish are only five cents apound, herring are half a cent each. ever hear of such a thing this time of the year. What are they going to be when things get plentiful this summer.

    We see Betty almost every day.. She had supper over here Monday and helped Barbara up at the new house a while. I guess Barbara is writing you all this news.

    You be good, take care of yourself and I'll write again when I can. Dont bother to write me, I'll read the letters you writ Barbara and think they are mine too. Ok.

Best of Luck

Warfield

Appendix F
COLLAGE OF FAMILY PICTURES

Daddy and Cousins

Left: Nemma's King finished first and had the fastest heat for the week.

Below: Mr. Hinson accepts Winner's Cup from fair princess, Janet Barrack.

Note:
Close Ties; Richmond County Intermediate School, 1991; Page 74, 75.

Appendix F, Collage of Family Pictures 387

Great Day Fishing

WARSAW OLD TIMERS—Kneeling front row left to right, Jimmy Messick, Billy Omohundro, Jimmy Sanders, Robert Croxton, Coach Kermit Sanders, Buddy Delano, standing left to right, Stanley Mothershead, Paul Rock, Leon Douglas, Harvey Hinson, Aubrey Lee Edwards, Wellford Courtney, Bobby Yeatman, Donald Douglas, and Bobby Wilson. Not pictured is J. A. Christopher.
—Debbie Bowen Photo

Old Timers' Team in the Beginning

Richmond County Old Timers

Hinson Team - ROMAS

Appendix F, Collage of Family Pictures 389

Second Cousins

Harvey Lee, Brian and Karen

**Robinson Sisters
Second Cousins**

Aunt Dollie, Uncle Bob Wedding

Made in the USA
Monee, IL
20 May 2024

58702200R00236